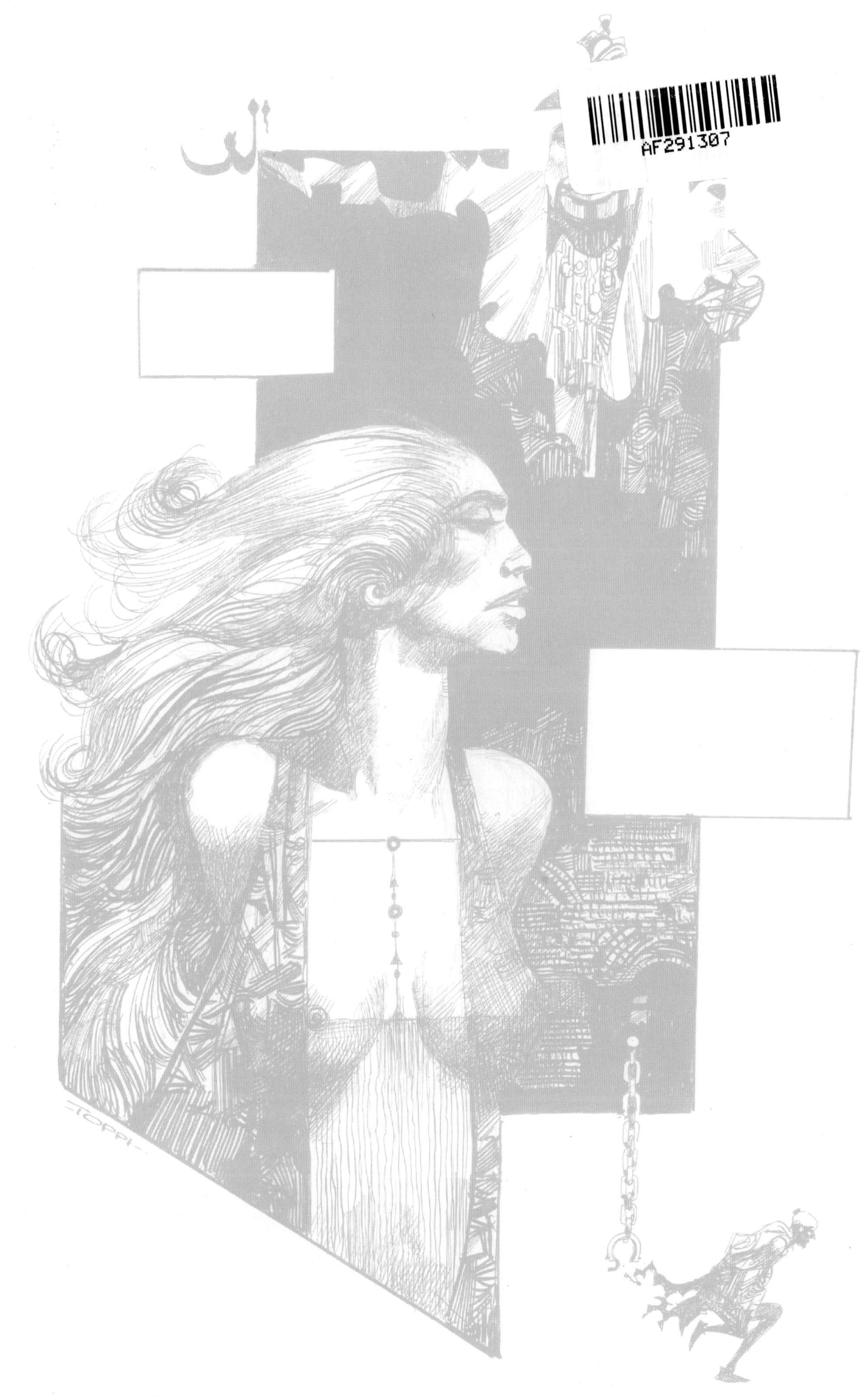

Sergio Toppi's
Harlots and Mercenaries

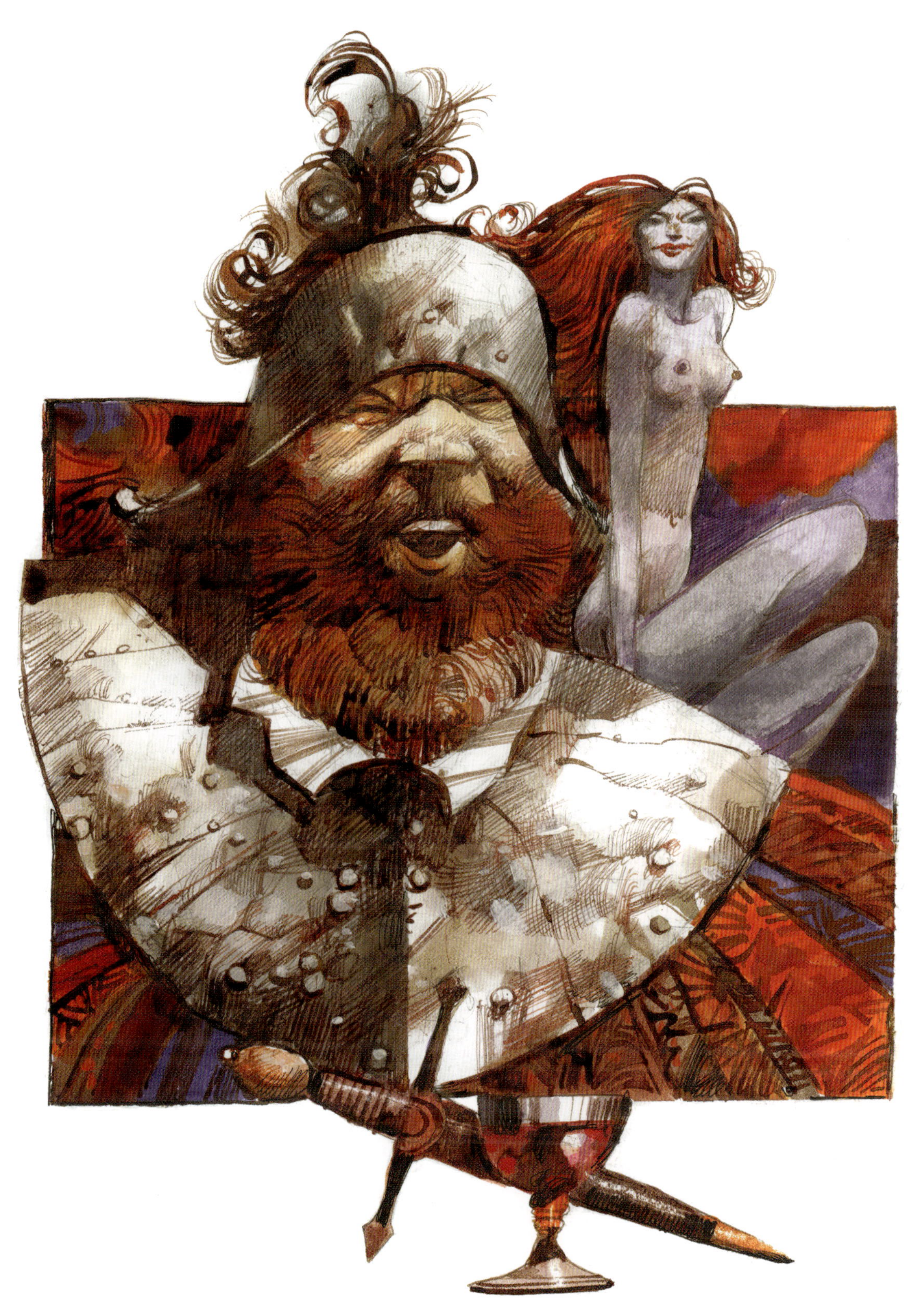

Translation by Dan Christensen
Editing by Mike Kennedy
Layout by Chris Northrop

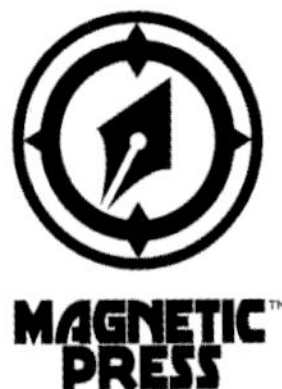

ISBN: 978-1-951719-67-8
Library of Congress Control Number: 2022916505

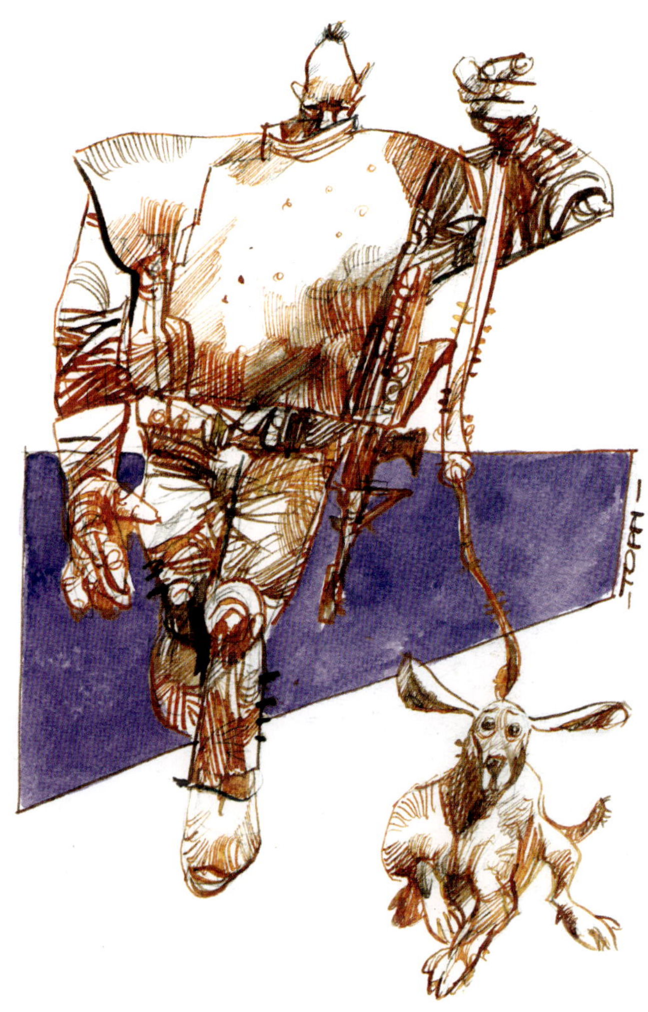

"Dog of War" unpublished drawing for the Soudards project, Mosquito 2008.

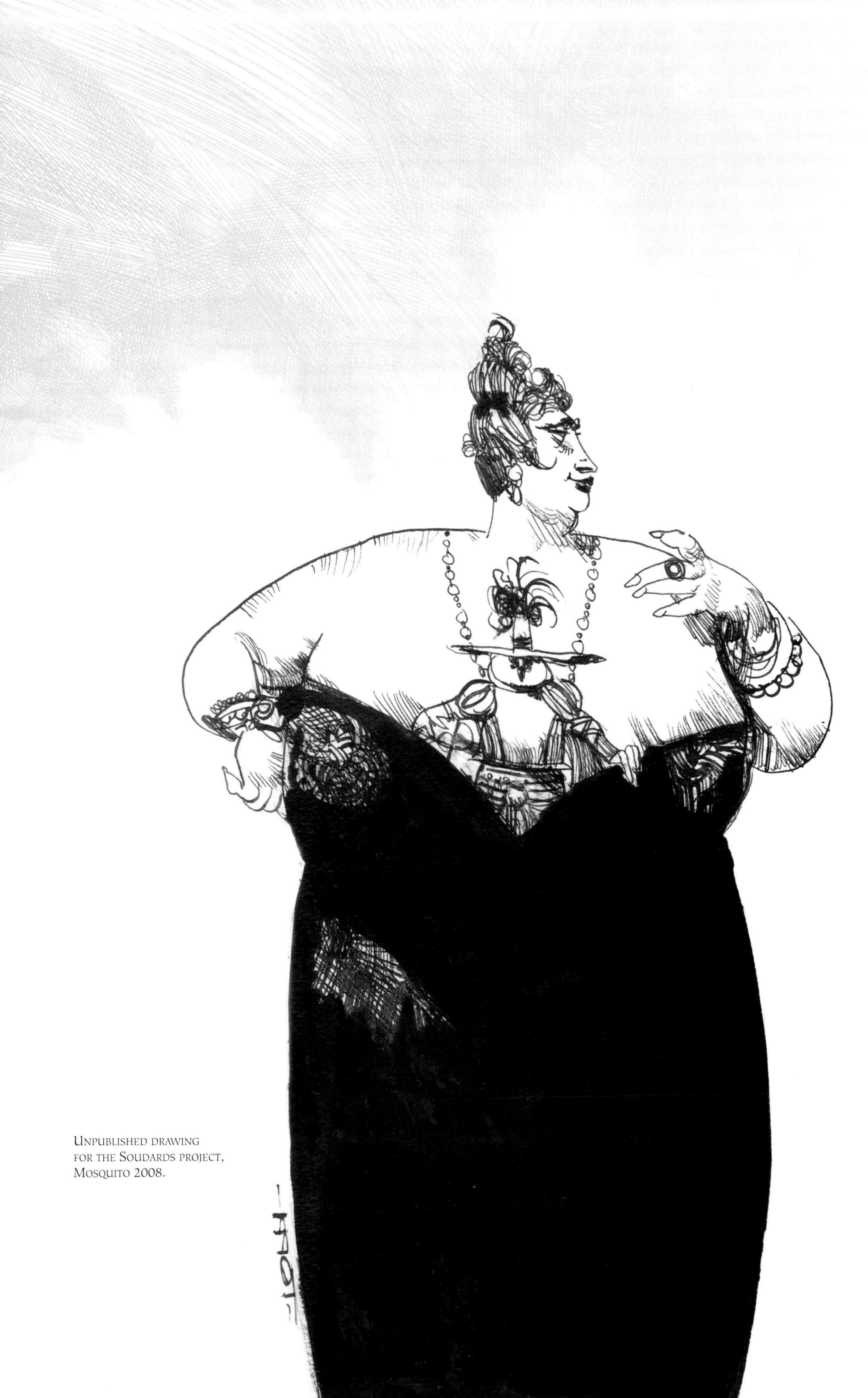

Unpublished drawing
for the Soudards project,
Mosquito 2008.

Dudes and Chicks

It will probably come as no surprise to anyone that the human race is separated into two categories: Dudes and Chicks. Dude, or "mec" in French, a masculine noun that is an altered version of the word "mac," which is itself a diminutive of the term "maquereau," or pimp. Chick, or "nana" in French, is a feminine noun, named after the courtesan Nana, the eponymous heroine from the famous Zola novel. Does this mean that all human relations are nothing more than prostitution and pimping? Certainly not! I merely suggest that everyone tries to get through life as best they can, one step at a time. The rugged sex would indeed like to be considered vigorous (the virile boyfriend, tough hustler, real man, real dude, hard guy), while the so-called weaker sex uses their supposed fragility as a strength (chick, broad, vamp, tease, flirt, femme fatale, hot babe, doe-eyed vixen). Each one chooses his or her weapons; each one chooses his or her arguments. Choose your side!

Eros and Thanatos, Mars and Venus, Beauty and the Beast, the Bear and the Doll, the Woman and the Puppet… the whole of humanity's history has been built by antagonistic and famous couples such as these. There is no archangel without a dragon, no moon without a sun, no day without night, no heat without cold, no sugar without salt, no charm without monstrosity, no refinement without vulgarity, no gentleness without brutality. You will have to opt for either the curves of good manners, or the hard edges of character.

Love, death. L'amour, la mort. LAMOUR ≠ LAMOR: a single U and everything changes. A variation of U, like a T-square ruler. The curved U faces off against the angular T. All of this is rather visual, a question of pen strokes. The caress is a curve, since it follows the roundness of the body and arouses excitement, while the fatal thrust is direct, since it penetrates the body and delivers death. And yet, there is little more than the space of a single pen stroke that divides the mercenaries from the beautiful harlots: blackest intentions entirely contained within the black ink of the drawing.

I maintain that Sergio Toppi's characters already bear their fates in the very shadows of their silhouettes. The laconic pen strokes hints at a terse destiny, while the incisive pen strokes foreshadow a tale that cuts like a scalpel. Sharp drawings tell sharp tales. Considering Toppi's keen style, I played along with the scathing intensity of the story. Derision and sarcasm seem to be the perfect match to such cutting visuals. For the pitiful mecs and the beautiful nanas born from Toppi's implacable artwork, I imagined blade-hewn fates. The guillotine is an invitation to cut short, so I will kept this brief, imagining destinies painted with the blade of a knife.

—Jean-Louis Roux, 2008
Journalist, poet, and artist

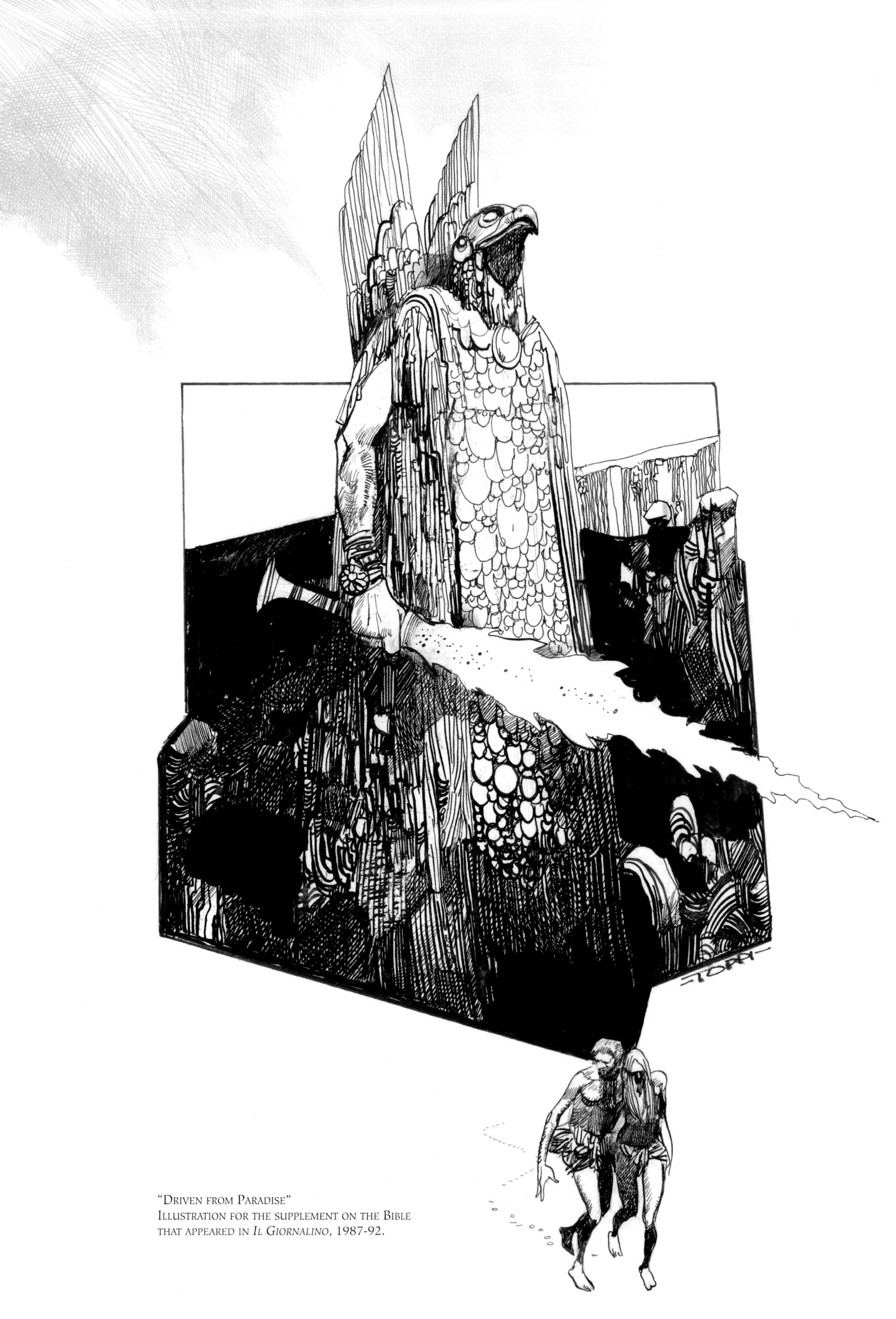

"Driven from Paradise"
Illustration for the supplement on the Bible
that appeared in *Il Giornalino*, 1987-92.

At the Dawn of Time

According to recent research, cavemen didn't live in caves.

In fact, as cavernous as they may have been (in our fantasies, at least),
they were no more obscure than we are.

And if we consider them savages, what does that say about us?
That, perhaps, we are the savages…

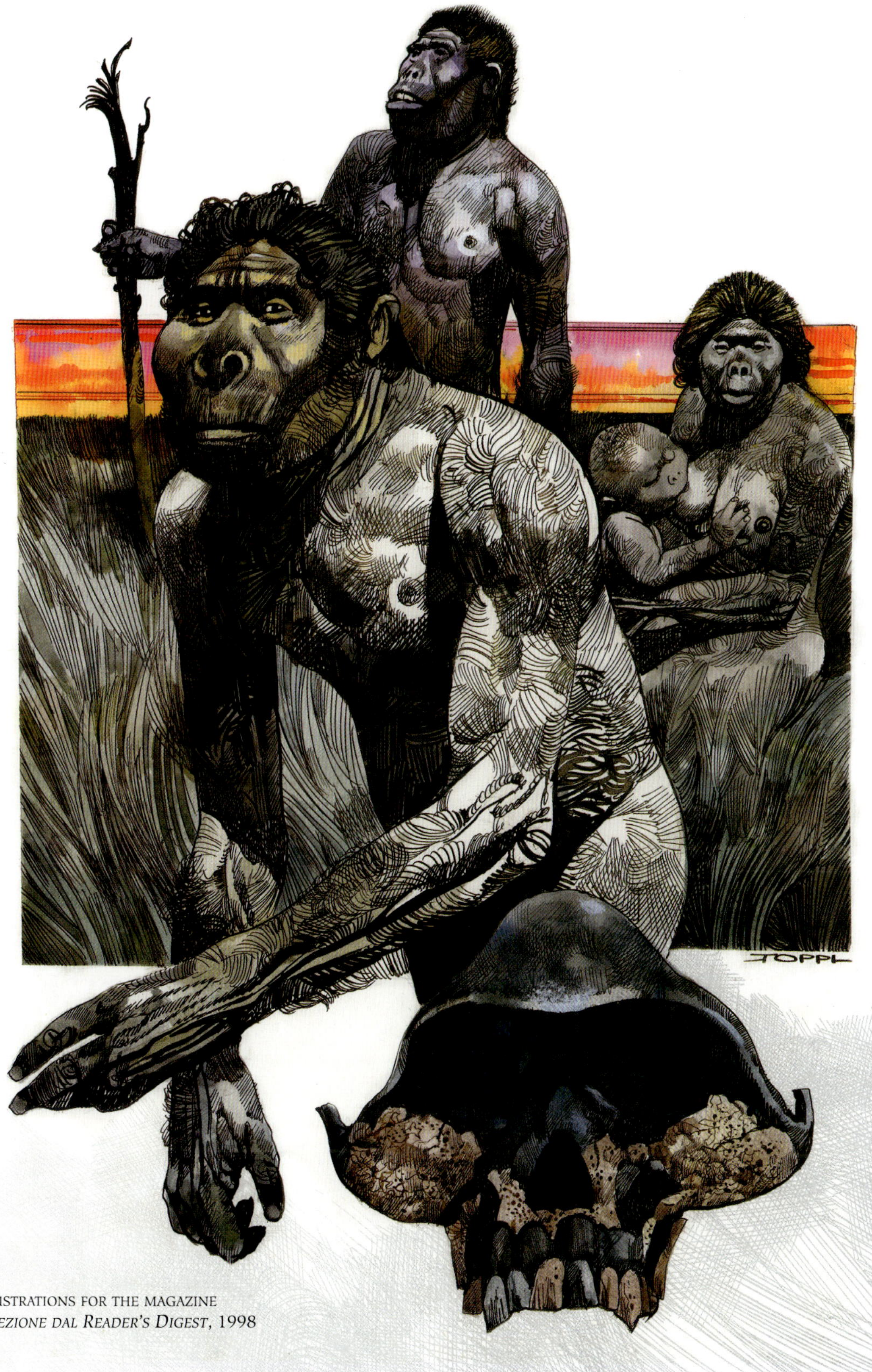

ILLUSTRATIONS FOR THE MAGAZINE
SELEZIONE DAL READER'S DIGEST, 1998

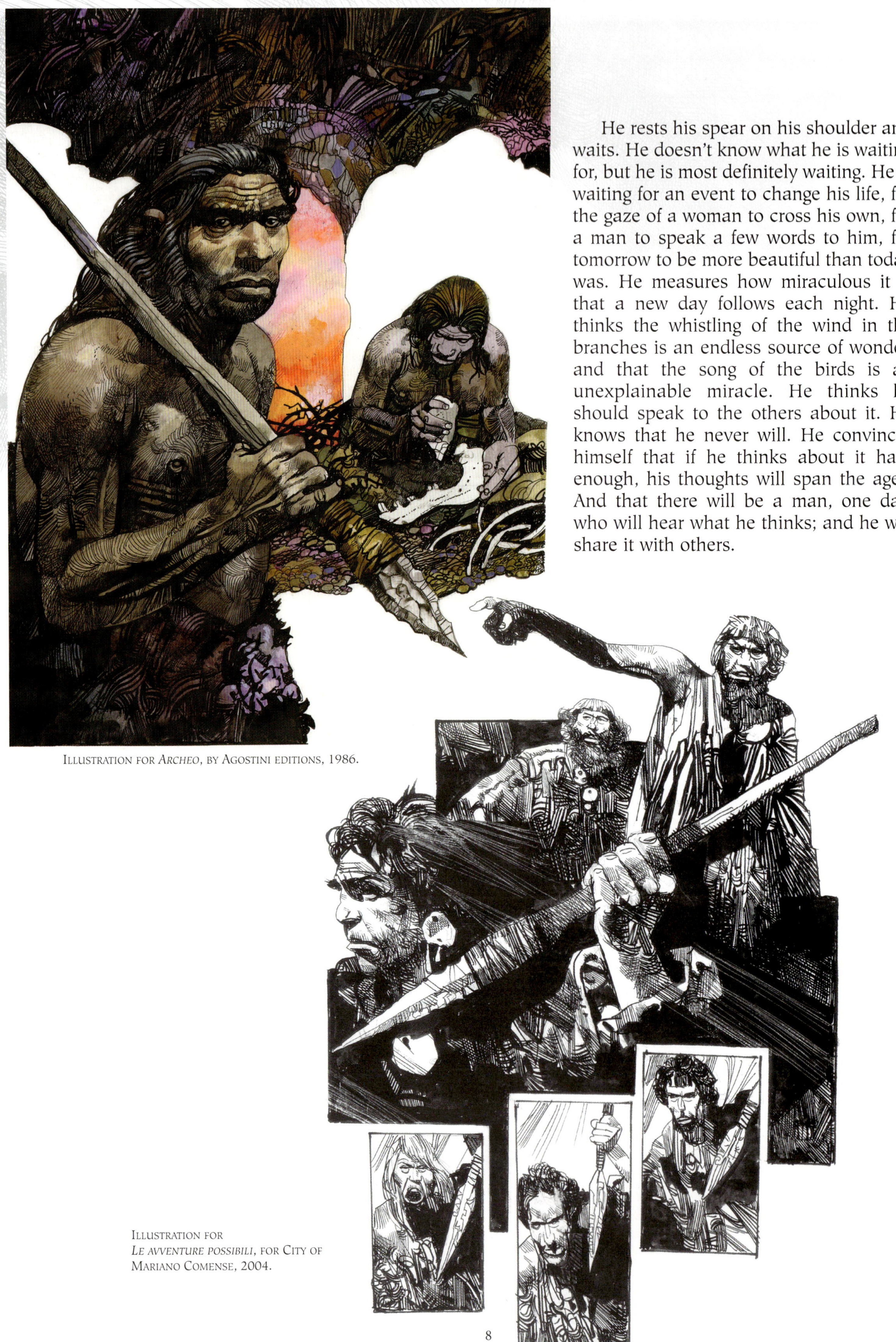

He rests his spear on his shoulder and waits. He doesn't know what he is waiting for, but he is most definitely waiting. He is waiting for an event to change his life, for the gaze of a woman to cross his own, for a man to speak a few words to him, for tomorrow to be more beautiful than today was. He measures how miraculous it is that a new day follows each night. He thinks the whistling of the wind in the branches is an endless source of wonder, and that the song of the birds is an unexplainable miracle. He thinks he should speak to the others about it. He knows that he never will. He convinces himself that if he thinks about it hard enough, his thoughts will span the ages. And that there will be a man, one day, who will hear what he thinks; and he will share it with others.

ILLUSTRATION FOR *ARCHEO*, BY AGOSTINI EDITIONS, 1986.

ILLUSTRATION FOR
LE AVVENTURE POSSIBILI, FOR CITY OF
MARIANO COMENSE, 2004.

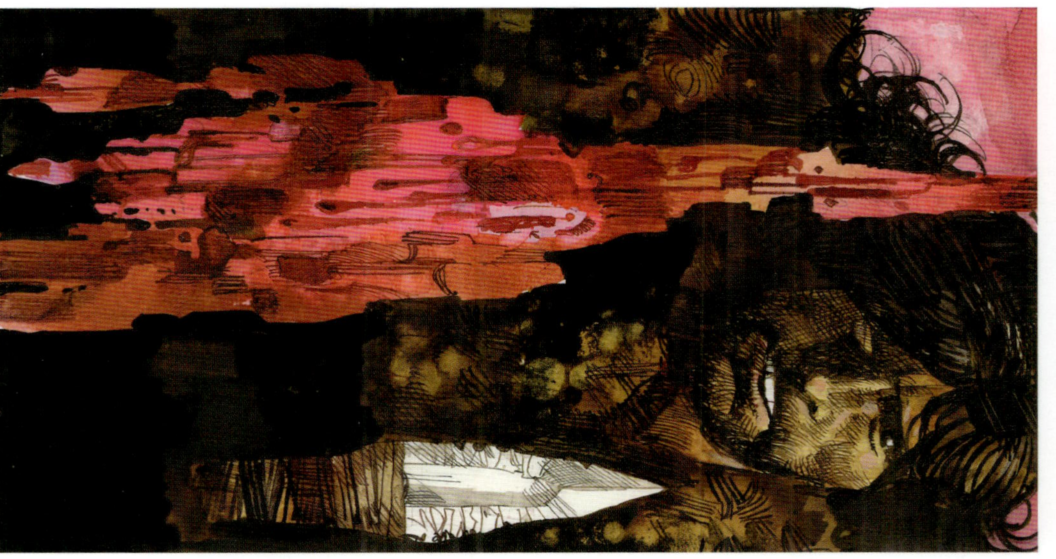
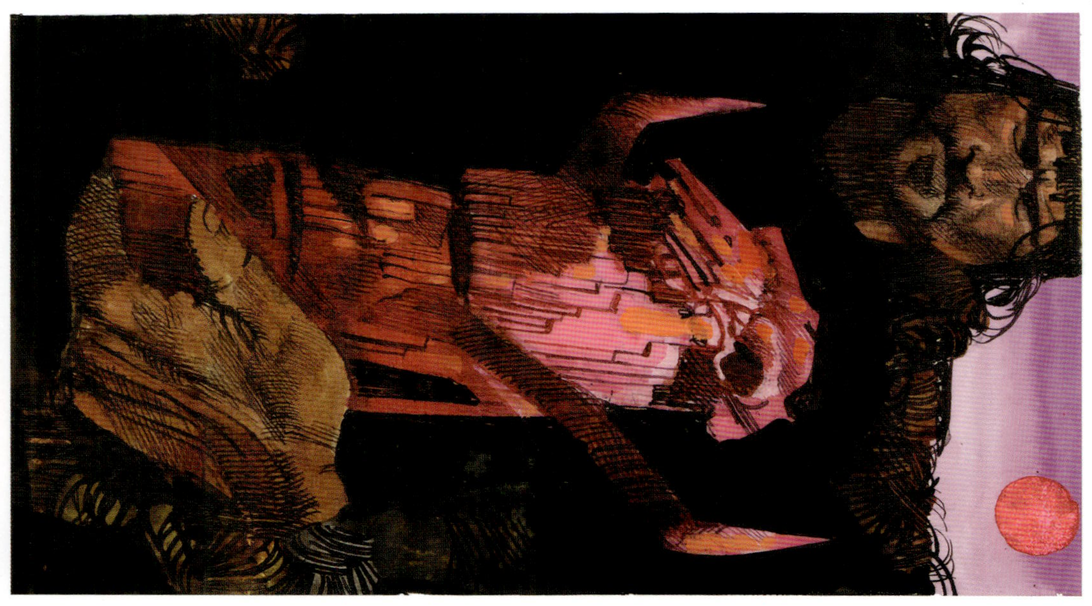
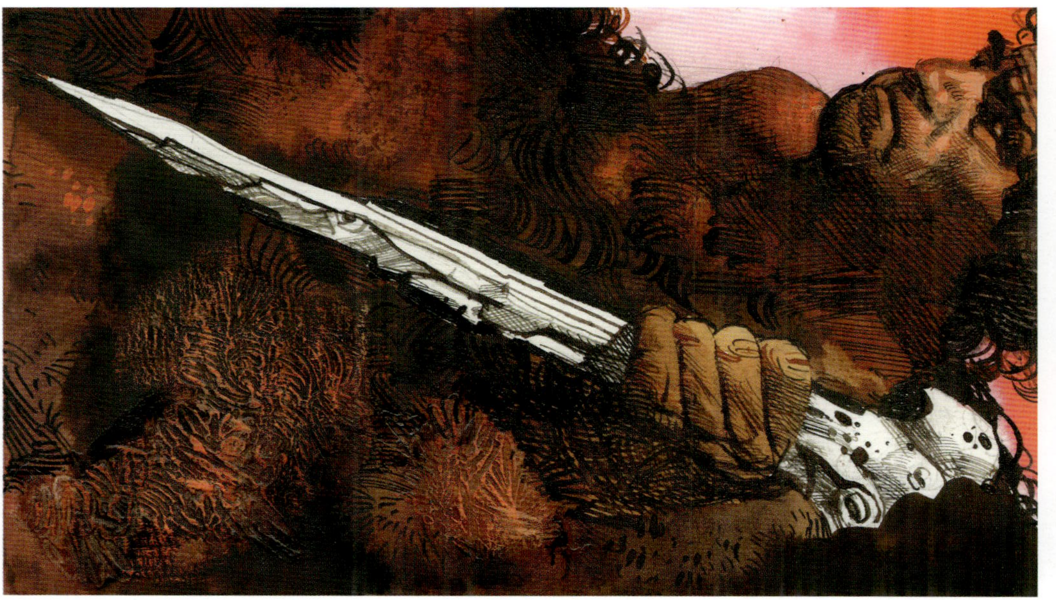
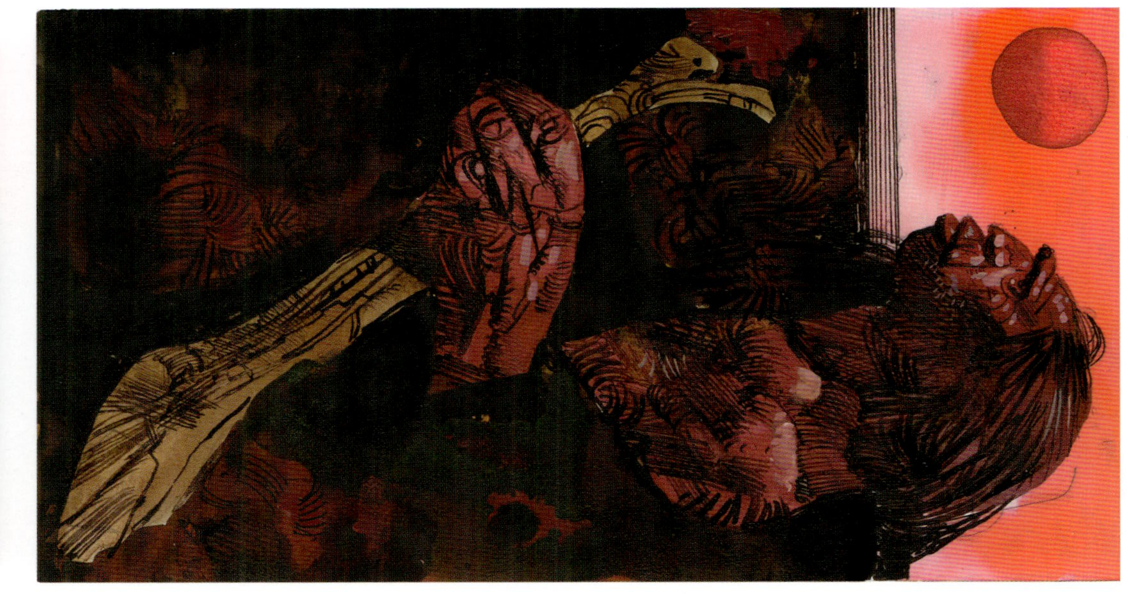

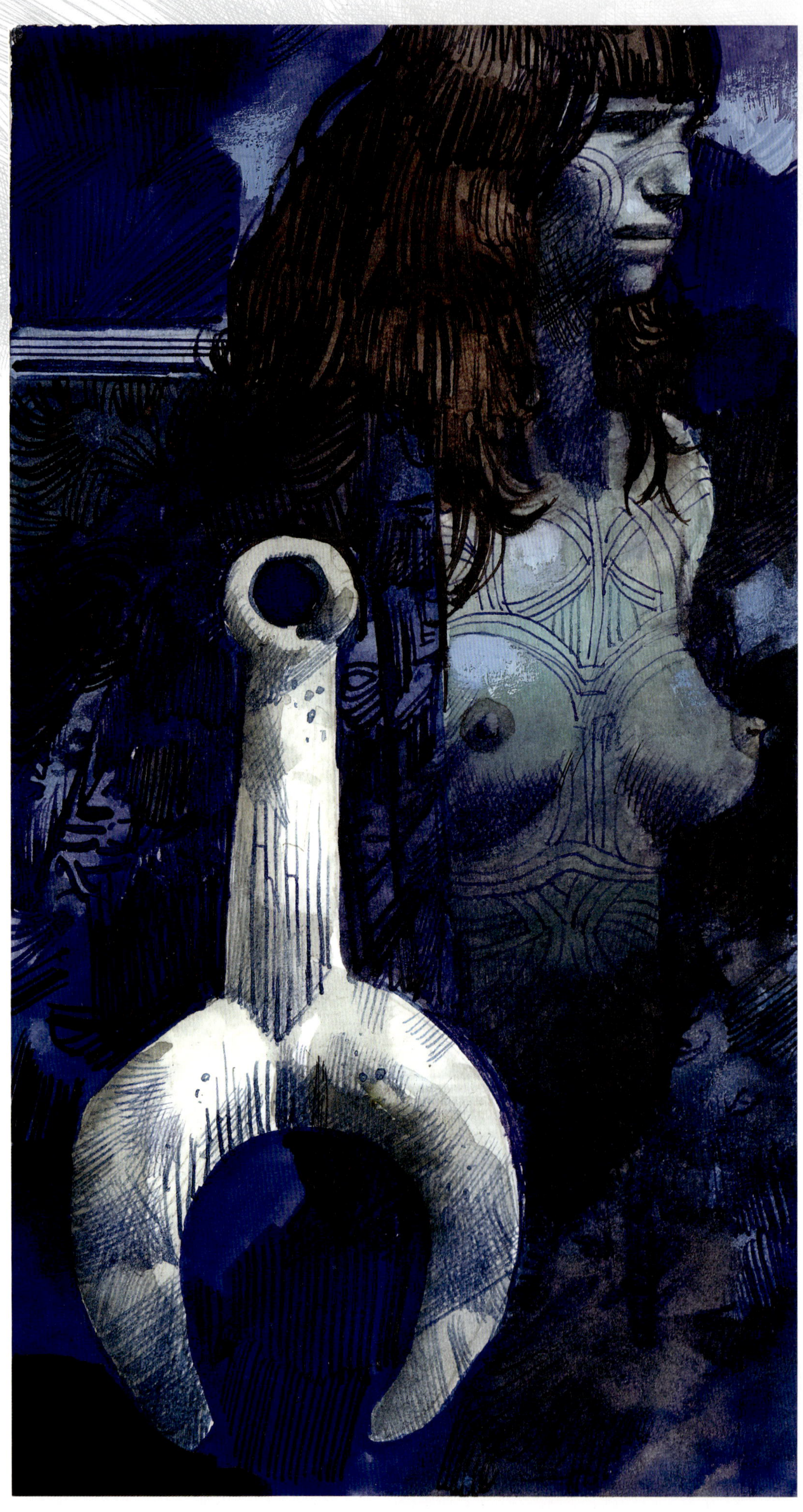

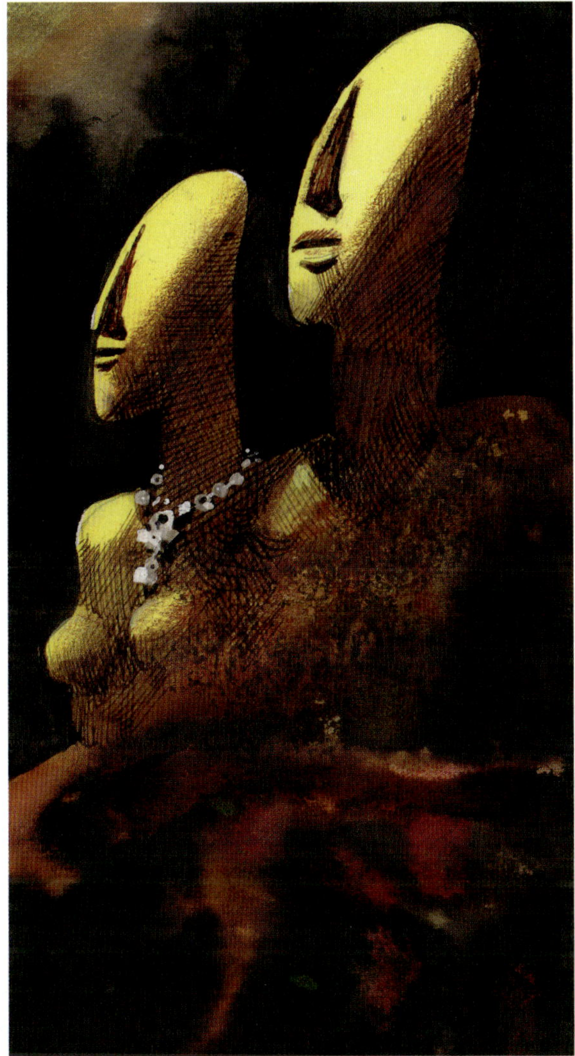

Their idols were blind. They explained that their deities had no need for eyes since they had better things to do than to judge mankind. They ensure the proper transition from day to night, the rhythm of the seasons, the coolness of running water, the rustling of wind-blown leaves, the position of stars in the heavens, the beating of the waves, the greenness of the grass, the roundness of the raindrops falling upon summer-scorched soil. Their gods were devoid of eyes, since they refused to keep a close watch over men. Their gods had little use for men, for in those days, men were responsible for their own actions. A very strange word was used to describe this: it was said they were "free."

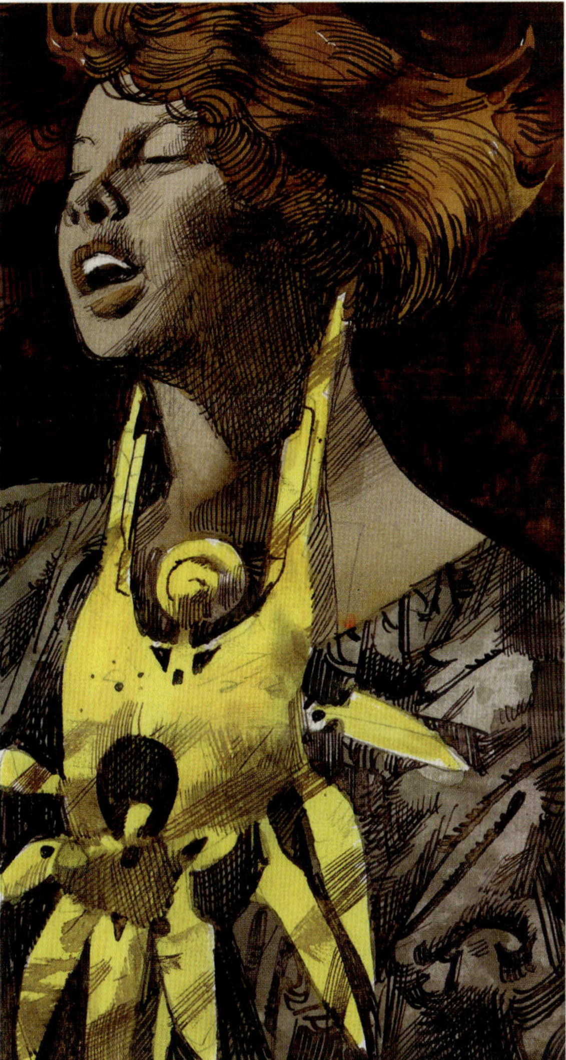

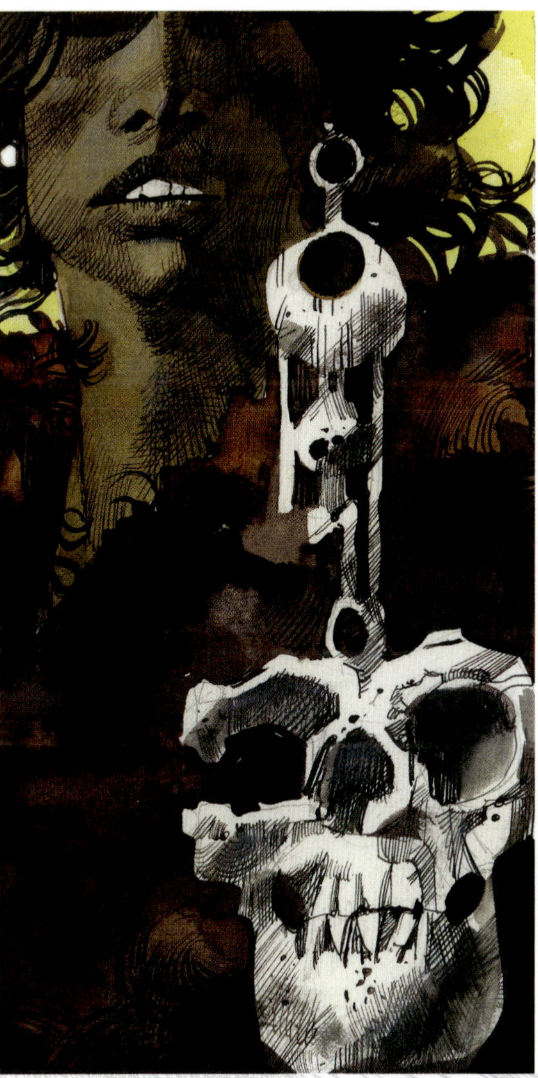

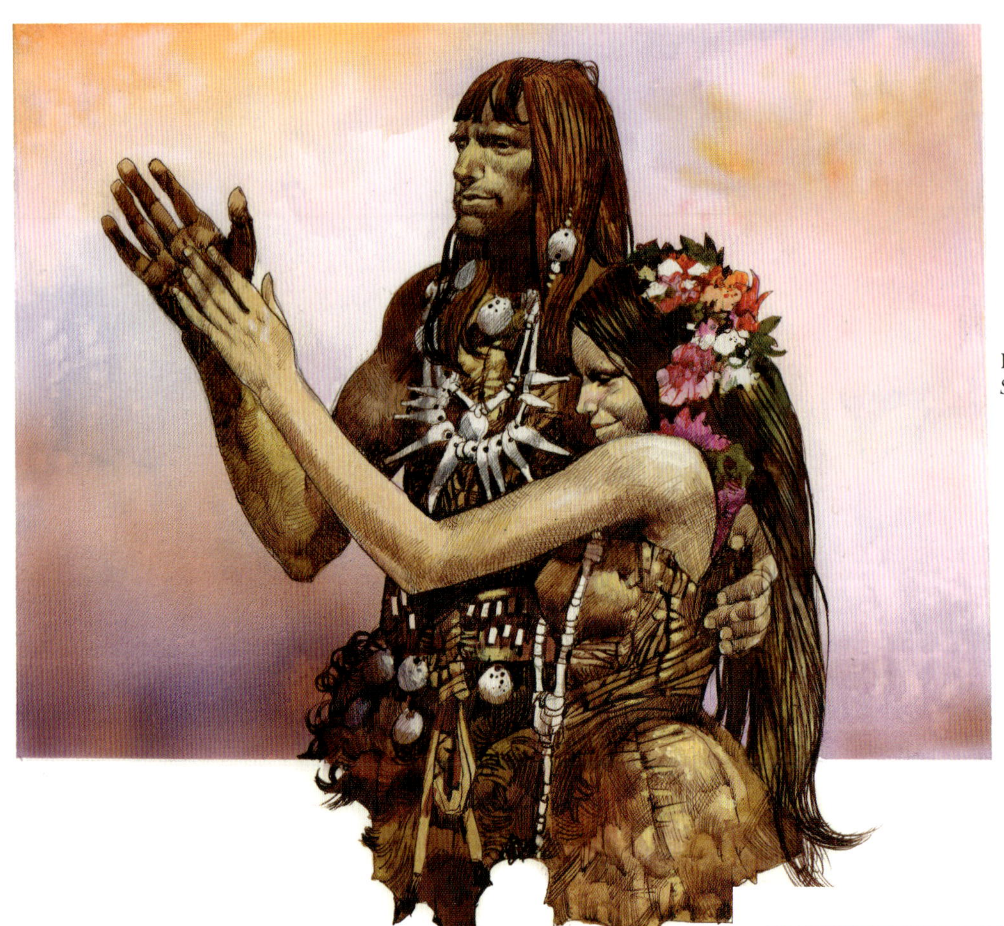

It was indeed foolproof. All we had to do was post a strong man on the top of the cliff overlooking the narrow path, position a large boulder balanced on a lever, and ask the strong man to pull the lever in question the moment those damned enemies of ours showed up. It was decided that this would be done. Except one may be strong of shoulder but weak of mind. That imbecile could not help but to preemptively test the lever's solidity and the satisfactory functioning of his muscles. By going about this far too soon, the numbskull pushed the boulder over before our enemies were beneath it, causing a hellish noise which got himself noticed. What happened next was, therefore, quite predictable: mostly annoyed, the soldiers scrambled over the boulder and skirted the cliff, which they climbed in a few great strides. The witless moron was then subjected to rather unpleasant treatment.

Meanwhile, anticipating what was about to unfold and, as a result, favoring caution, we had, of course, fled. Later, much later, after the horde had long since moved on, we buried the thick-skulled cretin.

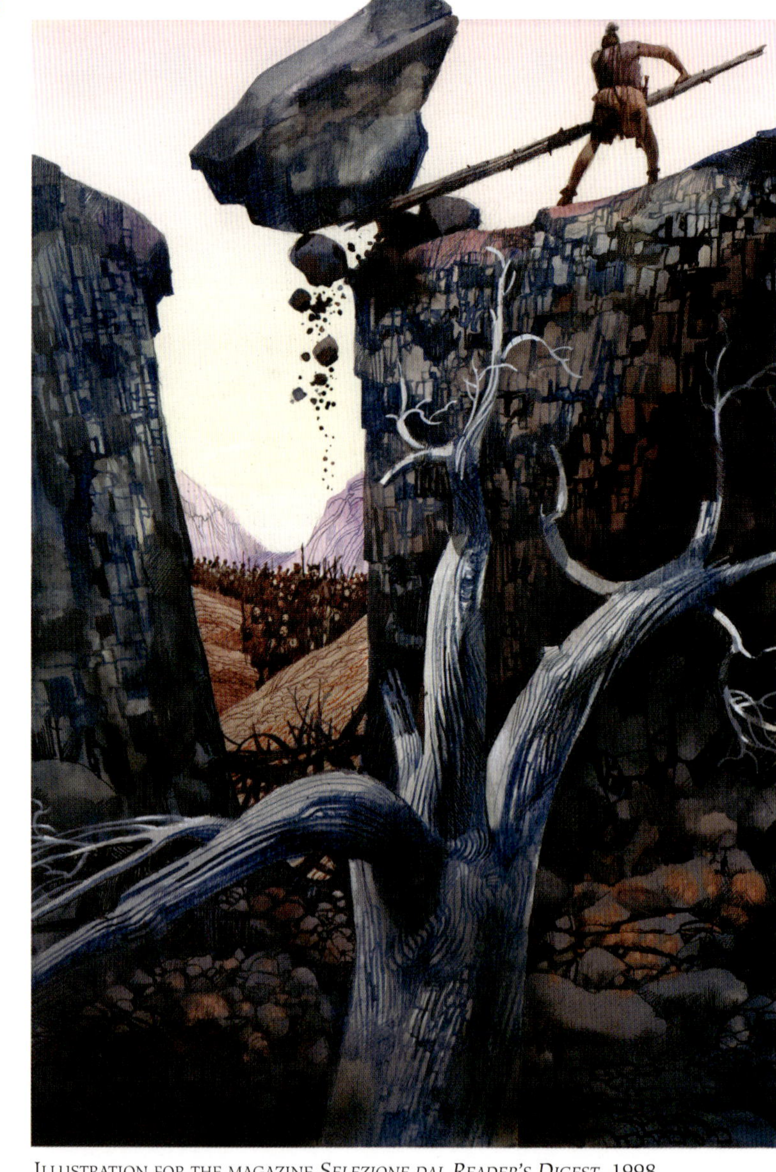

ILLUSTRATION FOR THE MAGAZINE *SELEZIONE DAL READER'S DIGEST*, 1998.

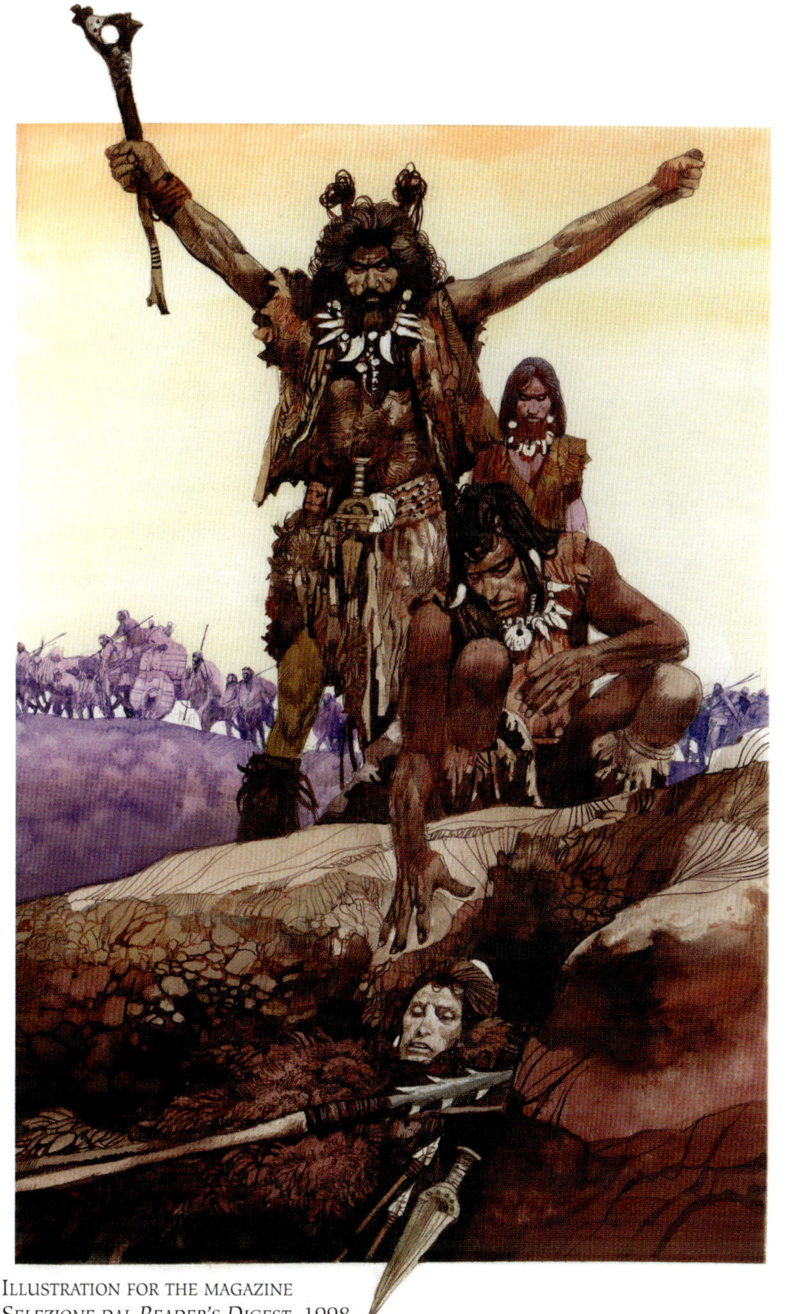

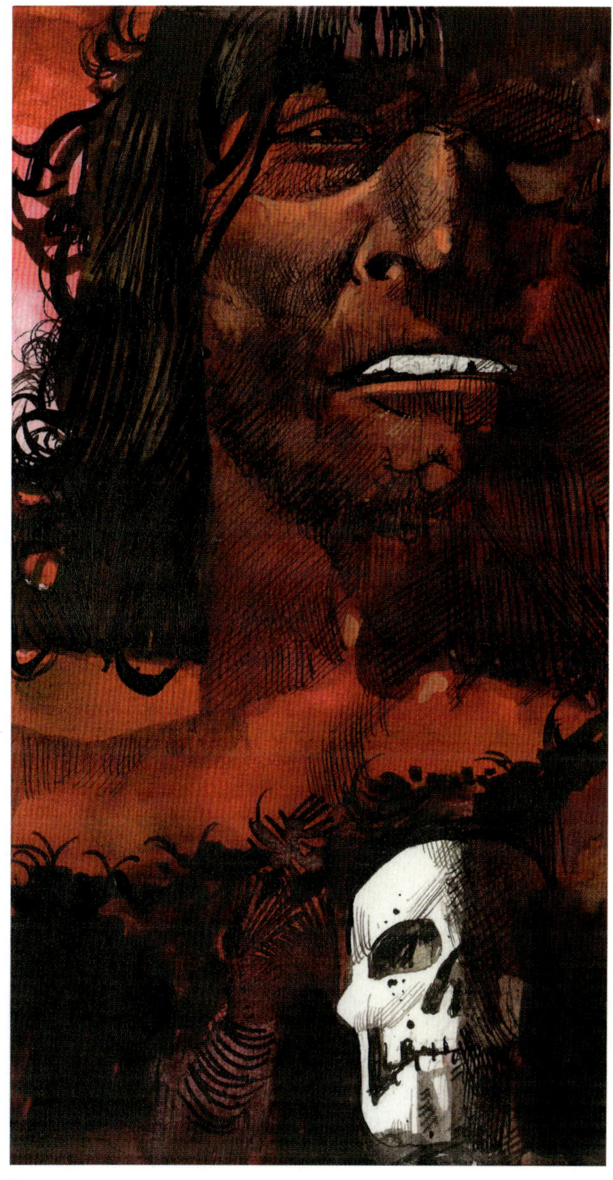

"Death shall make us immortal! Each of our deaths shall immortalize us all! When, a long time from now, in moons and moons, in seasons and seasons, when the sons of our sons, after generations and generations, find our skeletons resting in the ground, and the jade and onyx jewelry that adorn them, and our sepulchers laid out beneath stone slabs, transported by the living to honor the dead, then yes! When our distant descendants shall unearth our remains, they shall understand that they are dealing with the fathers of their fathers. They shall know that it was the anticipation of death that made men of us. And that it is death that keeps us alive forever."

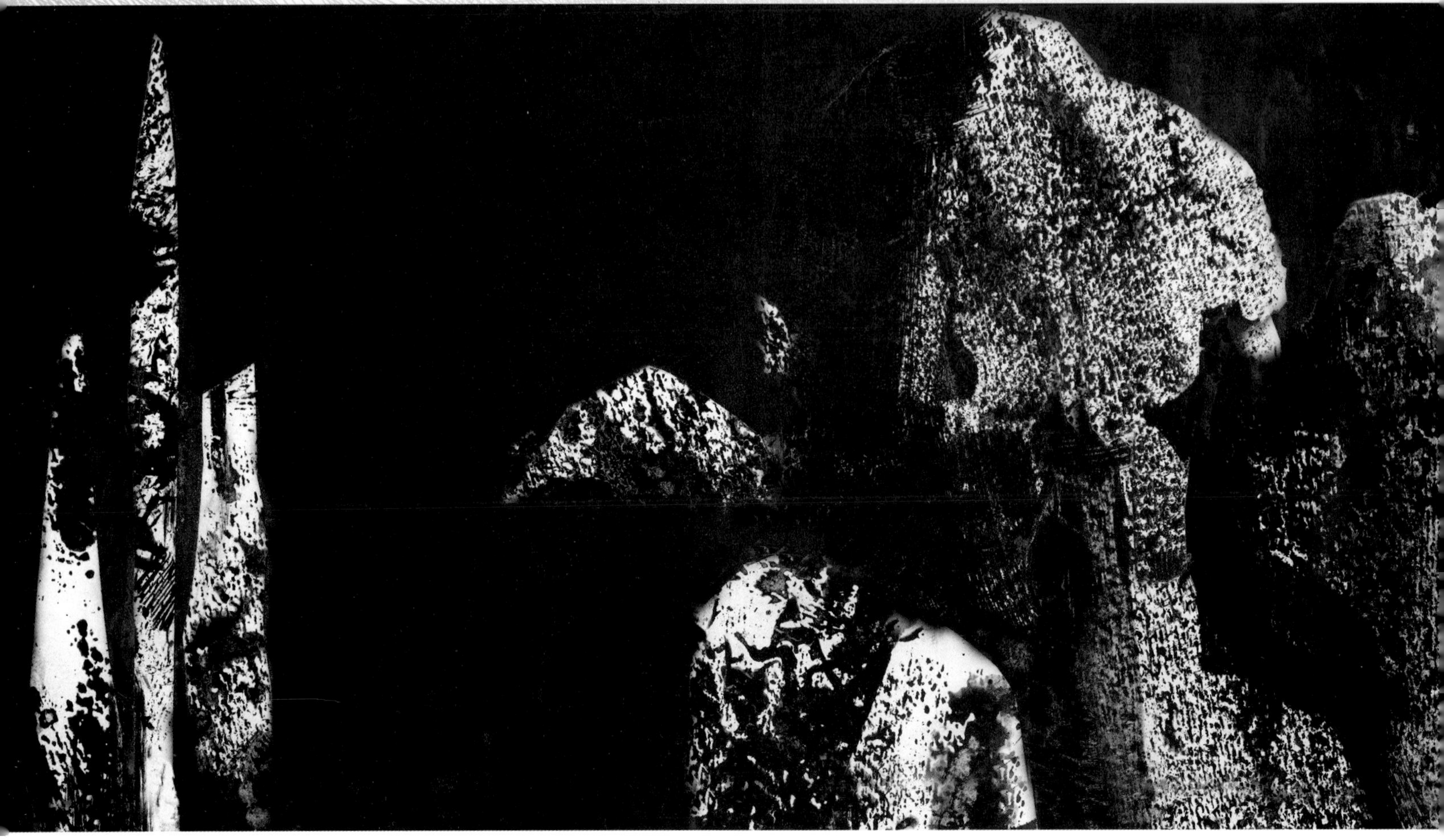

Mythical Times

Strange how that which does not exist is the same as that which does!
Our most extravagant fictions are nothing but pitiful plagiarisms of reality.
Our mythologies desperately resemble us.

And when inventing the gods of Olympus, men made them in their own image
while they were at it.

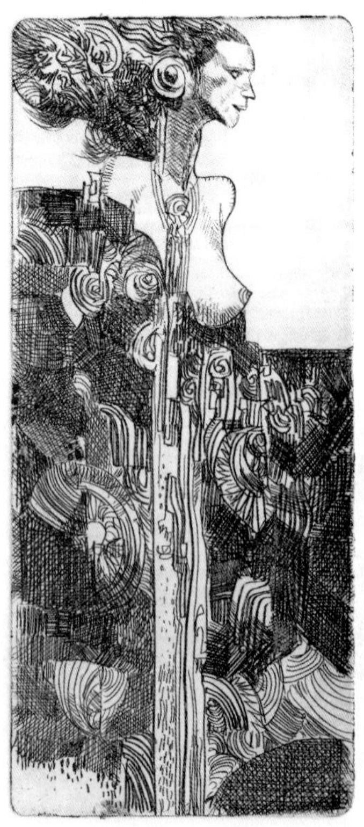

Unpublished illustrations on the theme of "falconers and flag-bearers", drawn in 2007

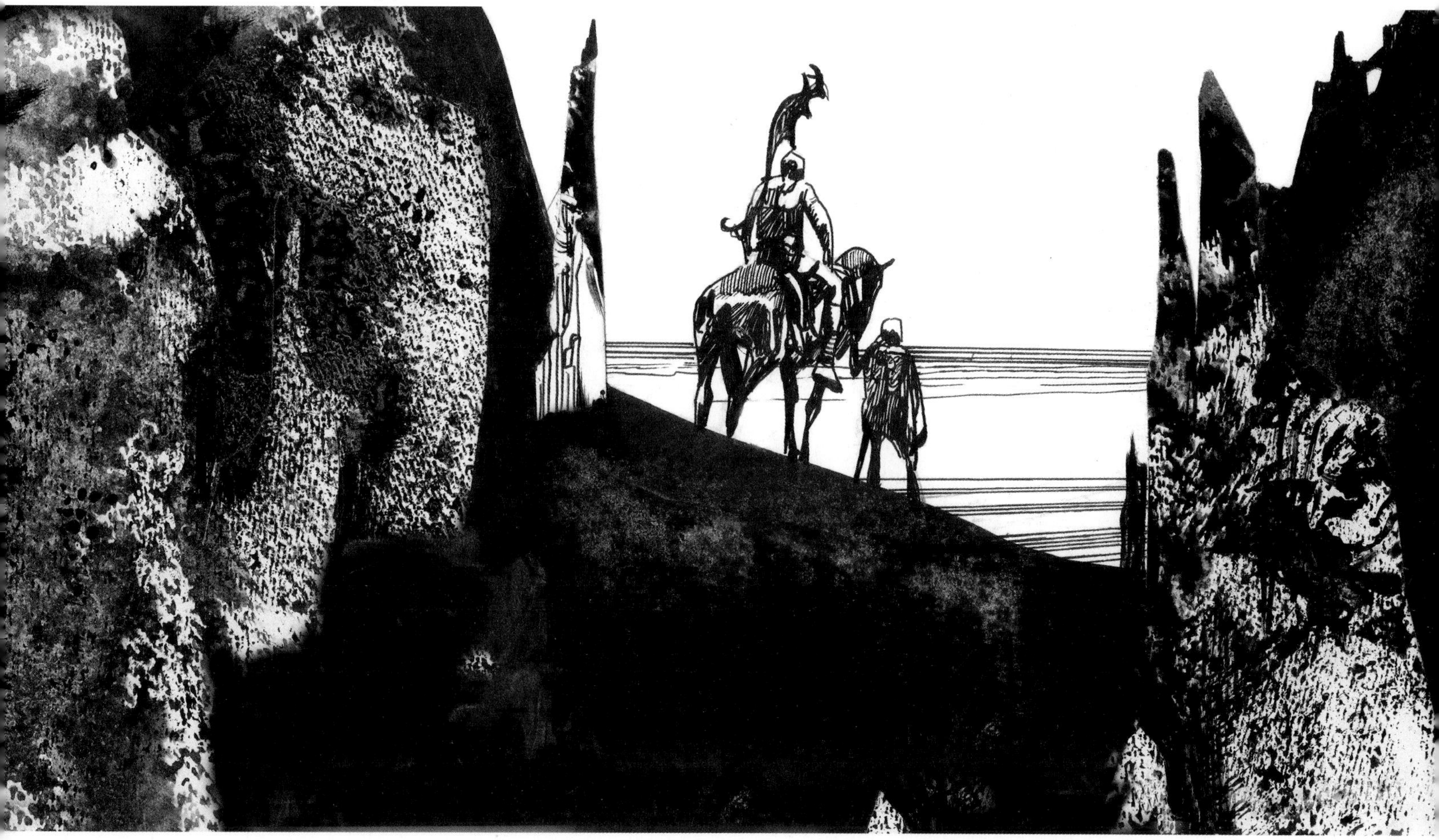

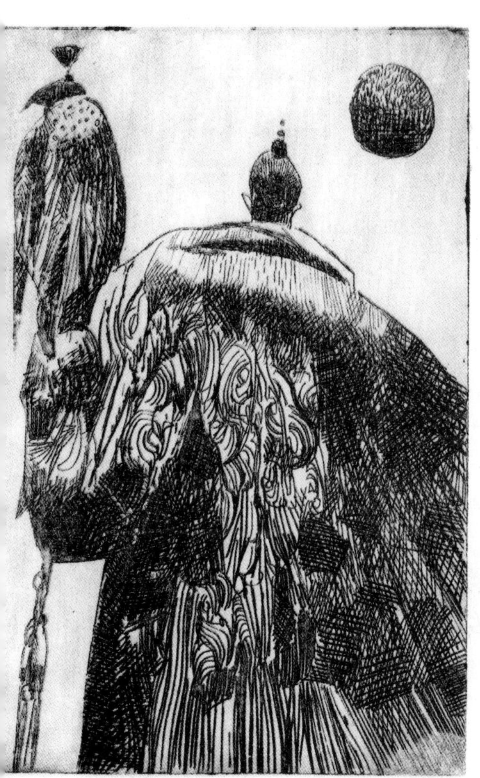

ILLUSTRATION FOR THE MAGAZINE *CORTO MALTESE*.

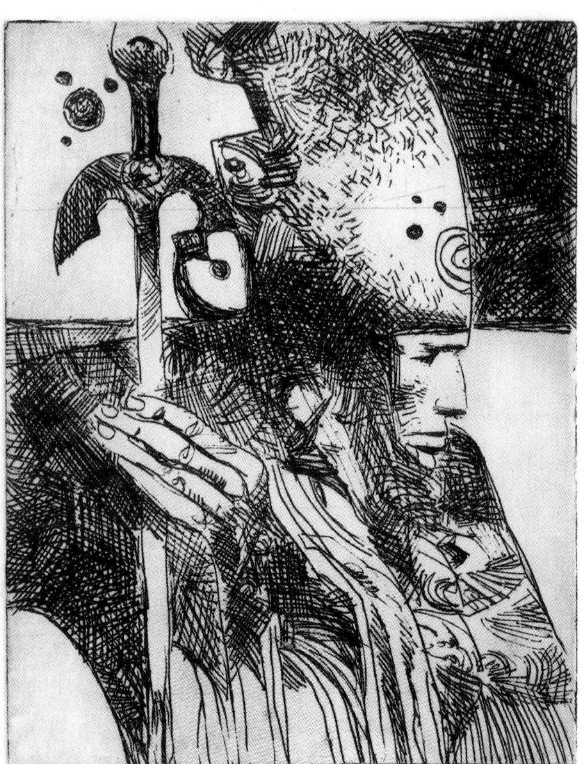

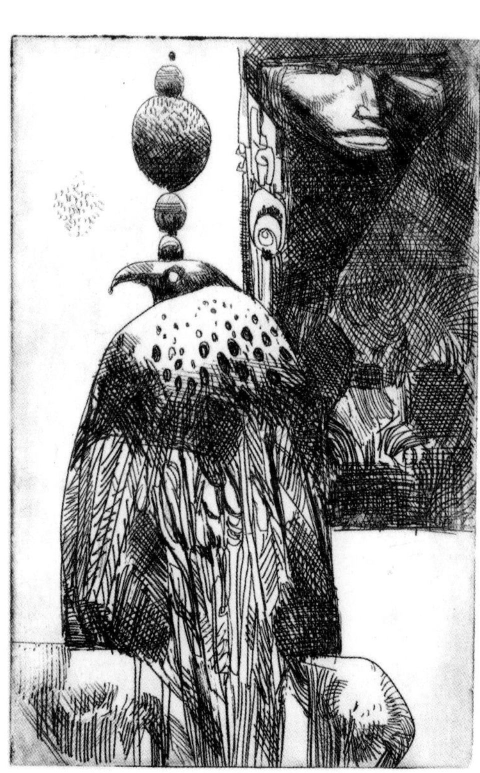

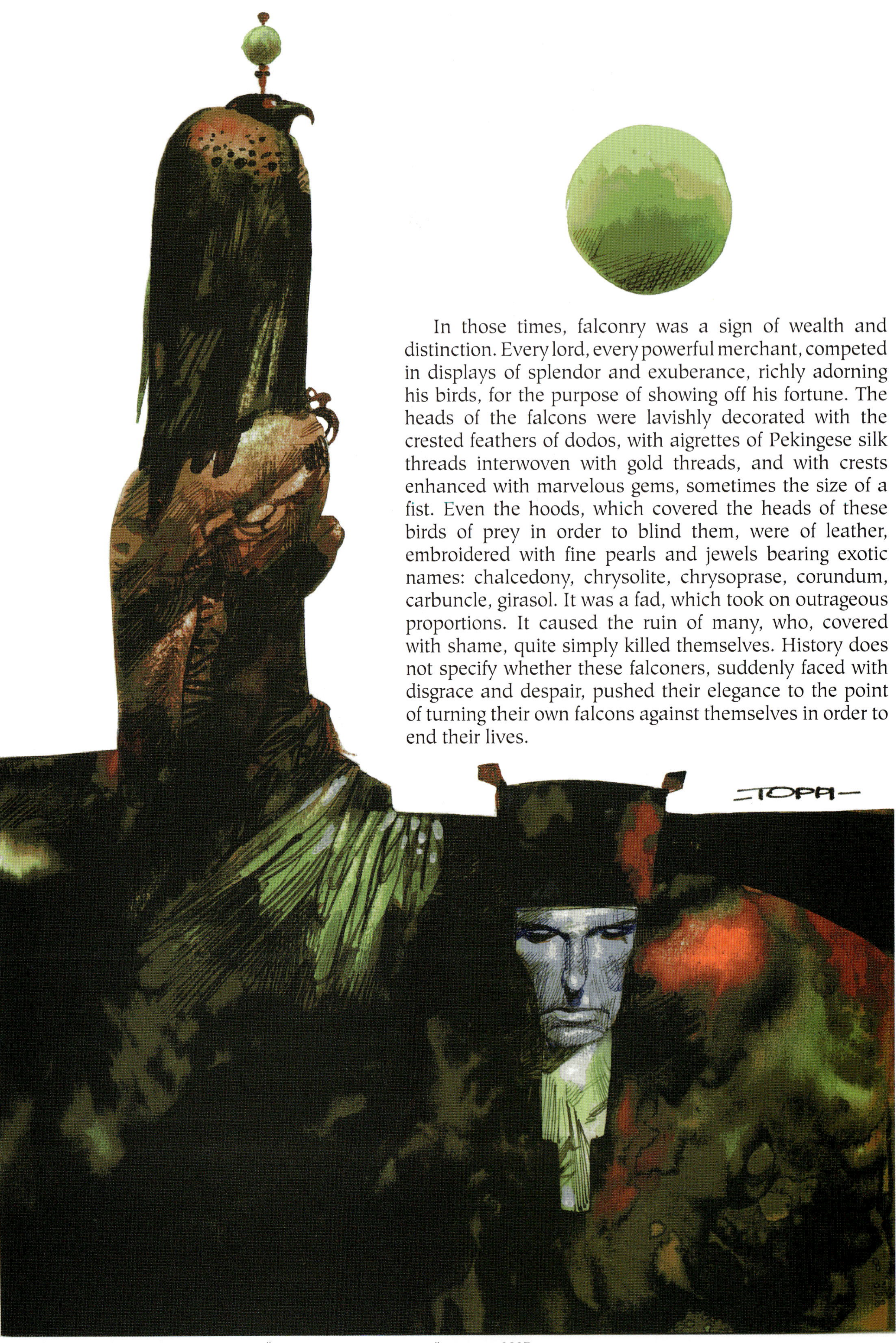

In those times, falconry was a sign of wealth and distinction. Every lord, every powerful merchant, competed in displays of splendor and exuberance, richly adorning his birds, for the purpose of showing off his fortune. The heads of the falcons were lavishly decorated with the crested feathers of dodos, with aigrettes of Pekingese silk threads interwoven with gold threads, and with crests enhanced with marvelous gems, sometimes the size of a fist. Even the hoods, which covered the heads of these birds of prey in order to blind them, were of leather, embroidered with fine pearls and jewels bearing exotic names: chalcedony, chrysolite, chrysoprase, corundum, carbuncle, girasol. It was a fad, which took on outrageous proportions. It caused the ruin of many, who, covered with shame, quite simply killed themselves. History does not specify whether these falconers, suddenly faced with disgrace and despair, pushed their elegance to the point of turning their own falcons against themselves in order to end their lives.

PAGES 16-22: VARIOUS PIECES ON THE THEME OF "FALCONERS AND FLAG-BEARERS," DRAWN IN 2007

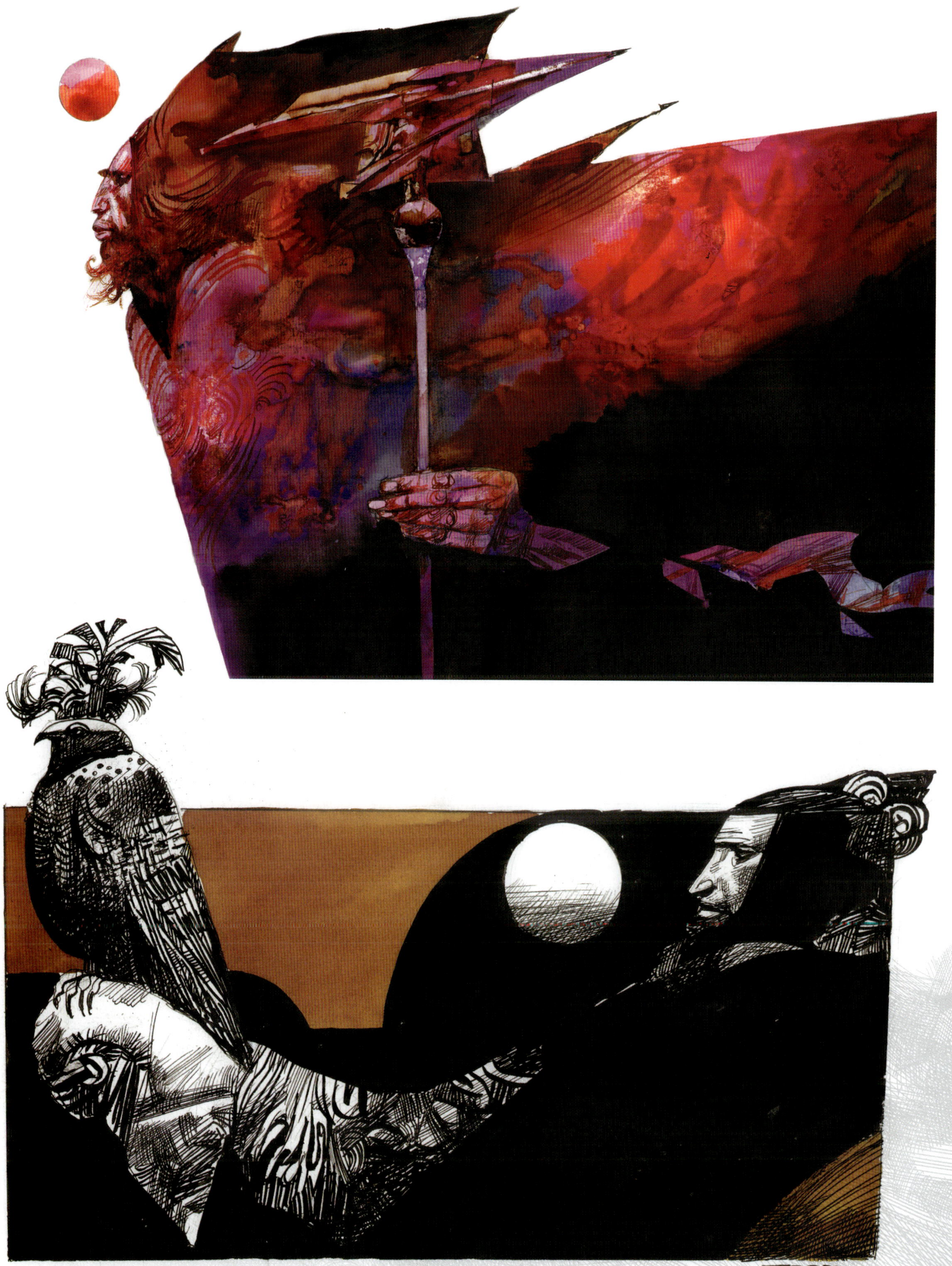

Bottom: Study for a silkscreen print intended for Mario Vigiak, end of the 1990s.

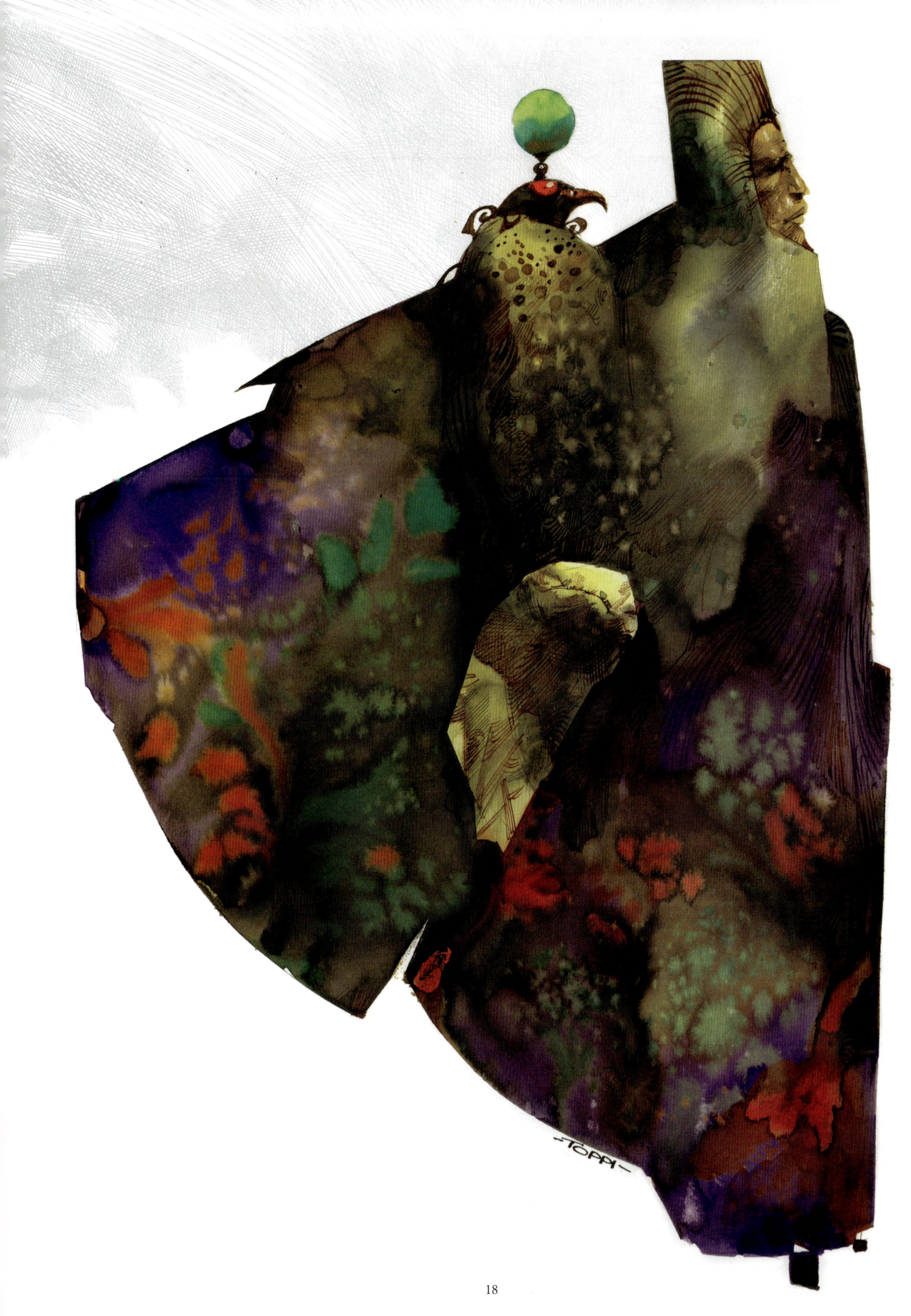

TOPPI

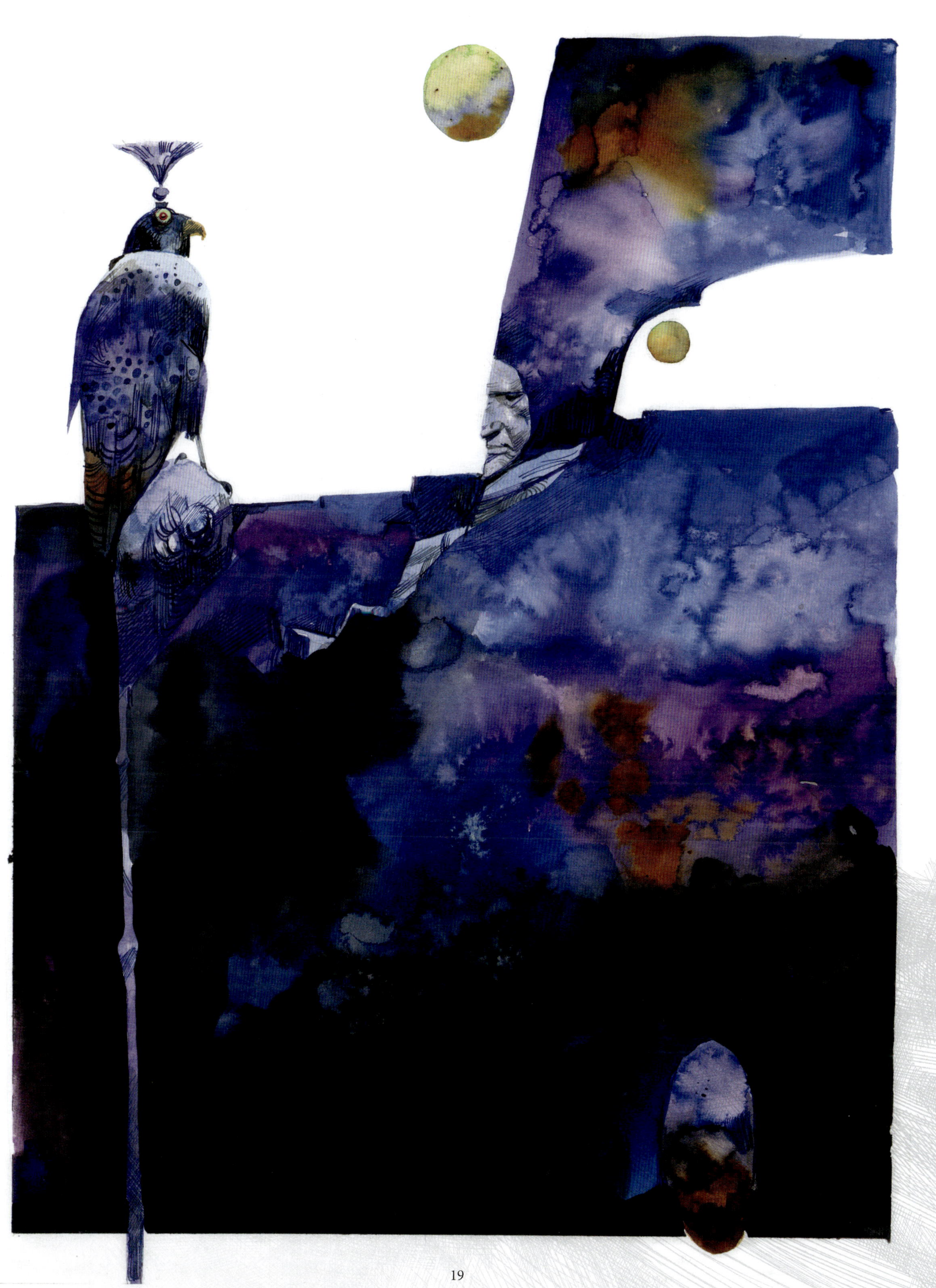

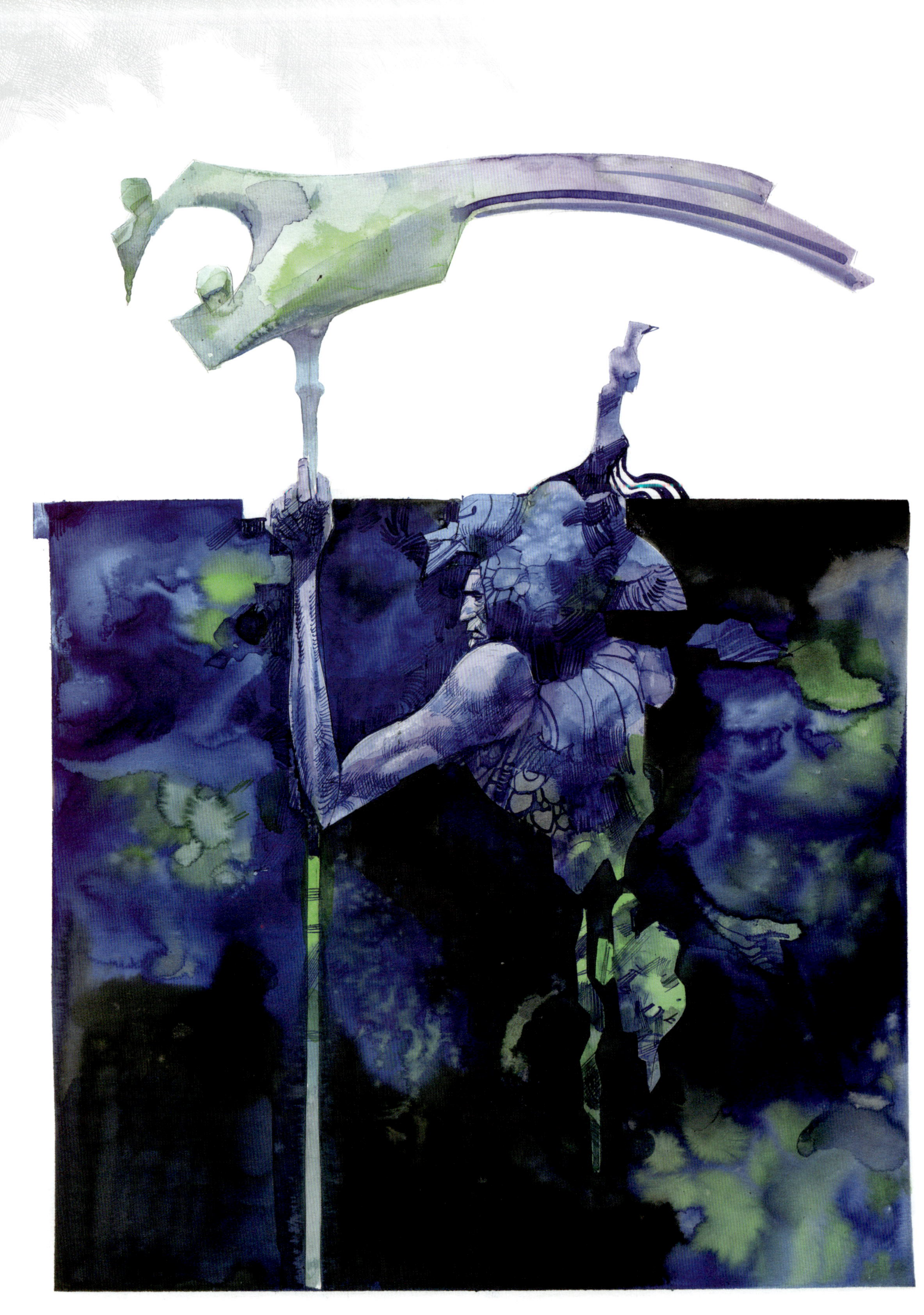

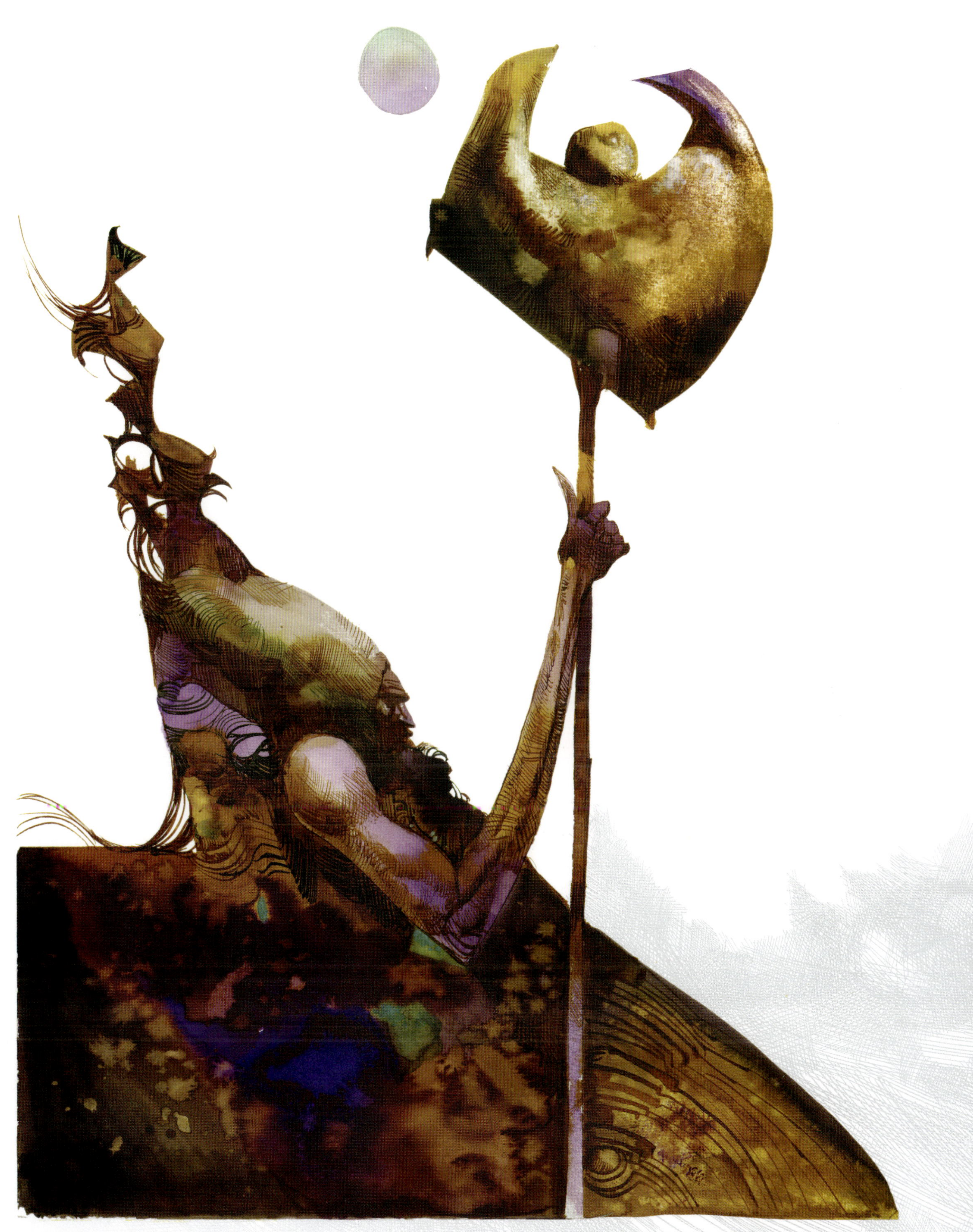

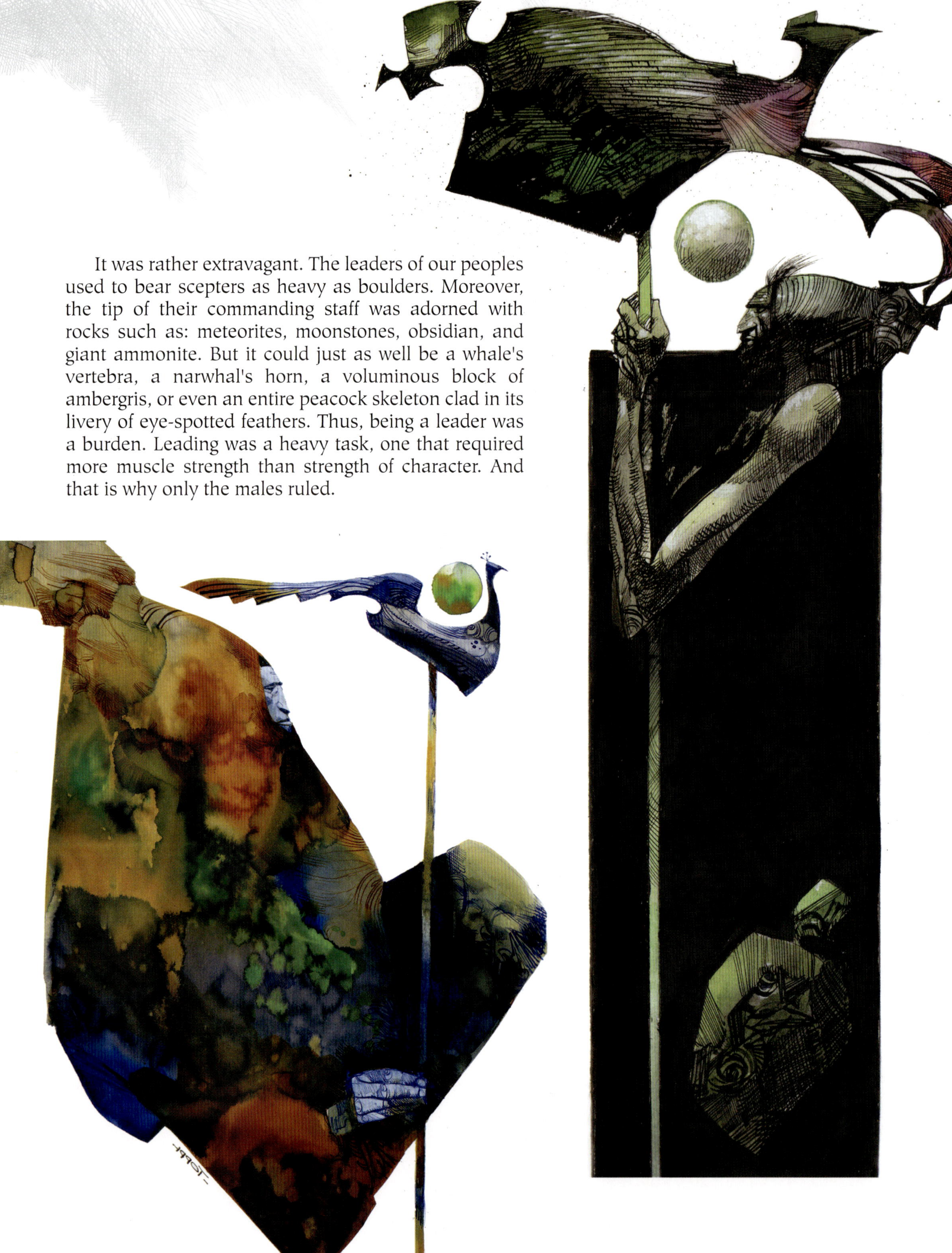

It was rather extravagant. The leaders of our peoples used to bear scepters as heavy as boulders. Moreover, the tip of their commanding staff was adorned with rocks such as: meteorites, moonstones, obsidian, and giant ammonite. But it could just as well be a whale's vertebra, a narwhal's horn, a voluminous block of ambergris, or even an entire peacock skeleton clad in its livery of eye-spotted feathers. Thus, being a leader was a burden. Leading was a heavy task, one that required more muscle strength than strength of character. And that is why only the males ruled.

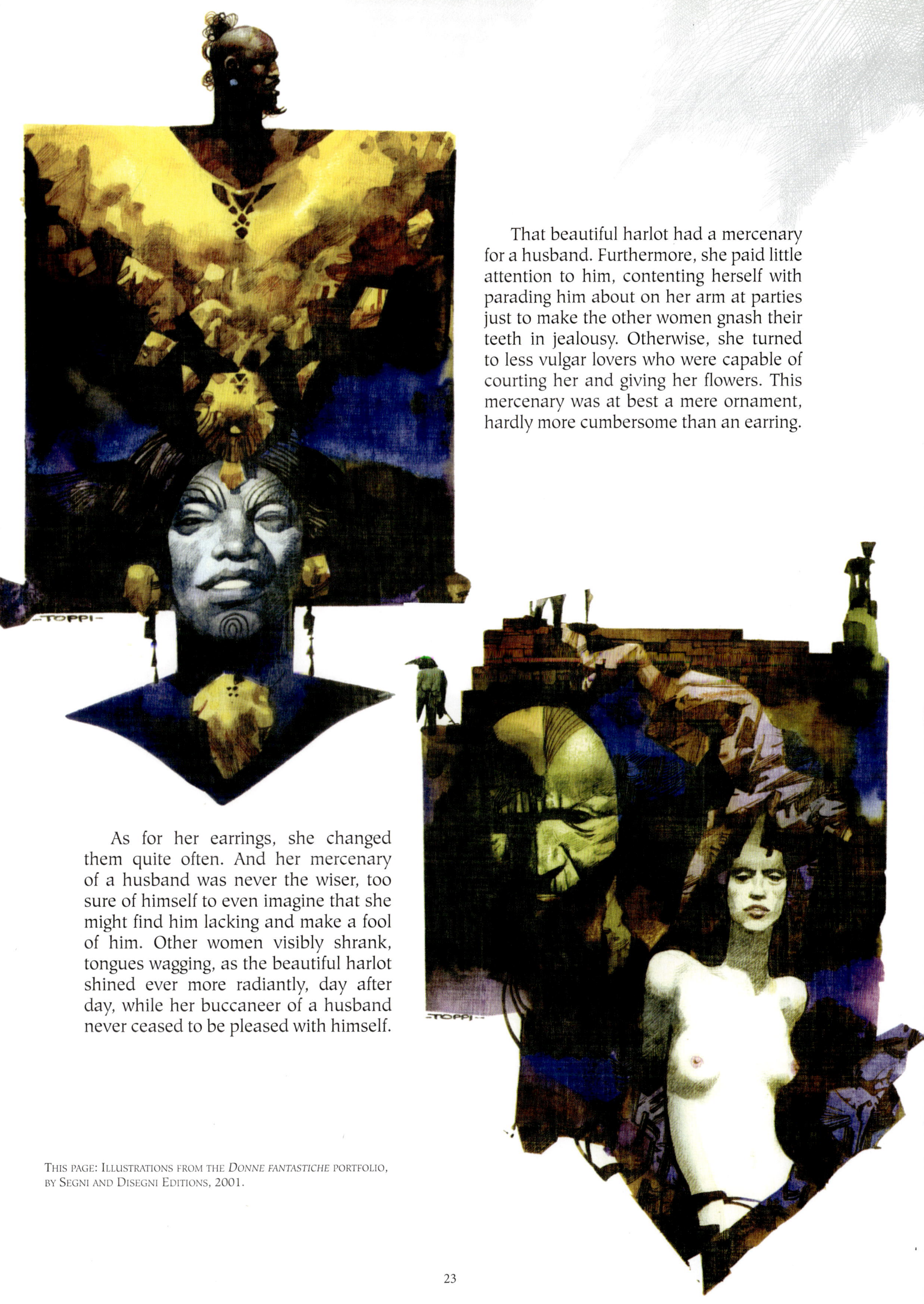

That beautiful harlot had a mercenary for a husband. Furthermore, she paid little attention to him, contenting herself with parading him about on her arm at parties just to make the other women gnash their teeth in jealousy. Otherwise, she turned to less vulgar lovers who were capable of courting her and giving her flowers. This mercenary was at best a mere ornament, hardly more cumbersome than an earring.

As for her earrings, she changed them quite often. And her mercenary of a husband was never the wiser, too sure of himself to even imagine that she might find him lacking and make a fool of him. Other women visibly shrank, tongues wagging, as the beautiful harlot shined ever more radiantly, day after day, while her buccaneer of a husband never ceased to be pleased with himself.

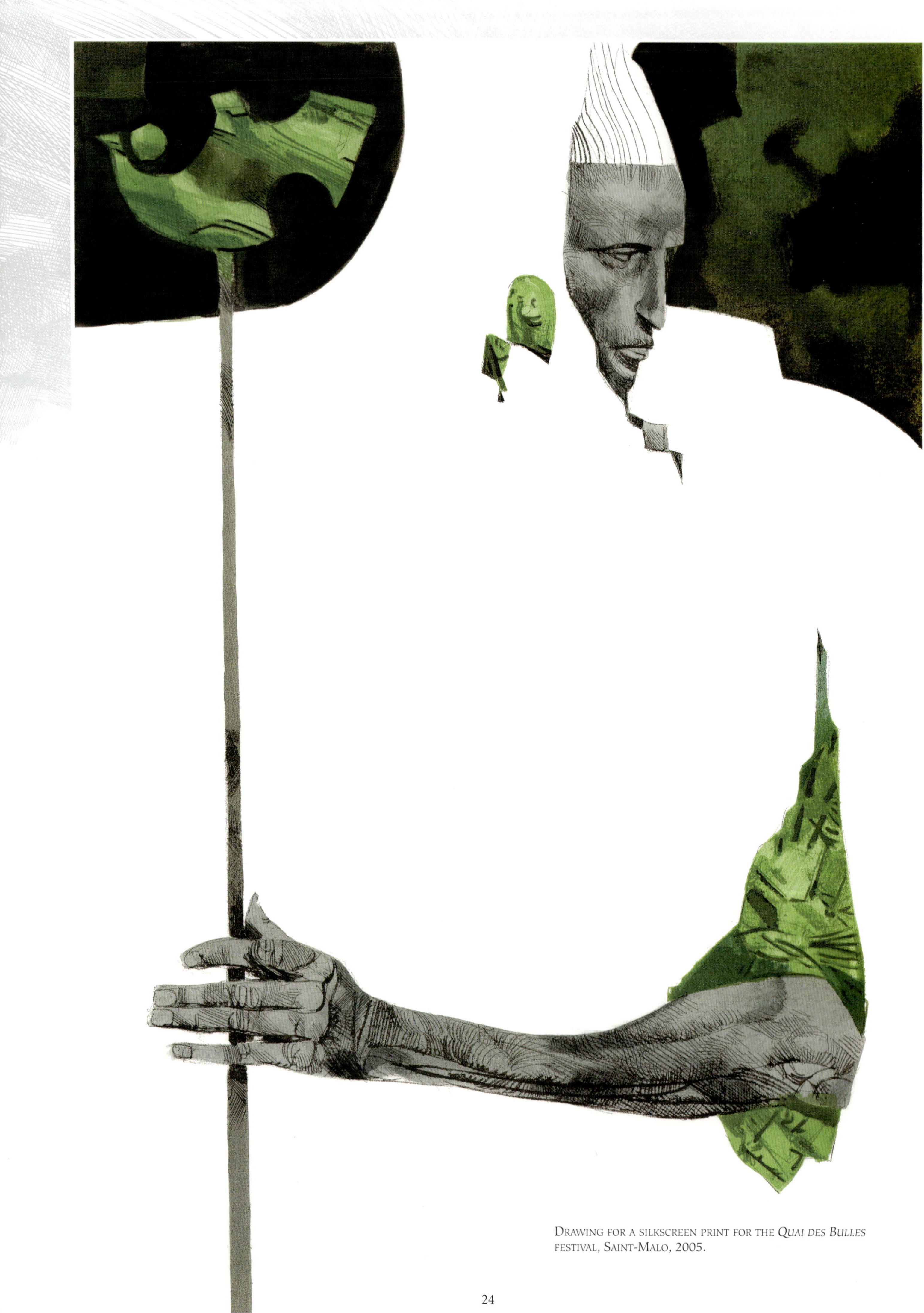

DRAWING FOR A SILKSCREEN PRINT FOR THE *Quai des Bulles*
FESTIVAL, SAINT-MALO, 2005.

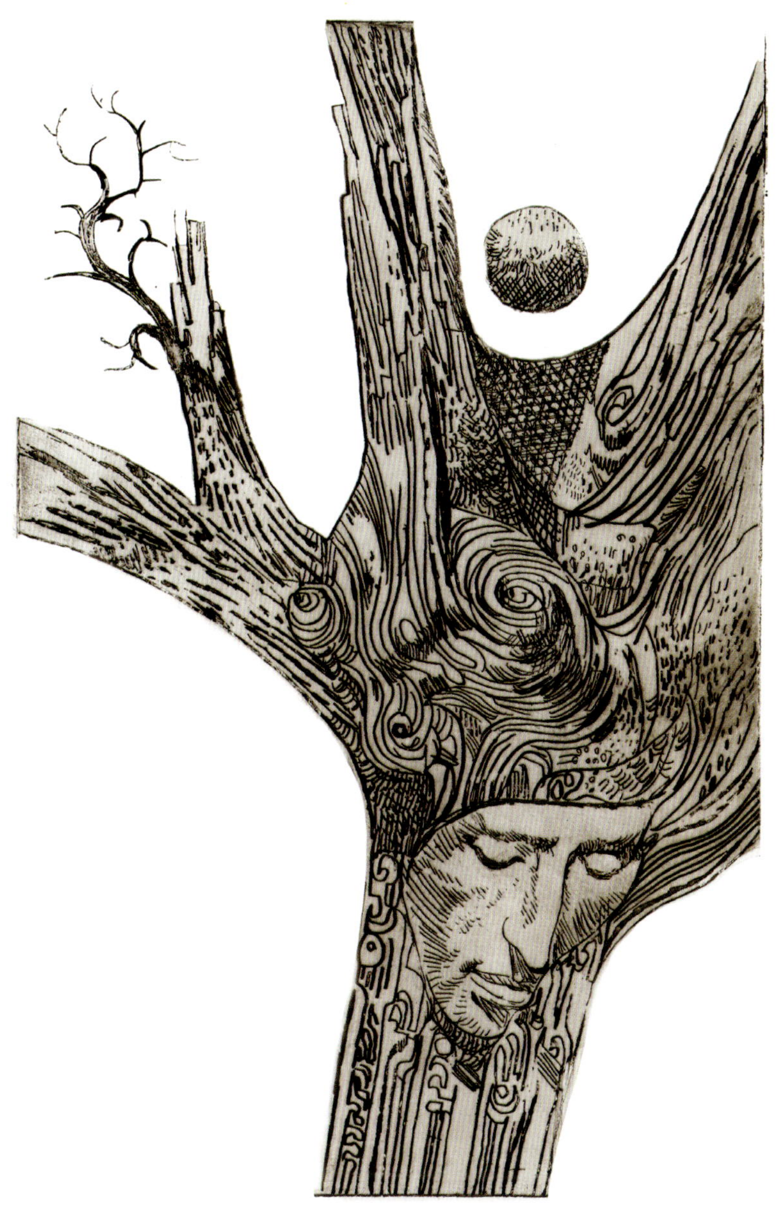

Was it his rugged disposition? Or his cracked skin? He made one think of tree bark. They called him the "Tree Man." They could have easily nicknamed him "stumpy" or "old wood"; but he was a touchy one… So people settled for that somewhat evasive sobriquet, neither too offensive nor overly familiar. Whenever he heard his nickname, some jokers would claim he'd "shake like a leaf." They would come to regret it; they can still recall the thrashing that ensued. He was quite imposing: he carried himself majestically. He moved little and seemed to have always been there. The older ones, however, claimed he wasn't from around here. Cowards came to the conclusion that he was from nowhere. "A tree without roots," they would cruelly whisper. Having become something of a philosopher, the tree man let them talk. For too long, perhaps. One day, he hung himself. From the highest branch of another tree.

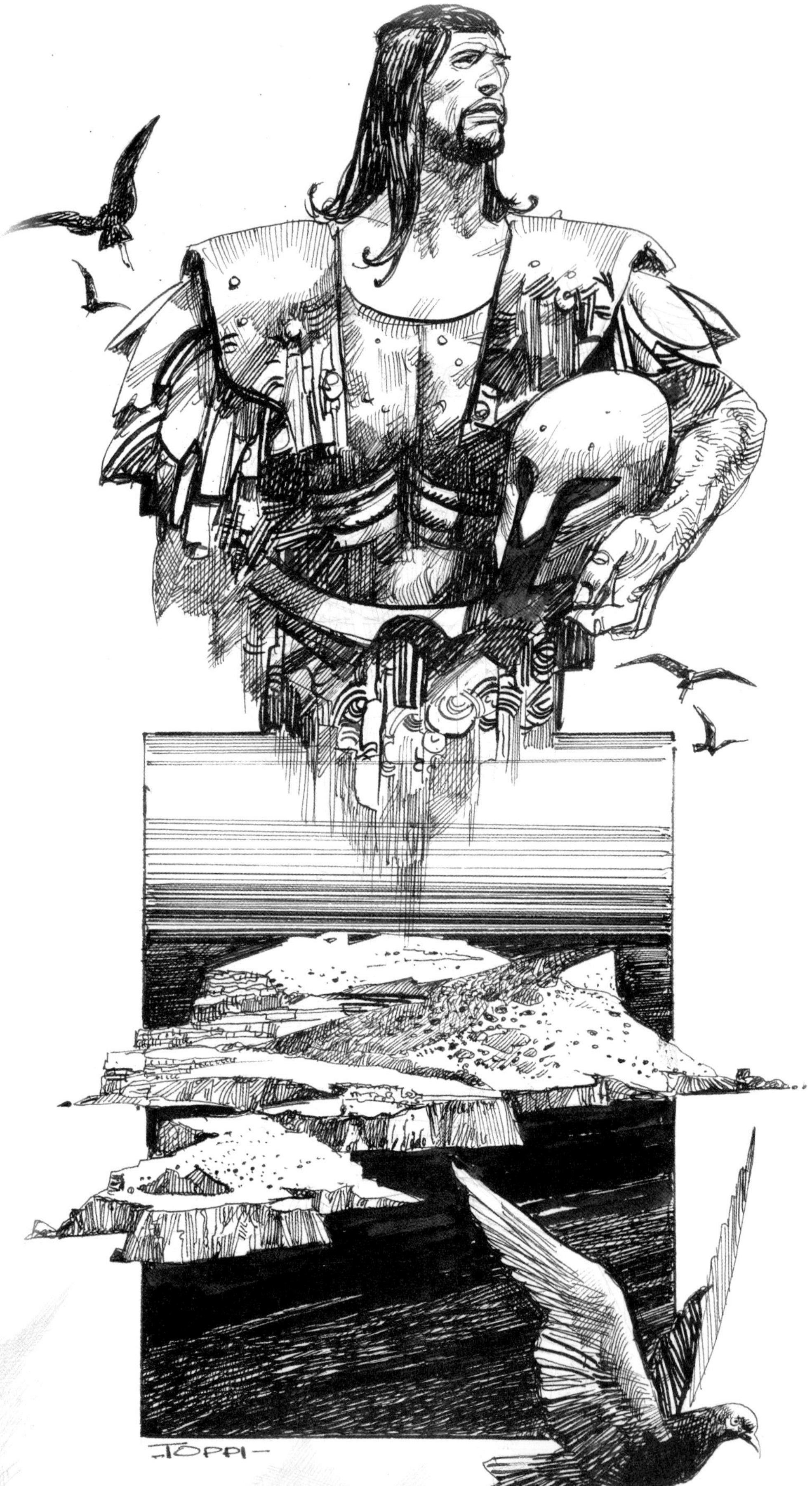

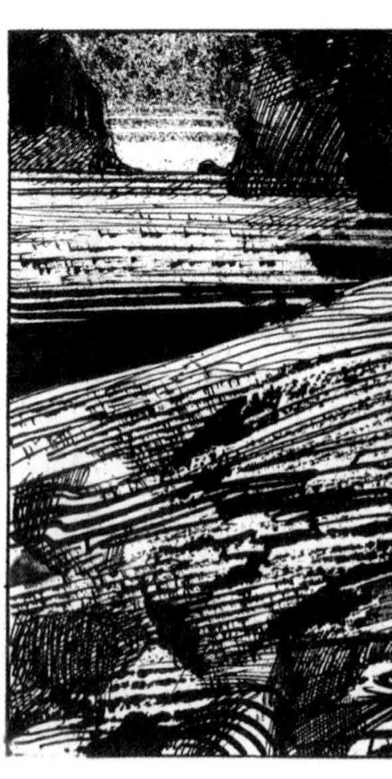

Illustration drawn for the Region of
Salento, an homage to Diomedes.

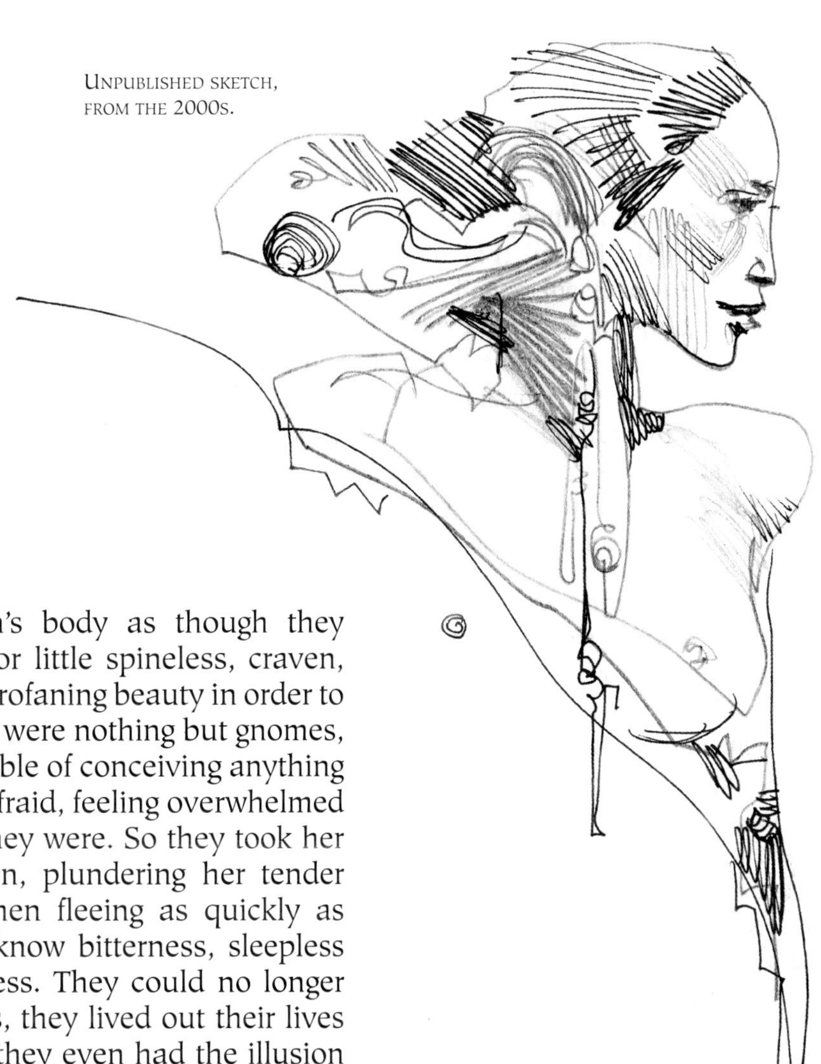

They fell upon the woman's body as though they were on conquered ground. Poor little spineless, craven, pusillanimous men, reduced to profaning beauty in order to believe themselves heroes! They were nothing but gnomes, counterfeit and cowardly, incapable of conceiving anything beyond themselves. They were afraid, feeling overwhelmed by someone more fragile than they were. So they took her together, trampling her soft skin, plundering her tender flesh, discharging their seed, then fleeing as quickly as possible. They would come to know bitterness, sleepless nights, alcohol-induced numbness. They could no longer feel themselves; but nonetheless, they lived out their lives as respectable fathers. Perhaps they even had the illusion of being worthy, while in reality they were only pathetic. Someone more fragile than they were had definitively overwhelmed them.

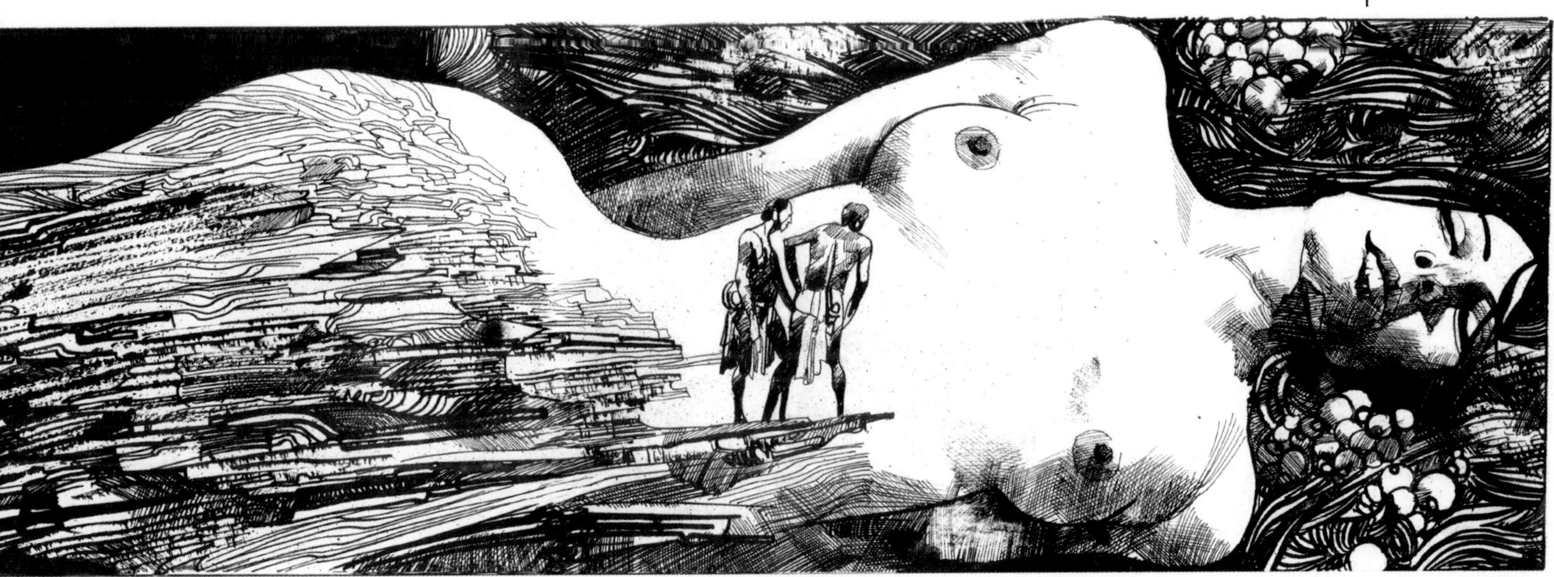

Illustration for a story written by Lucien de Samosate in the magazine *Corto Maltese*, no.7, 1984

A Few Barbarians

The ancient Greeks invented the term "barbarian" to designate those peoples whose language they could not understand. The word "barbarian" quite simply means "stranger".

Montaigne wrote defining words on the subject:
"Each man calls barbarism whatever is not his own practice."

Duly noted.

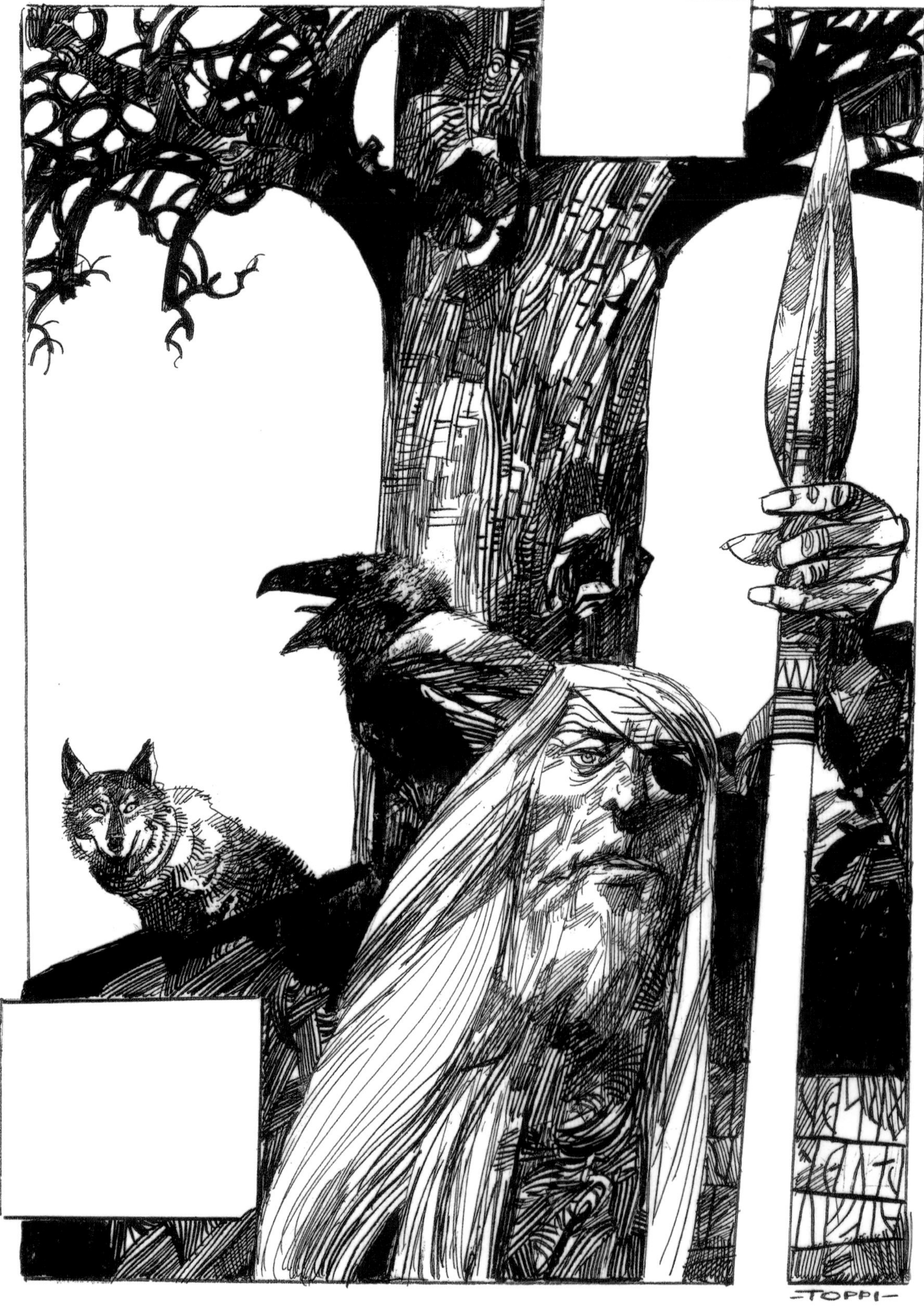

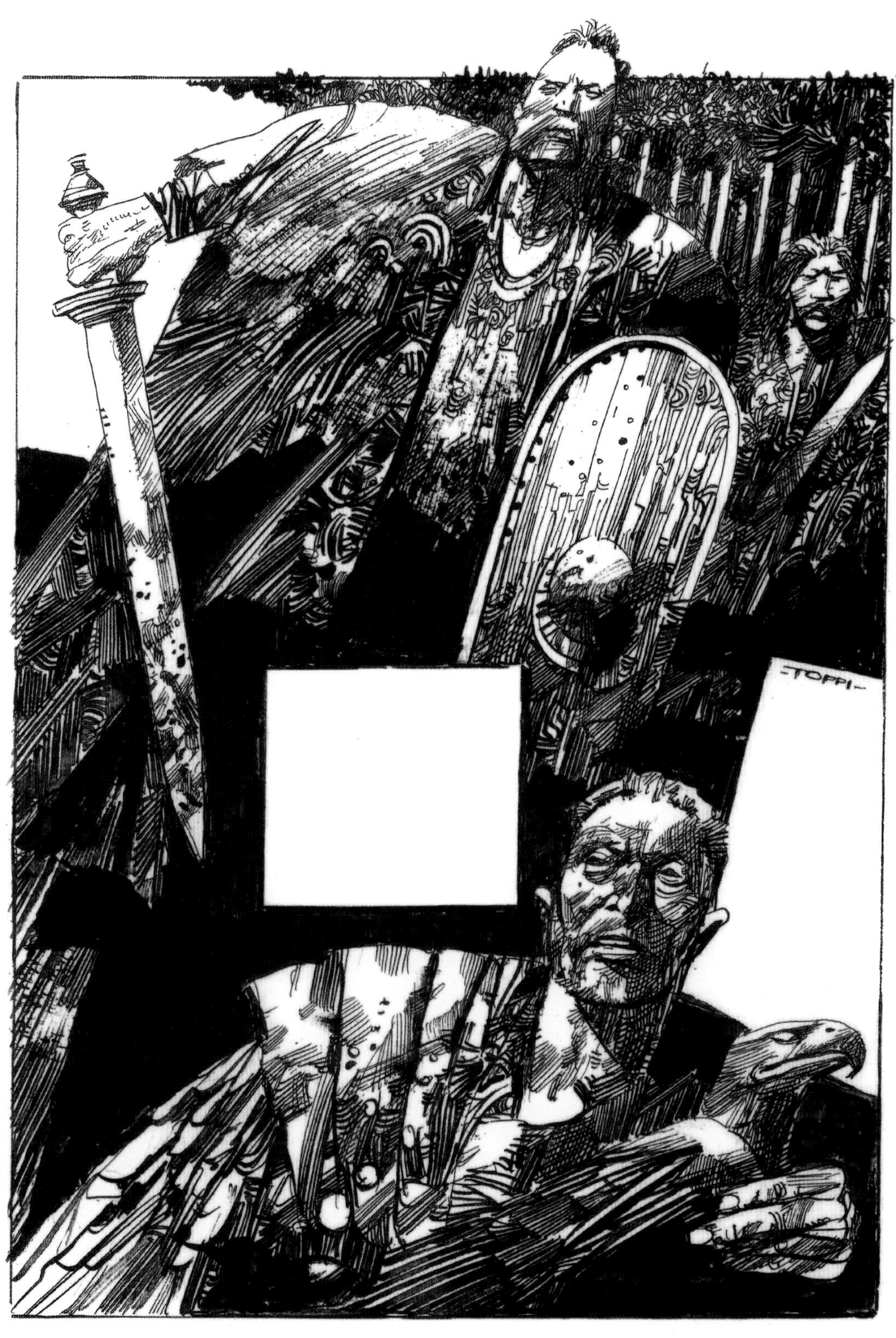

We called them the Sylvans, for they had come through the forest to reach the village. They had the pallid skin and dilated eyes of those who lurk in shadow. Their footsteps were heavy, they bore long coats, heavy swords, and gyrfalcons as their pets. They spoke little, staying for the most part at the edge of the woods staring at the horizon as a sailor surveys the ocean. They were not from around here; they were not here to stay. Once they had plundered our food reserves and regained their strength, they set off once more, but not without first taking time to carefully set fire to our homes. The Sylvans once more entered the forest and returned forever to the darkness of our legends, where they never should have left in the first place.

Pages 28 to 34:
Illustrations for the *Teutoburgo* portfolio, which tells of the defeat of the Roman legions of Varus in the forest of Teutoburg in 9 A.D. Portfolio published in Lucca by Angelo Nencetti in 2006.

"They cried wolf. So I became what they said. I was a wolf — to prove them right. They called me 'barbarian' so I became a complete stranger — a stranger to their reasons. They called me a savage, so I proved them right. I became a wild beast: constant in my savagery, impartial in my cruelty.

Predator by necessity, as all carnivorous animals are. But without hate, without spite. A criminal with equanimity."

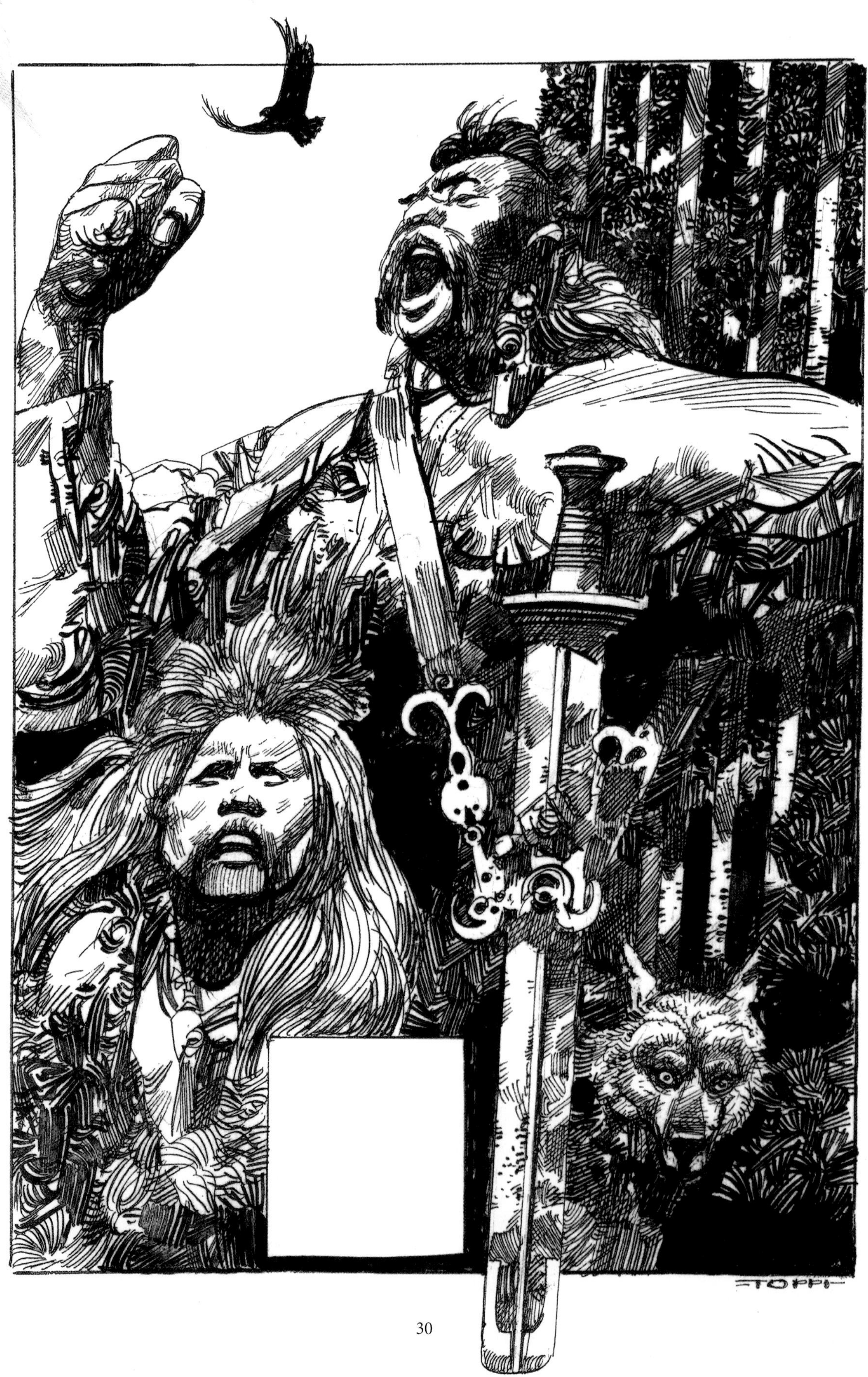

When the legionnaire first spied him, he had a crow perched on his head and an amulet suspended by a thread from the tips of his fingers. The legionnaire was not particularly moved, calmly throwing his spear, which cleanly pierced the old fool's belly. What happened next was beyond understanding: the old man's corpse swiftly transformed into a pile of precious stones. The legionnaire seized the heavy jewel and gave thanks to his blessed spear, which, with a single throw, had made him rich. Had he lived a few centuries later, he could have named a fable after it. The body beautiful and the lucky pilum.

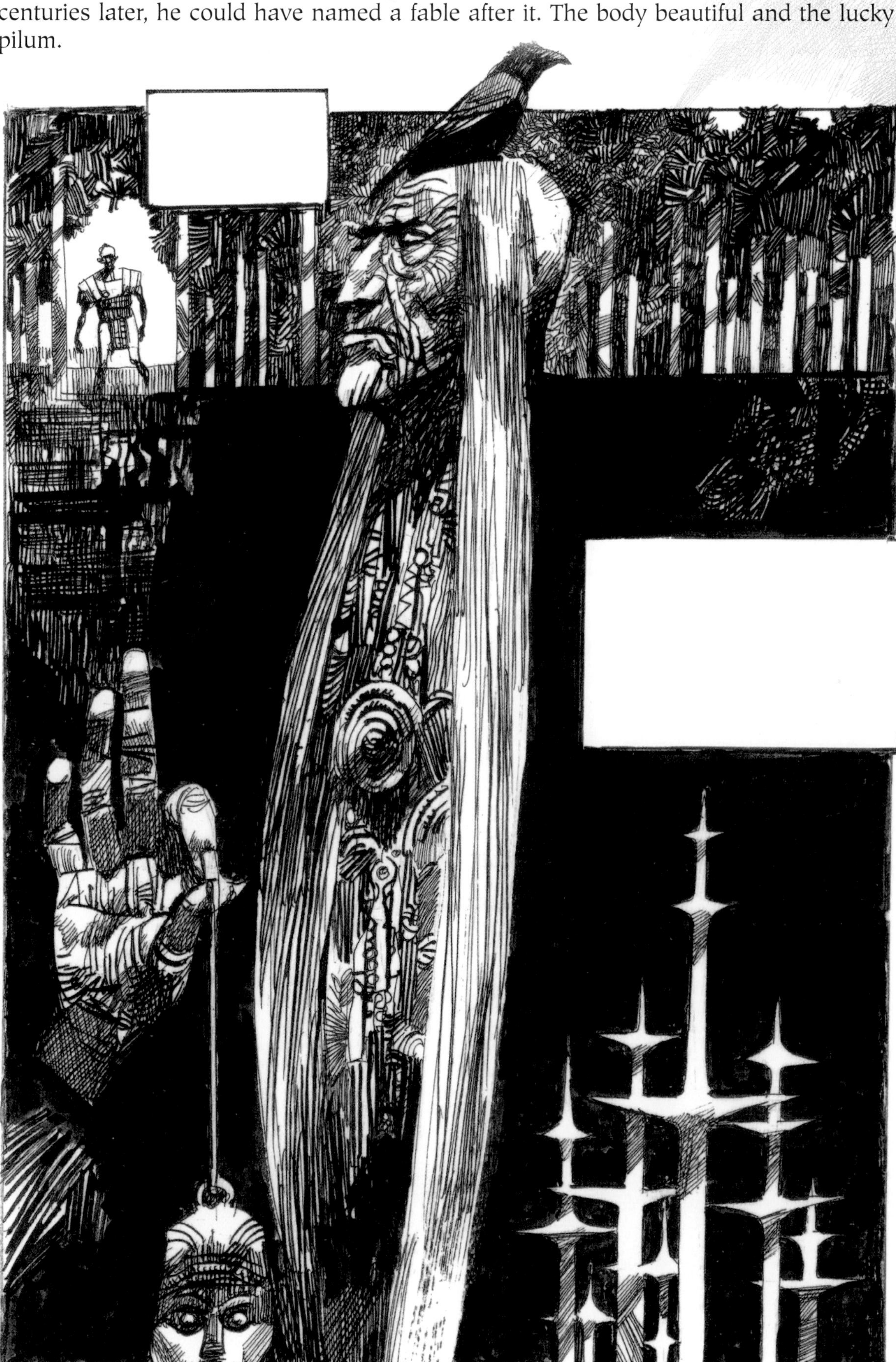

We hadn't even been dead four hours when we saw a half-naked young woman approach. At first, we believed her to be a kind of vanguard for the Valkyries, although we found the absence of a horse somewhat intriguing. But our amazement reached its peak when we realized that she was not alone. We were upset (although the onset of rigor mortis would hardly have allowed us to express our surprise): Odin himself had descended to earth in order to render tribute to two brave warriors who had perished with weapons in hand!

But the rest of the scene took a completely unexpected turn: Odin and his Valkyrie rushed to each other, tore their clothes off, and rolled about in the grass like lunatics. Gods fornicating so close to our corpses! Then they got up, straightened their clothes, and walked away laughing to return to the path, without ever realizing that we were there and that we had seen everything.

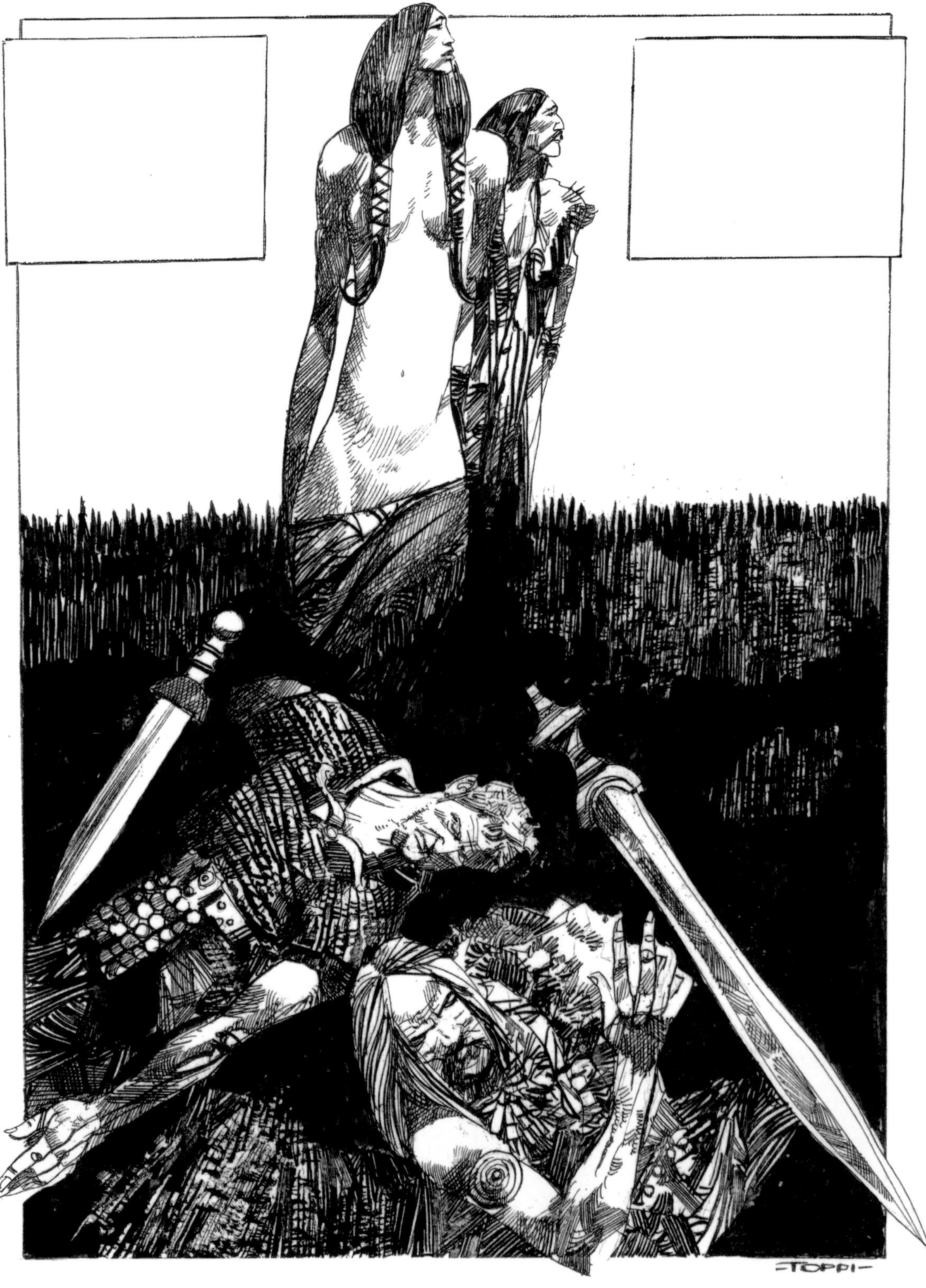

He was an aggressive fighter, as uncontrollable as a mad dog. He would invoke Odin with every breath and would daydream aloud about going to Valhalla. It became quite tedious after a while. But that day, in the midst of the fray, he suddenly exclaimed that the Valkyries were coming for him. Overcome by emotion, he forgot to fight. His enemies, who saw no naked woman mounted on a flying horse, were not so easily taken in, and, believing the poor devil to be frozen in fear, dealt him a fatal sword stroke in the back. Though vigorous and valiant, he immediately expired. Right away, the Valkyries swept him away and carried him to the paradise of warriors where only the dead have the right to feast. He shall soon be able to eat to his heart's content.

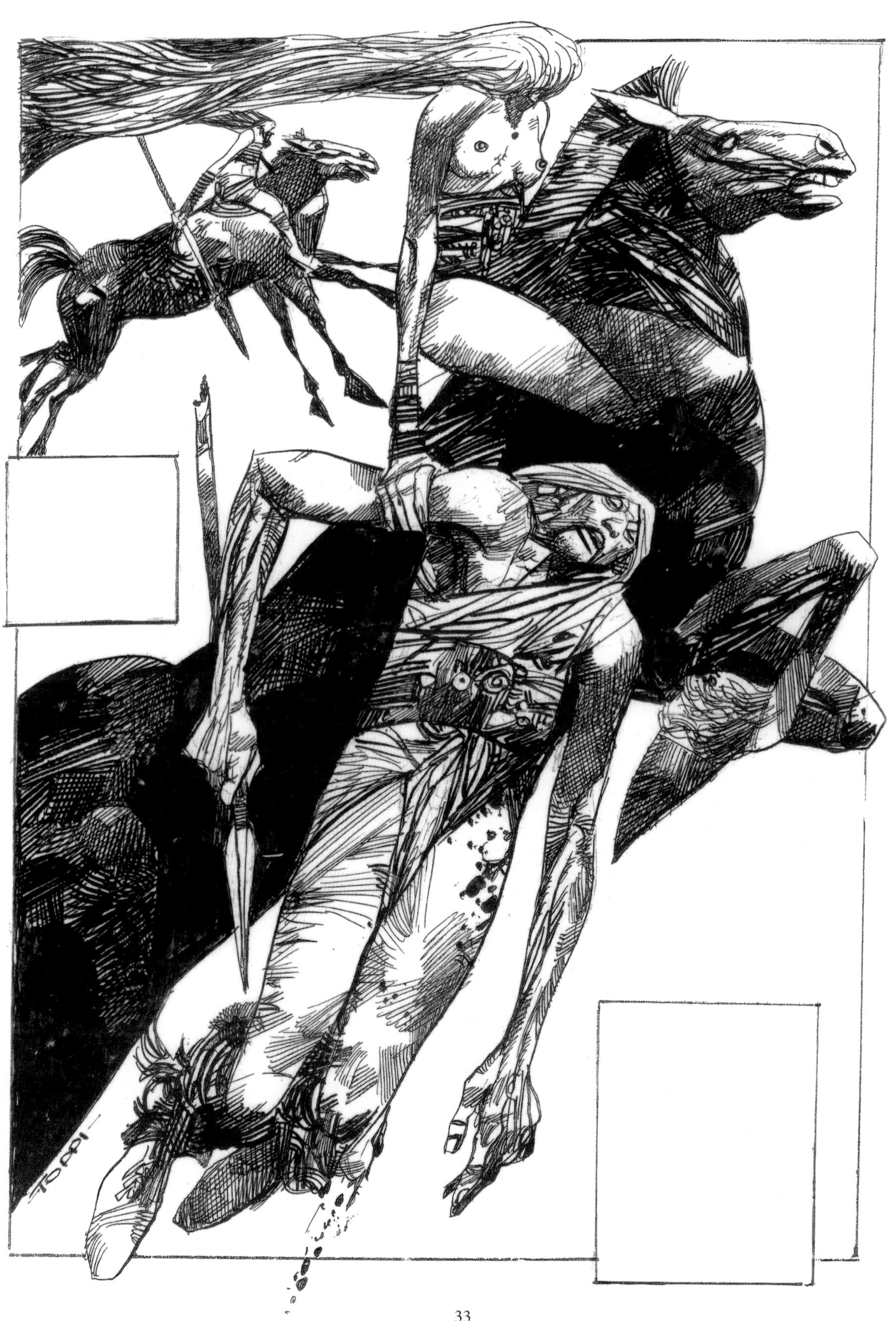

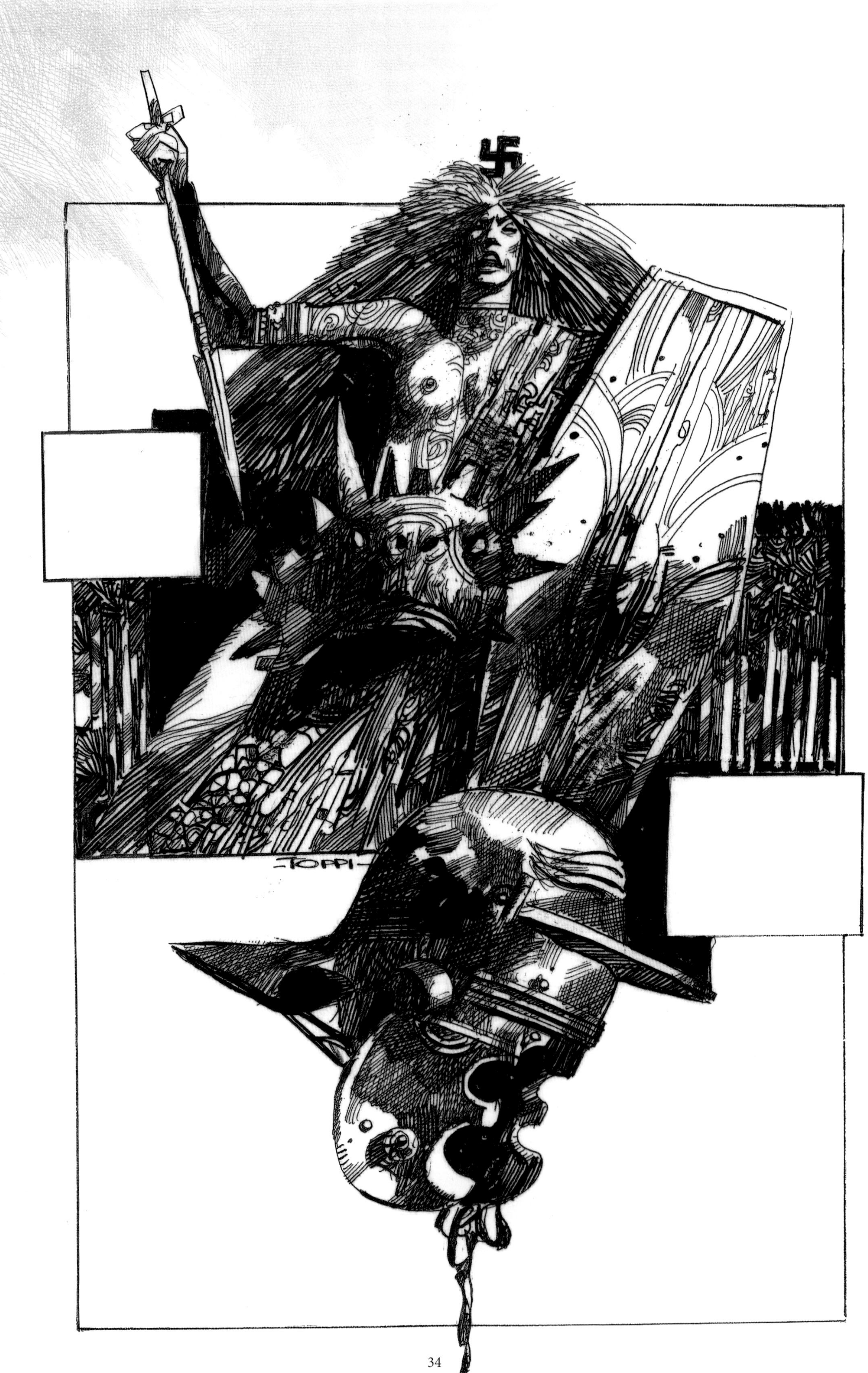

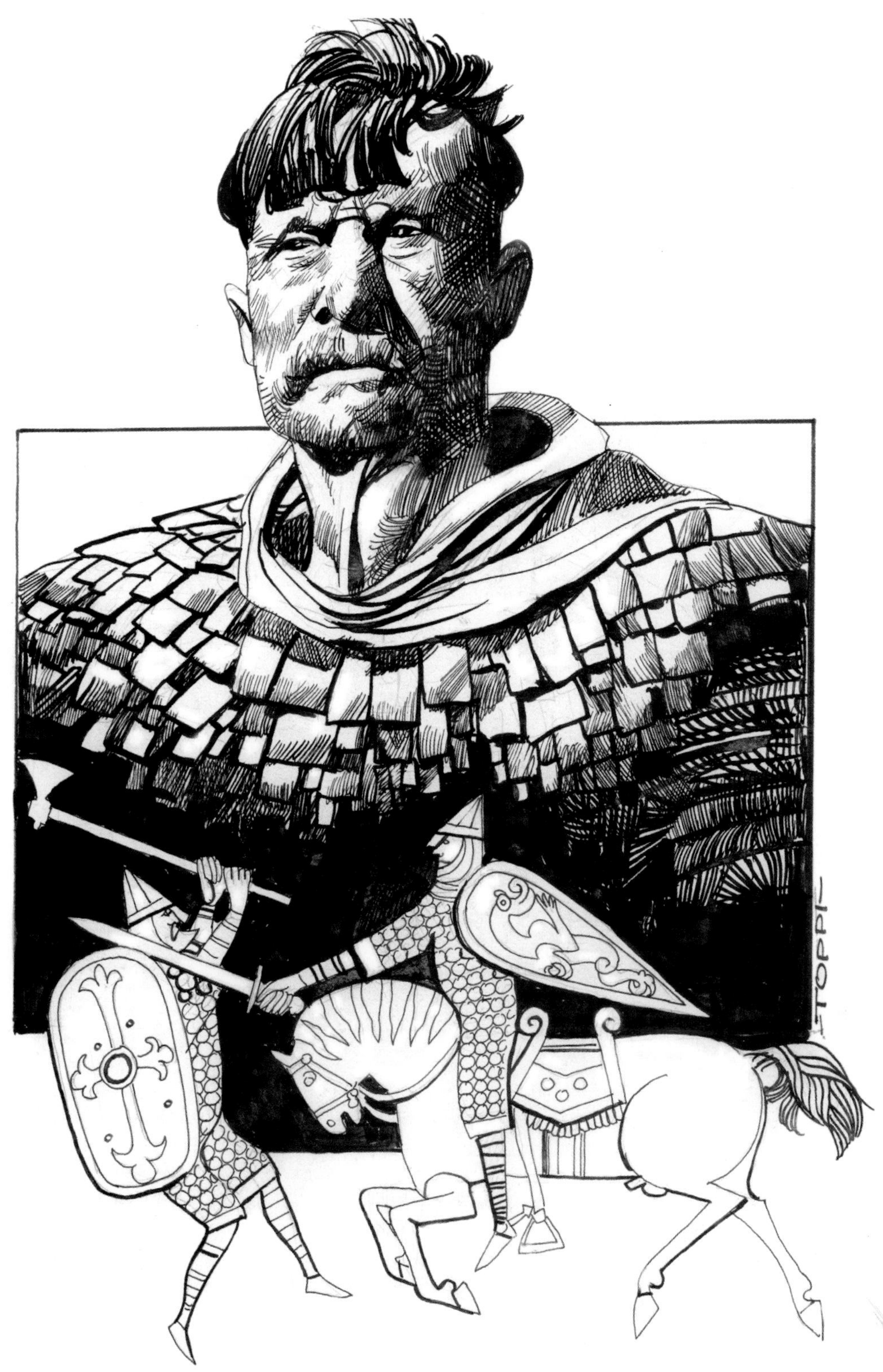

A Few Cutthroats

To each his own obscurantism. The Middle Ages had their crusades, but the Renaissance had its wars of religion, which were hardly more flattering to the reputation. As for the rest, feudal cutthroats were probably neither better nor worse than the ruffians of today. Brutality is timeless.

William the Conqueror, illustration for *Il Giornalino*, from the 1980s.

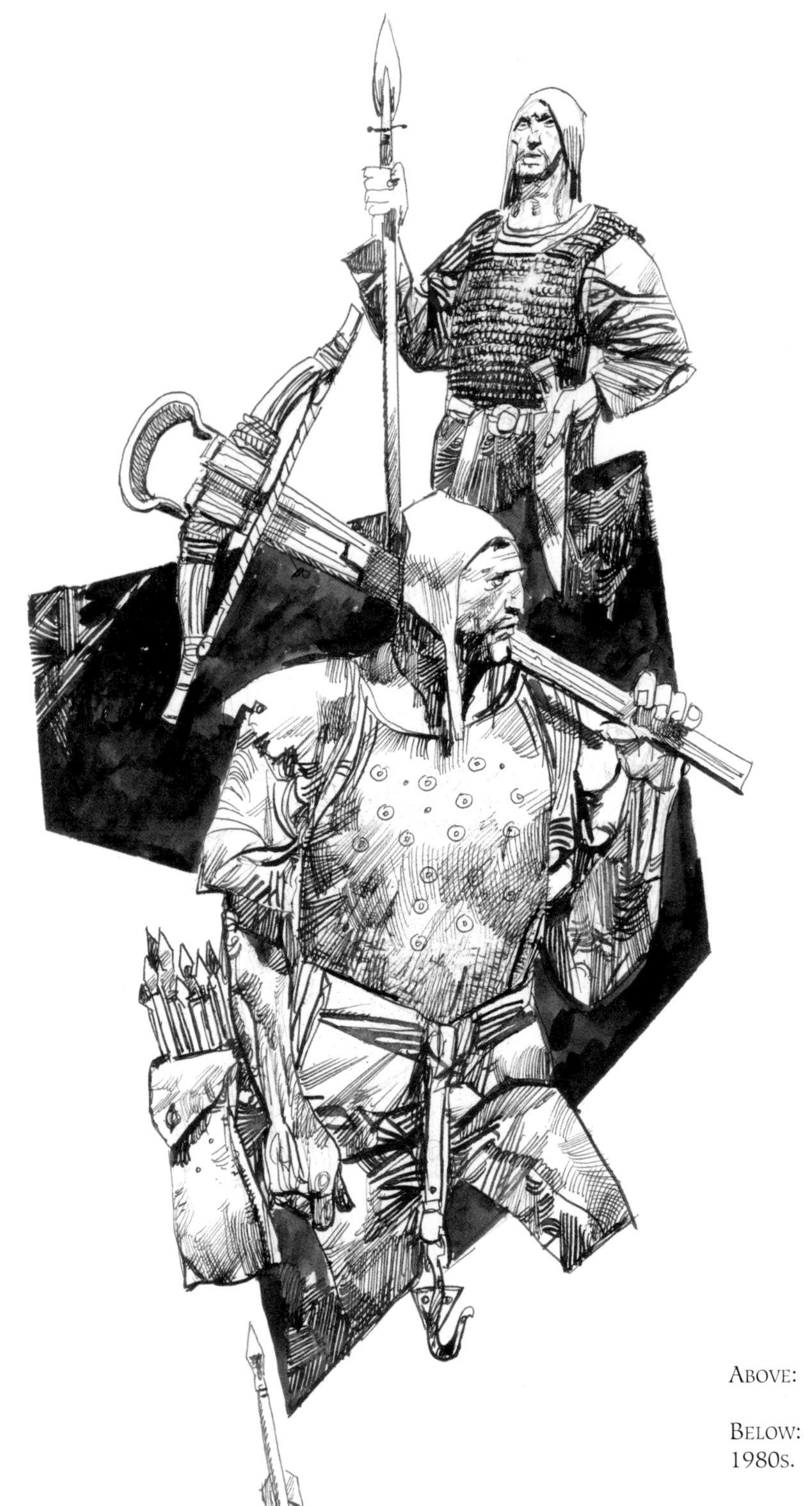

They bore many weapons, but very few worries. Their trousers were ill-fitting, their hats reeked of the manure they had trudged through, they hadn't washed in three weeks, and their digestive troubles never left them. They made a great deal of noise, trying to forget the deathly silence that ate away at their lives. They suffered from stomach pain and did not know why. They did evil out of ignorance of good. They knew not a single word for beauty. They took revenge on others for their own inanity.

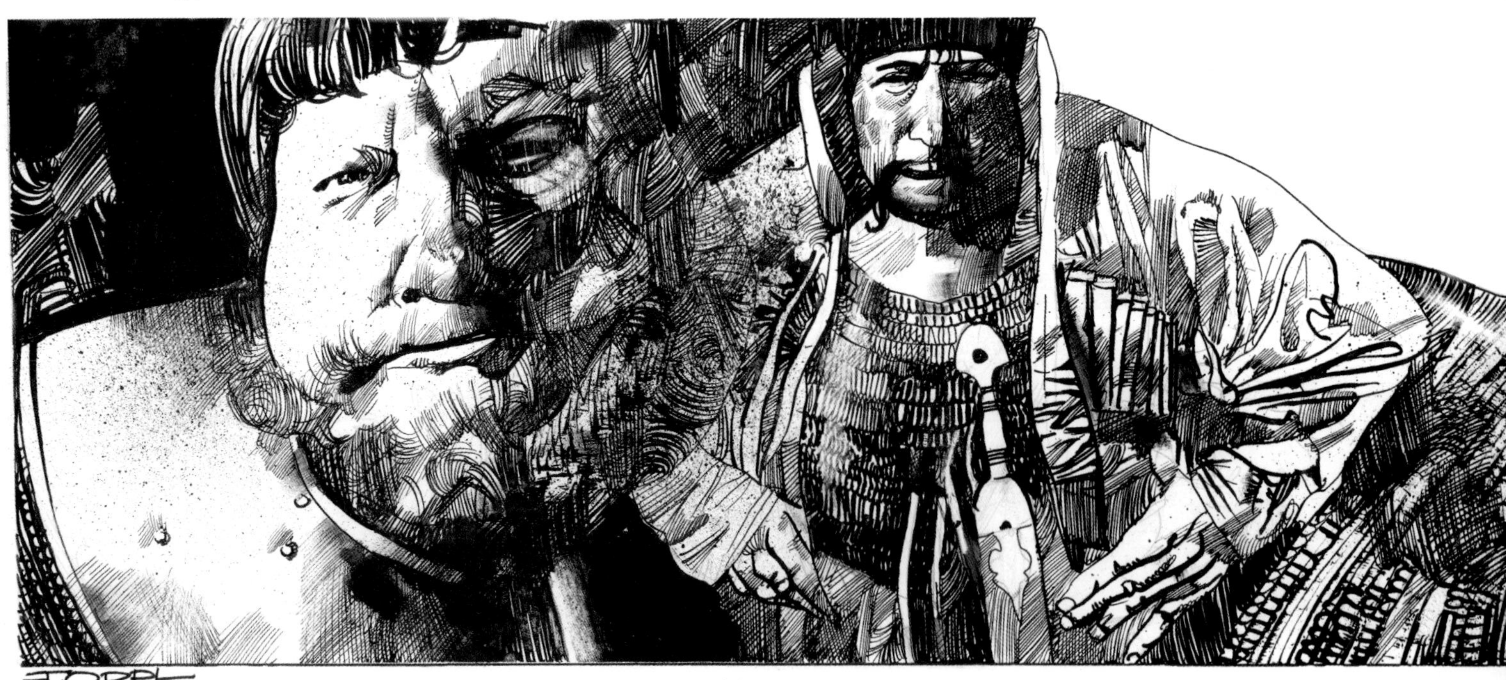

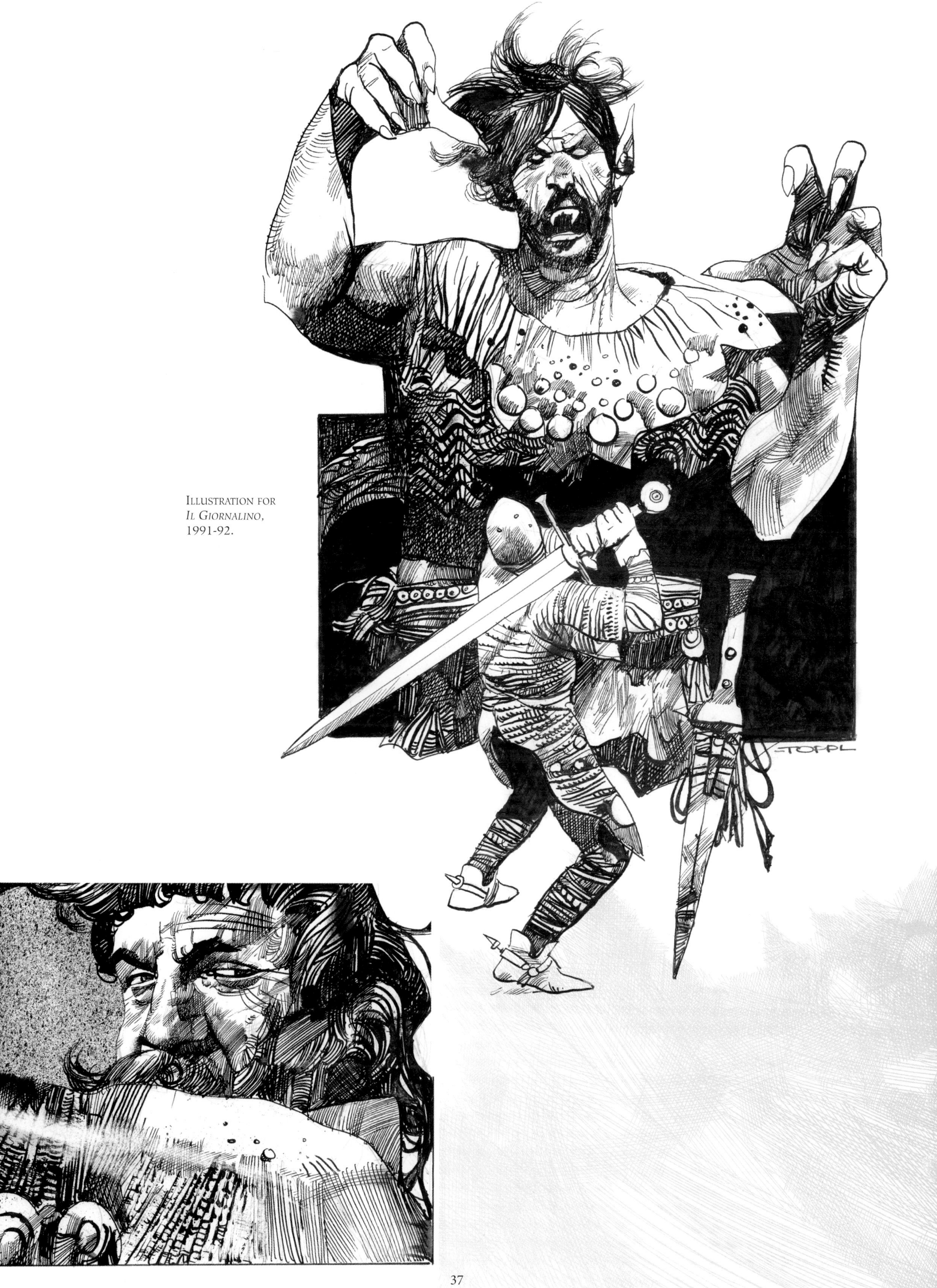

ILLUSTRATION FOR
IL GIORNALINO,
1991-92.

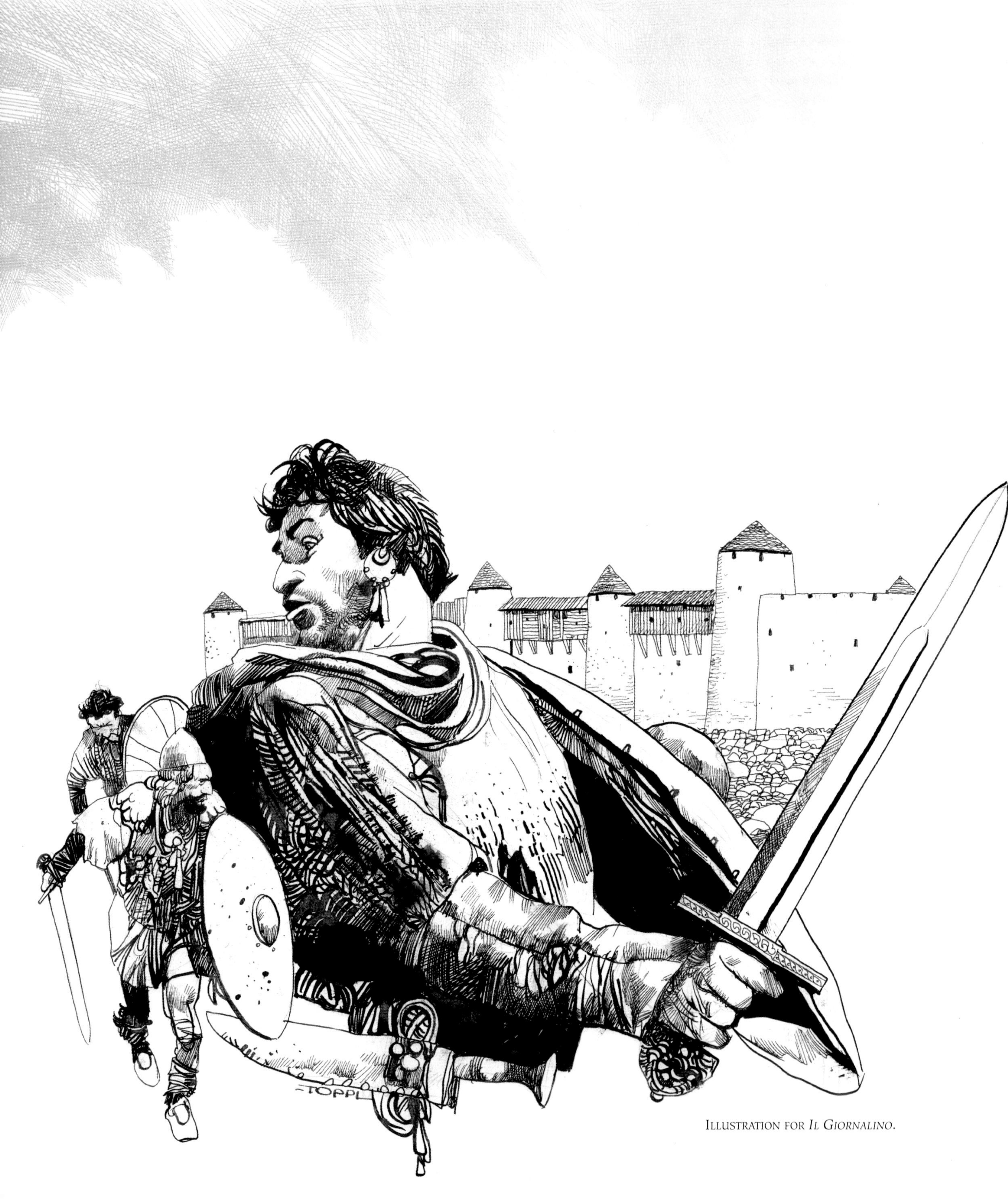

ILLUSTRATION FOR *IL GIORNALINO*.

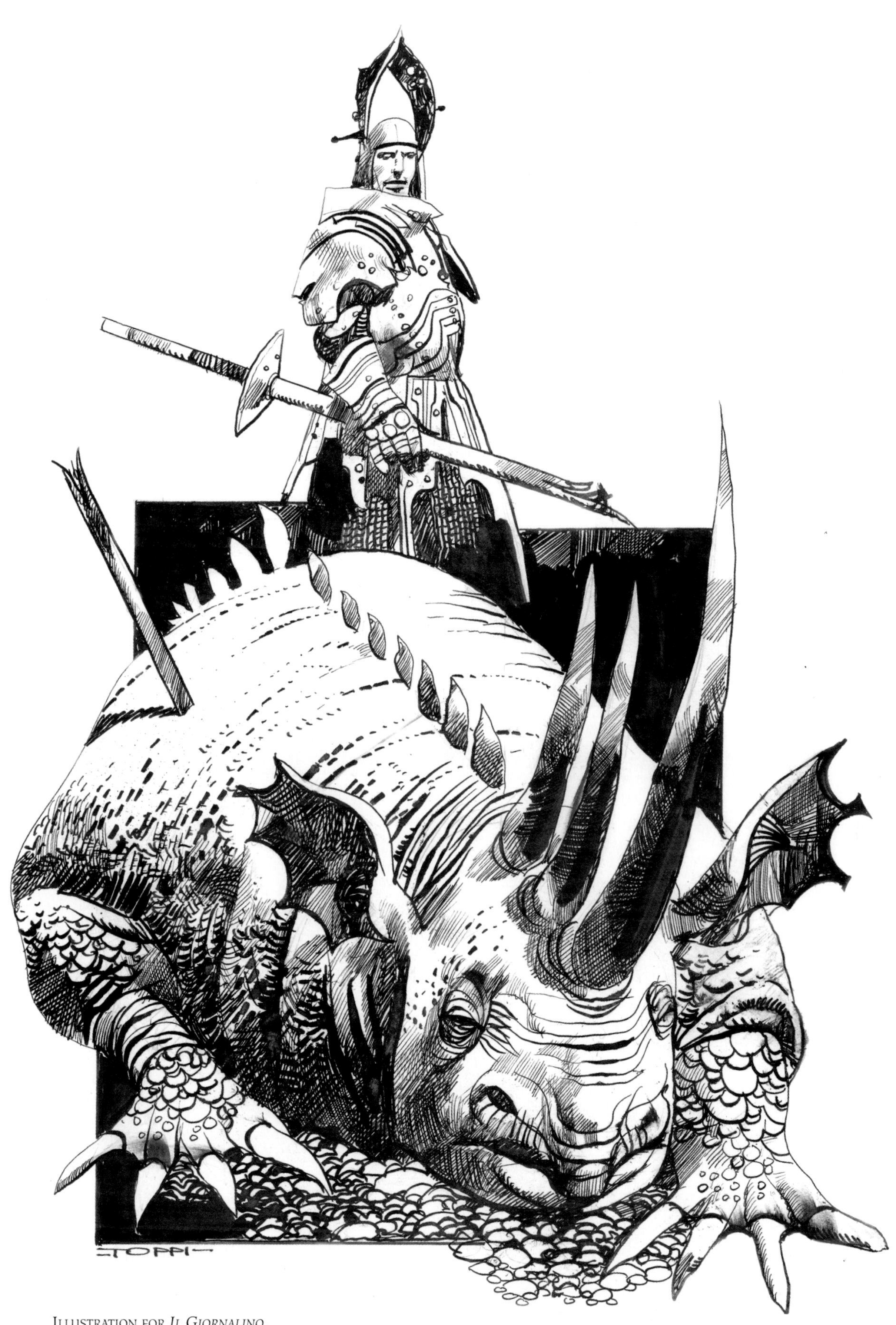

Illustration for *Il Giornalino*.

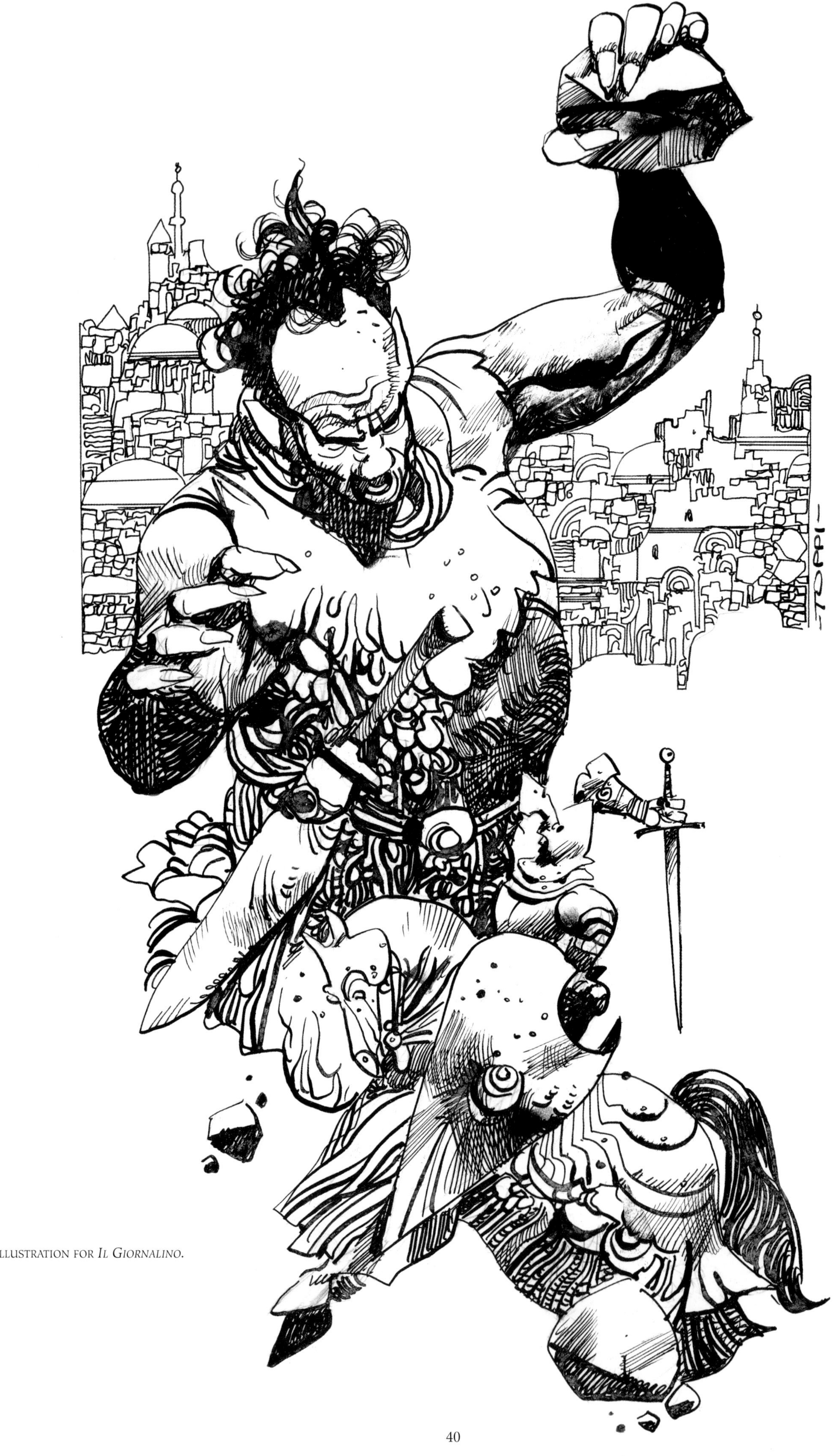

Illustration for *Il Giornalino*.

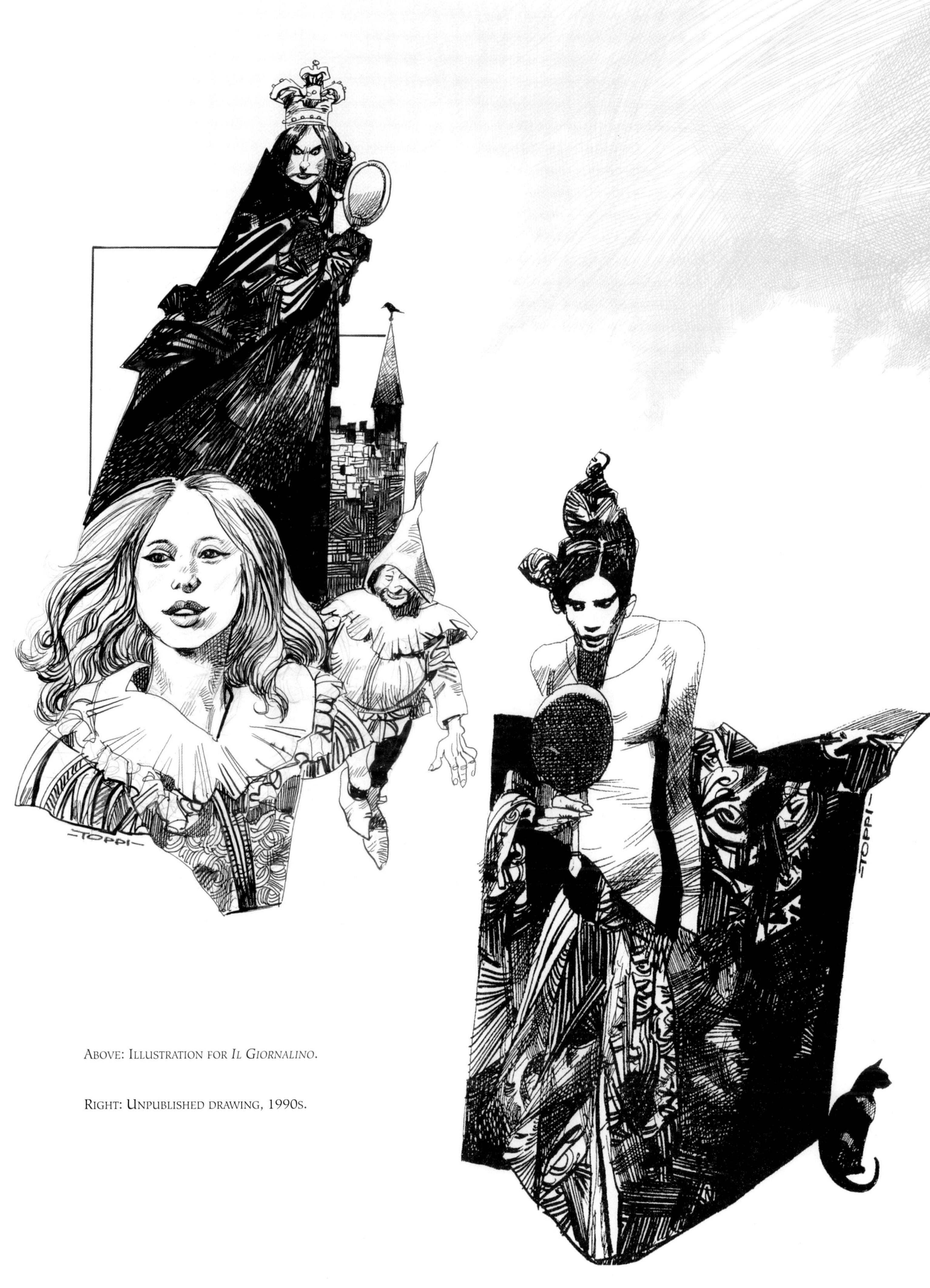

ABOVE: ILLUSTRATION FOR *IL GIORNALINO*.

RIGHT: UNPUBLISHED DRAWING, 1990S.

Sword of flame, fangs of wolf, helmet of iron: monsters emerge from the womb of night. They are born of our fears. They possess the weight of a nightmare as well as its immateriality. To defeat them, there is no need for an archangel with a glaive. We have but to arm ourselves with courage and look each of our terrors straight in the eye. Monsters are nothing more than acrid smoke; to be rid of them, perhaps all it takes is to simply open the window — and to air out our lives.

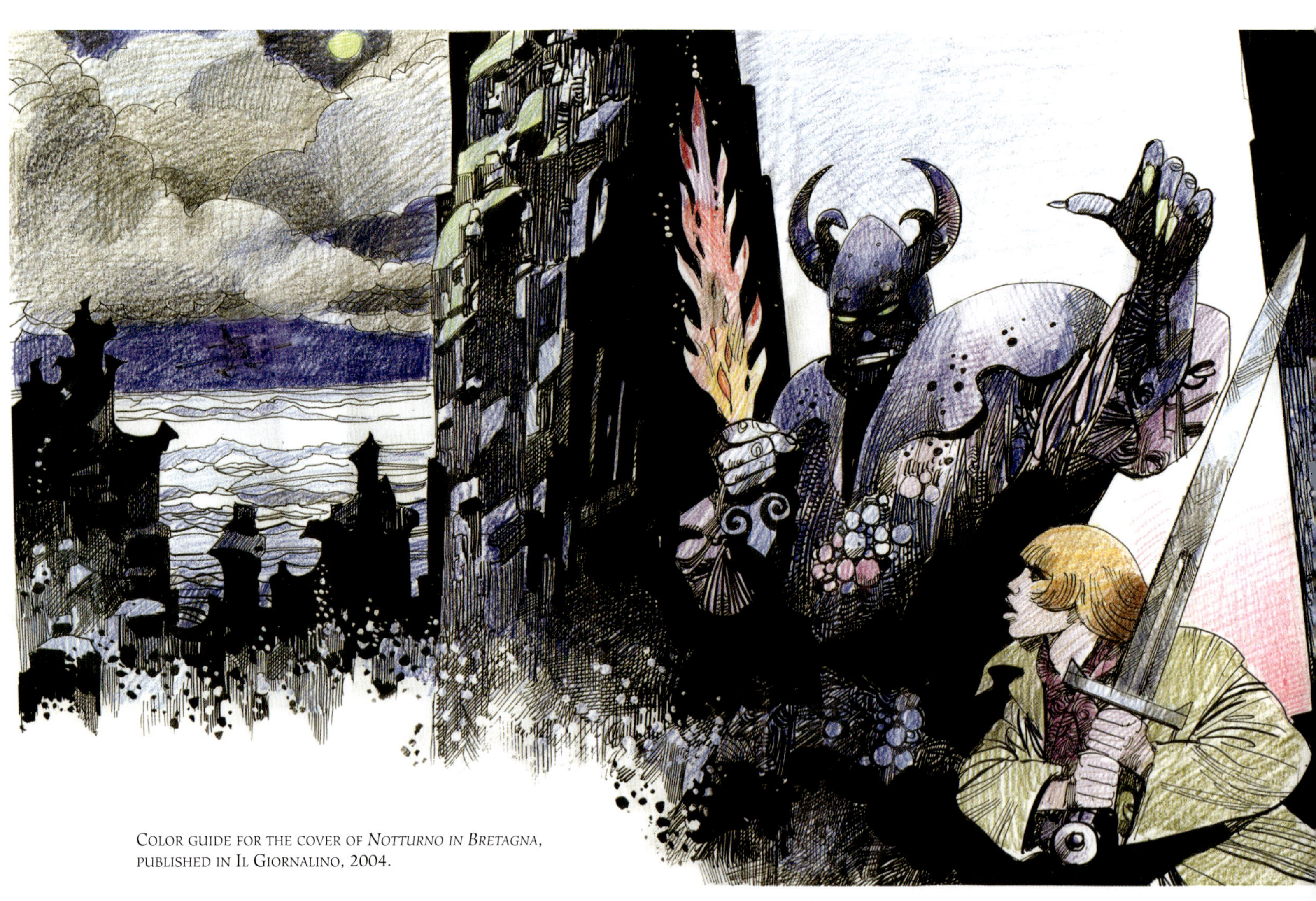

Color guide for the cover of *Notturno in Bretagna*, published in Il Giornalino, 2004.

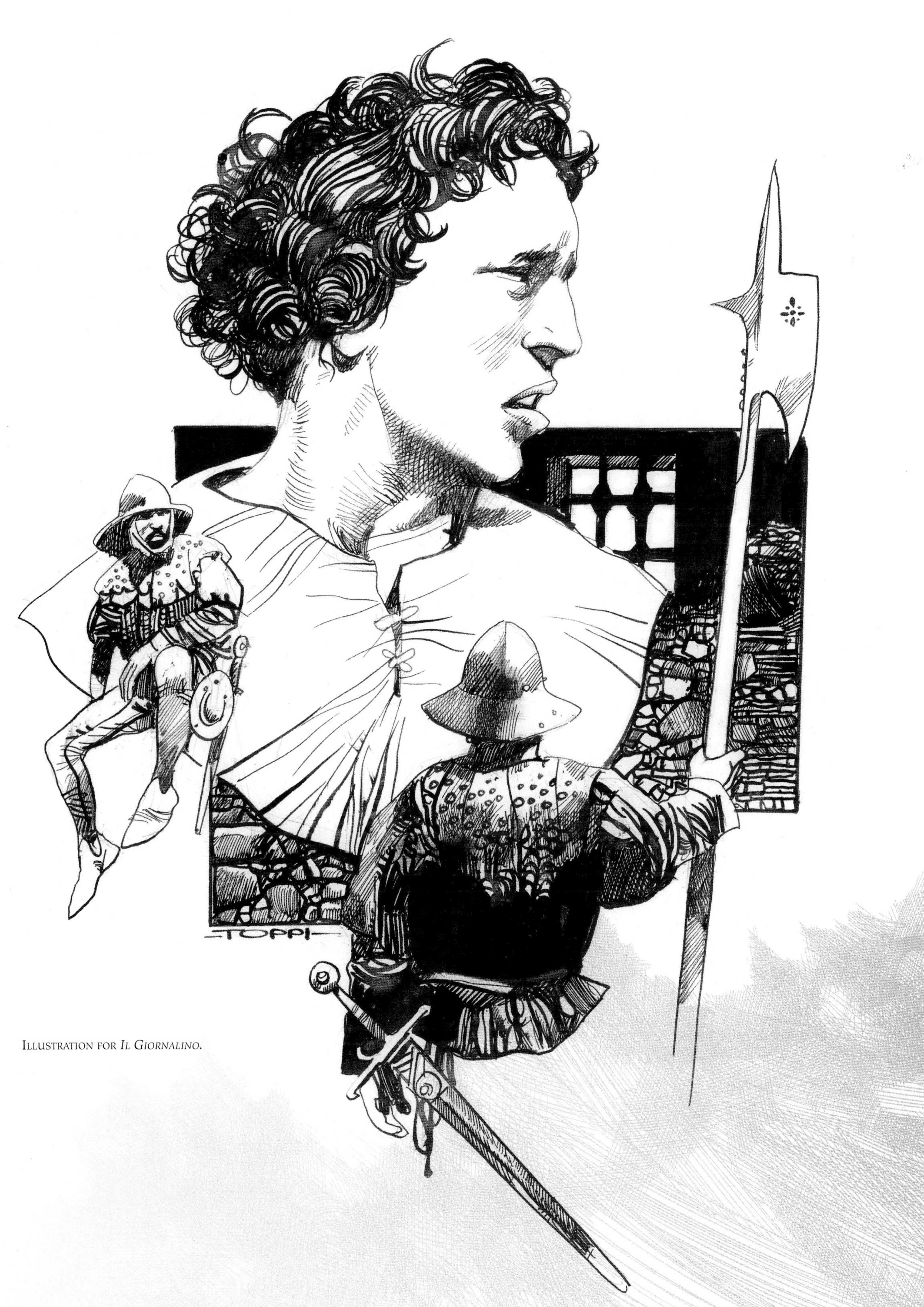

ILLUSTRATION FOR *Il Giornalino*.

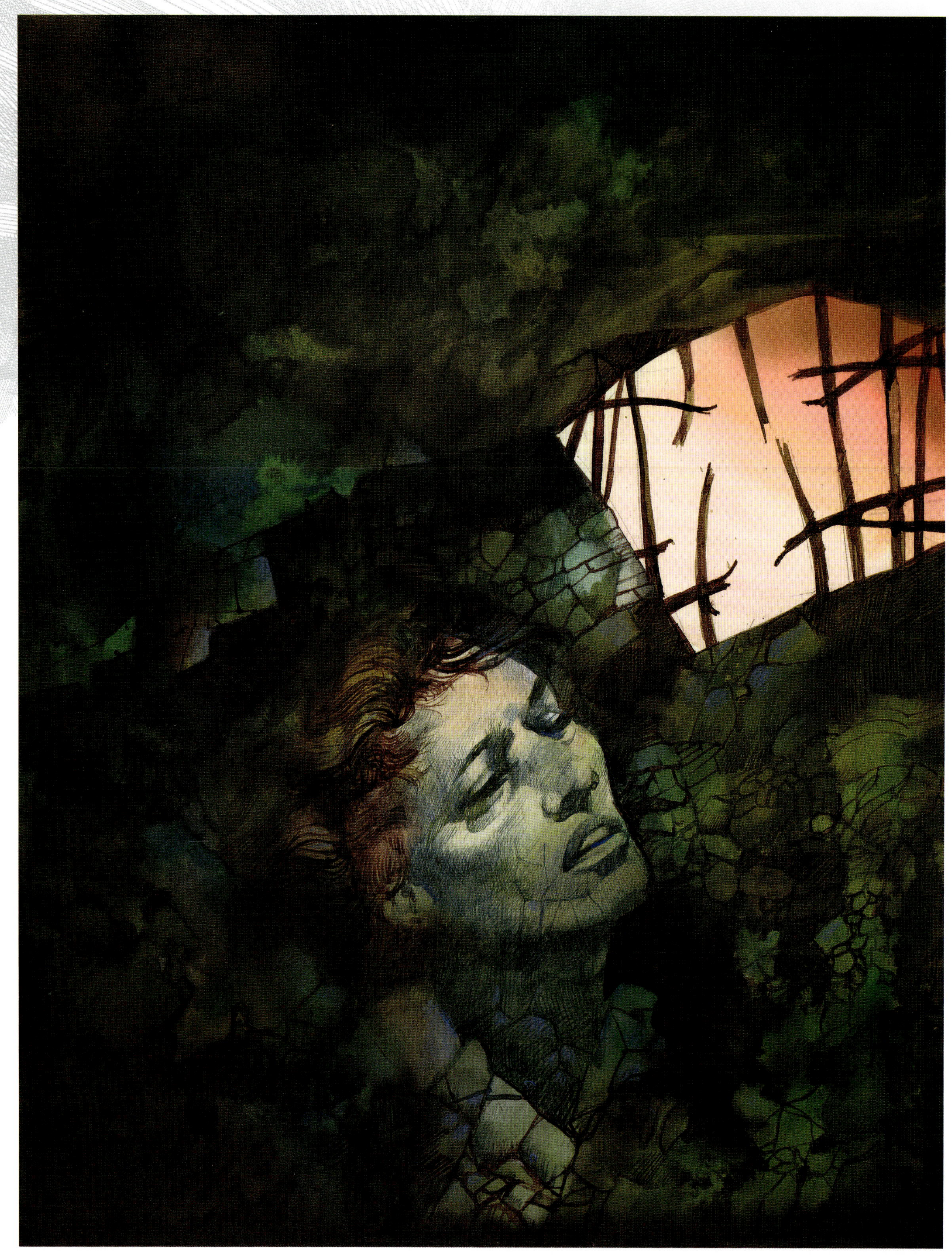

ILLUSTRATION FOR A MEDICAL JOURNAL, 2004.

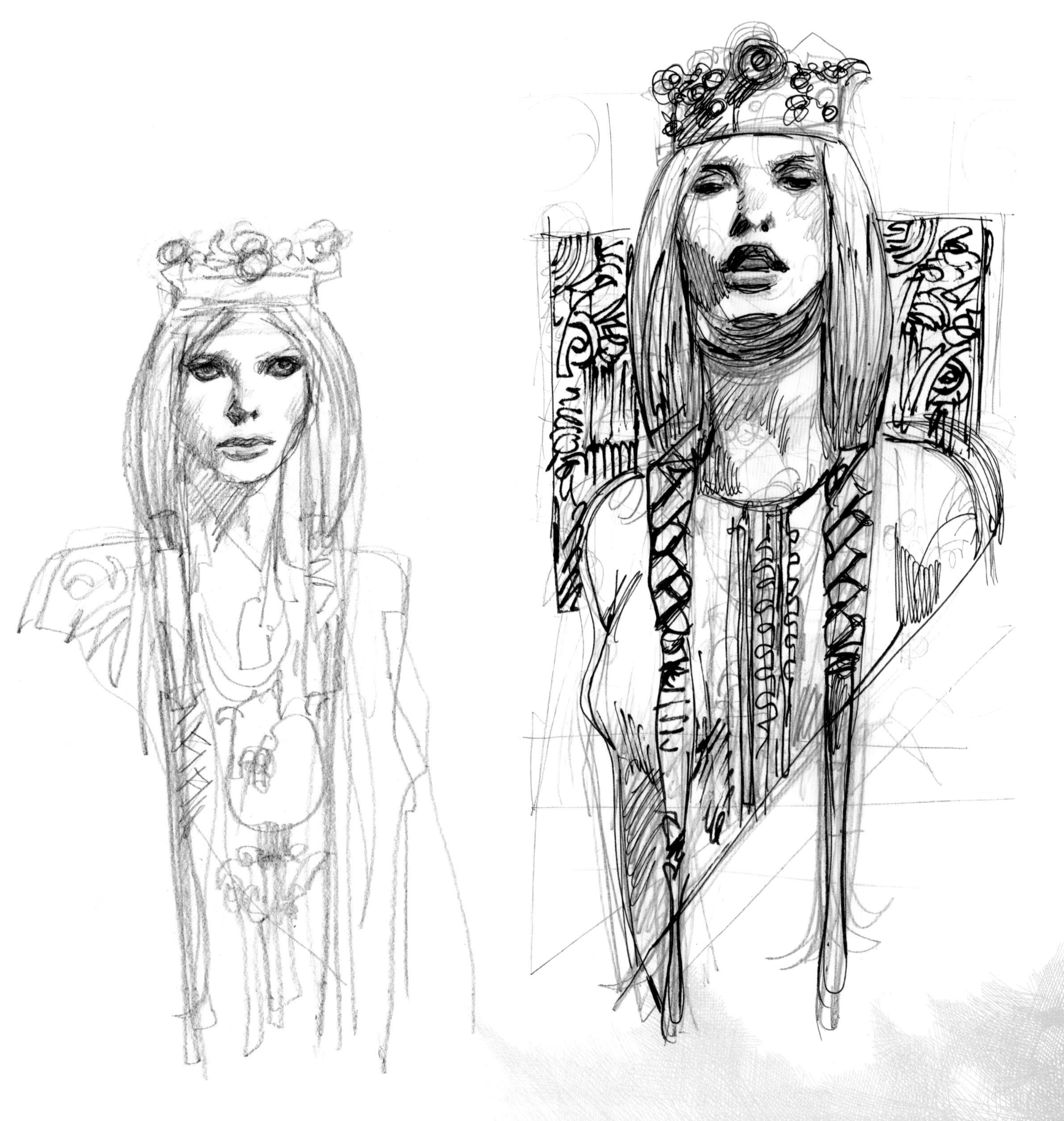

Pages 45-46: Character sketches of
Ermengarda de Manzoni and Matilde di Canossa,
for the Régiion of Salento, 2000's.

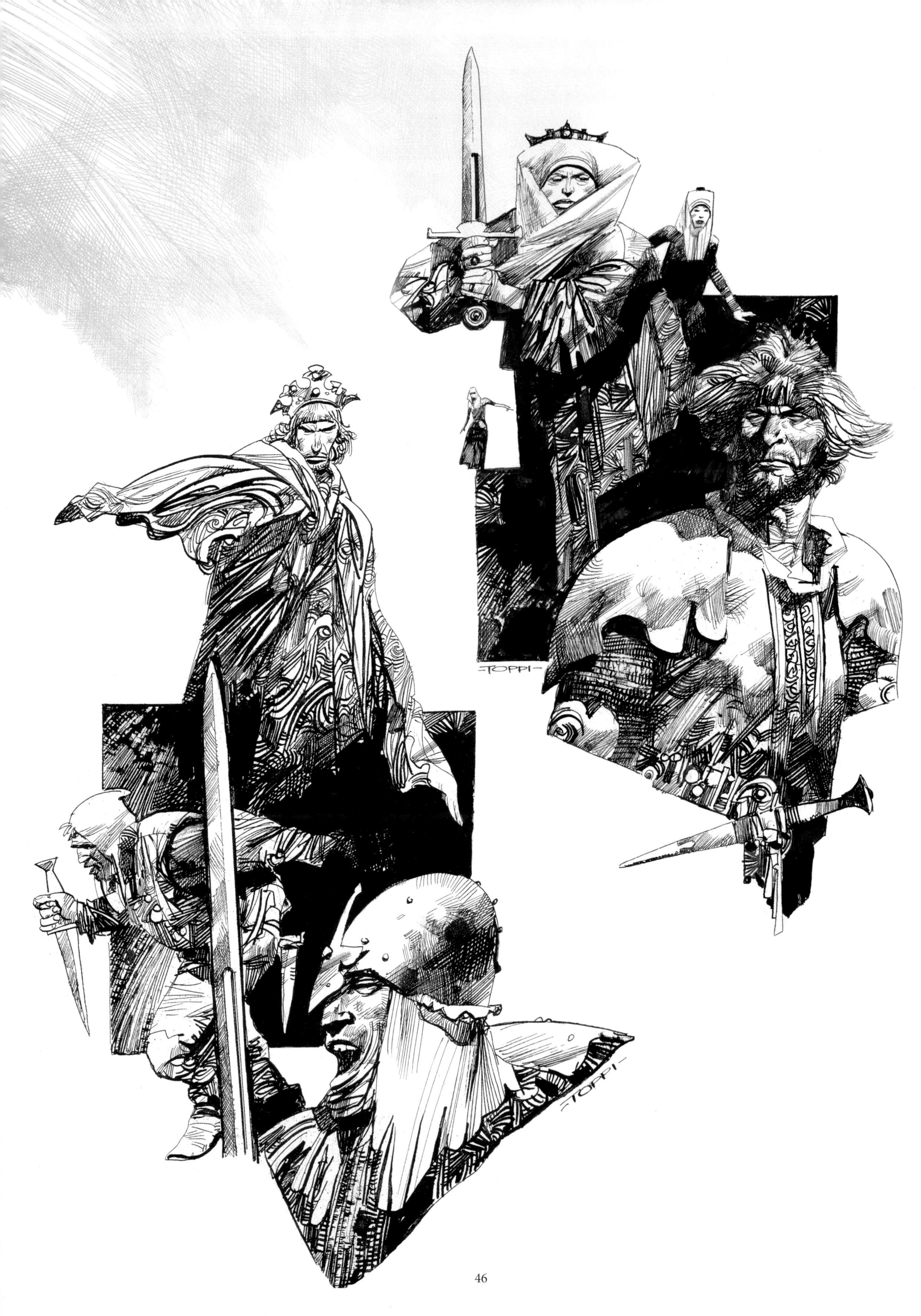

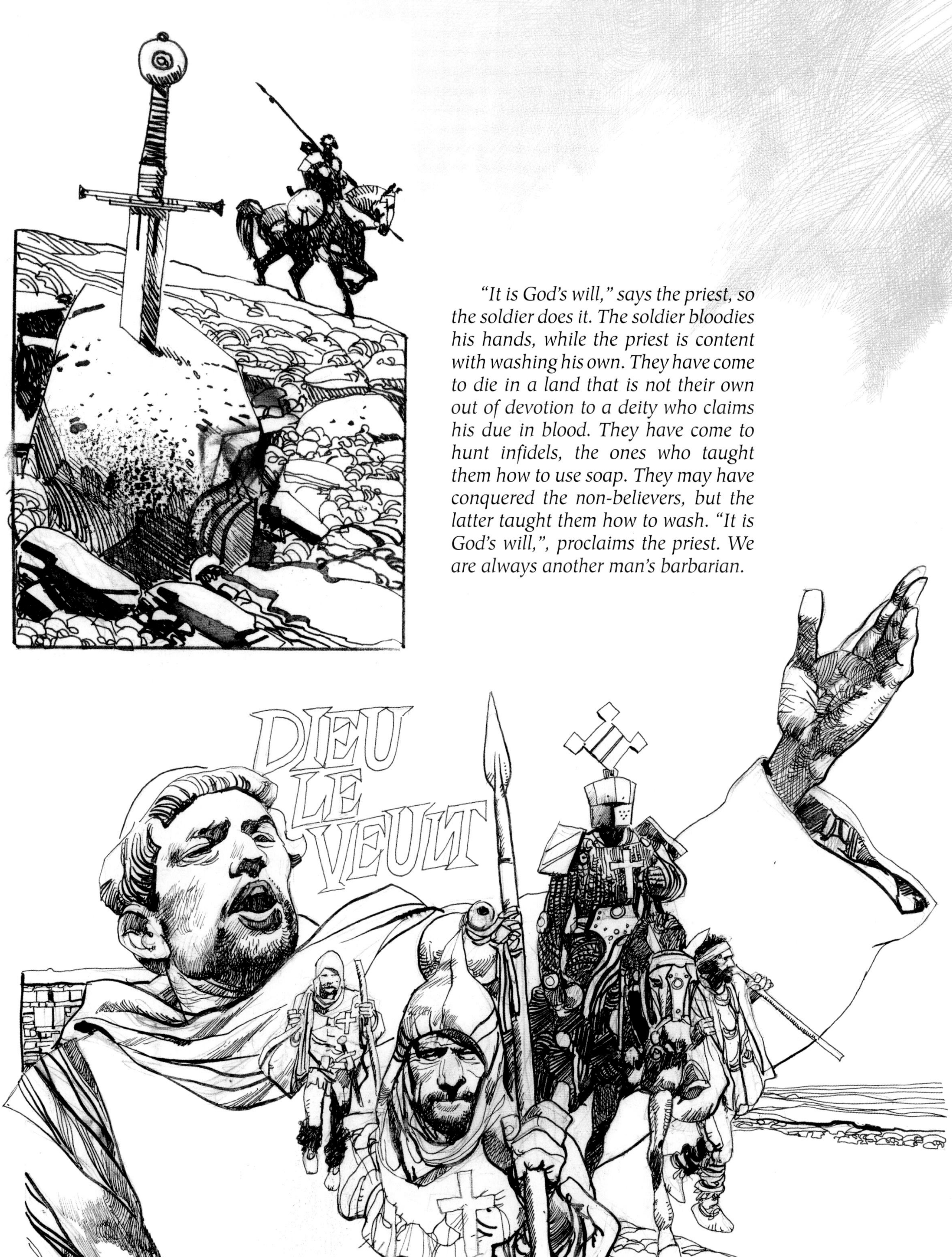

"It is God's will," says the priest, so the soldier does it. The soldier bloodies his hands, while the priest is content with washing his own. They have come to die in a land that is not their own out of devotion to a deity who claims his due in blood. They have come to hunt infidels, the ones who taught them how to use soap. They may have conquered the non-believers, but the latter taught them how to wash. "It is God's will,", proclaims the priest. We are always another man's barbarian.

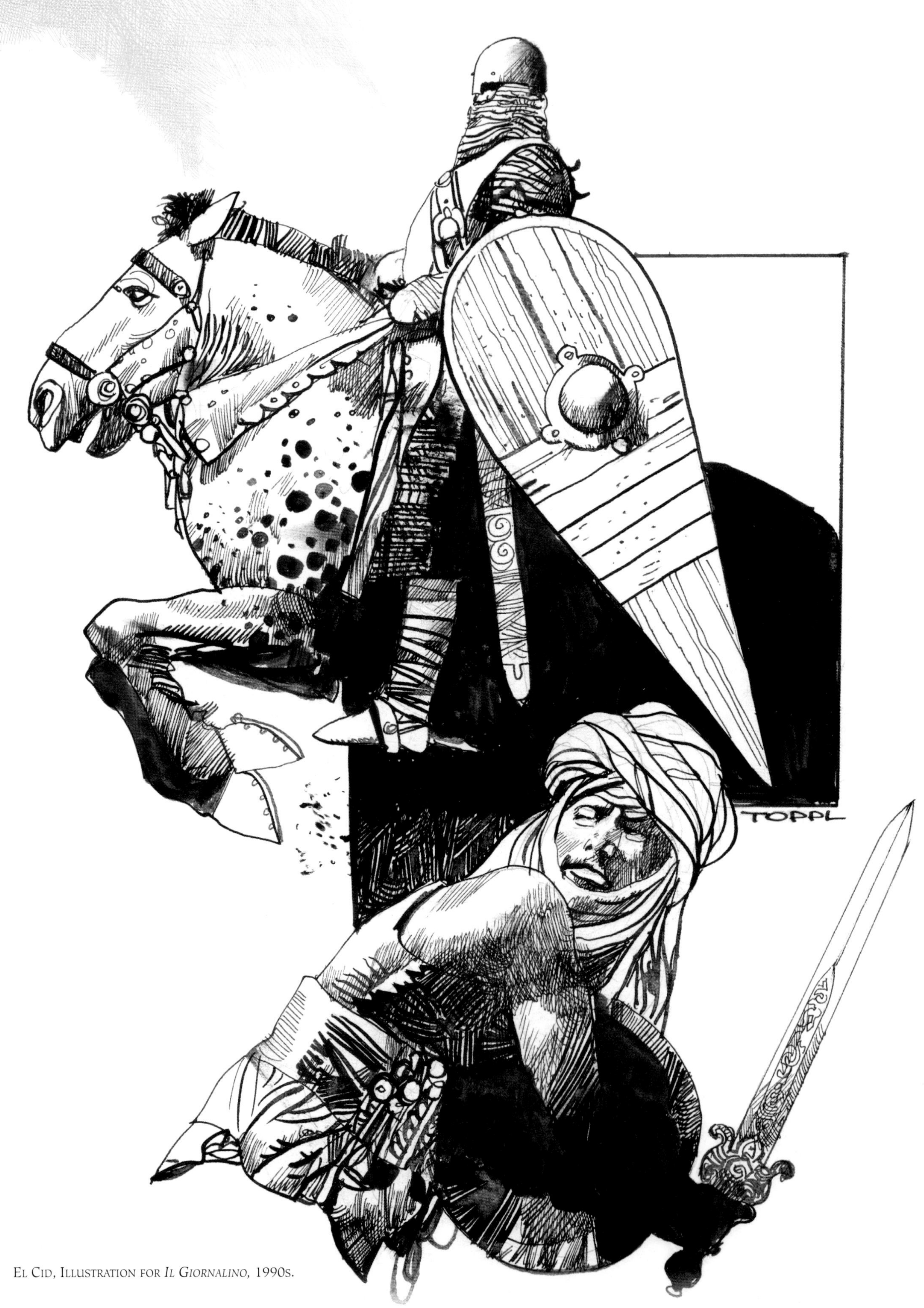

El Cid, Illustration for *Il Giornalino*, 1990s.

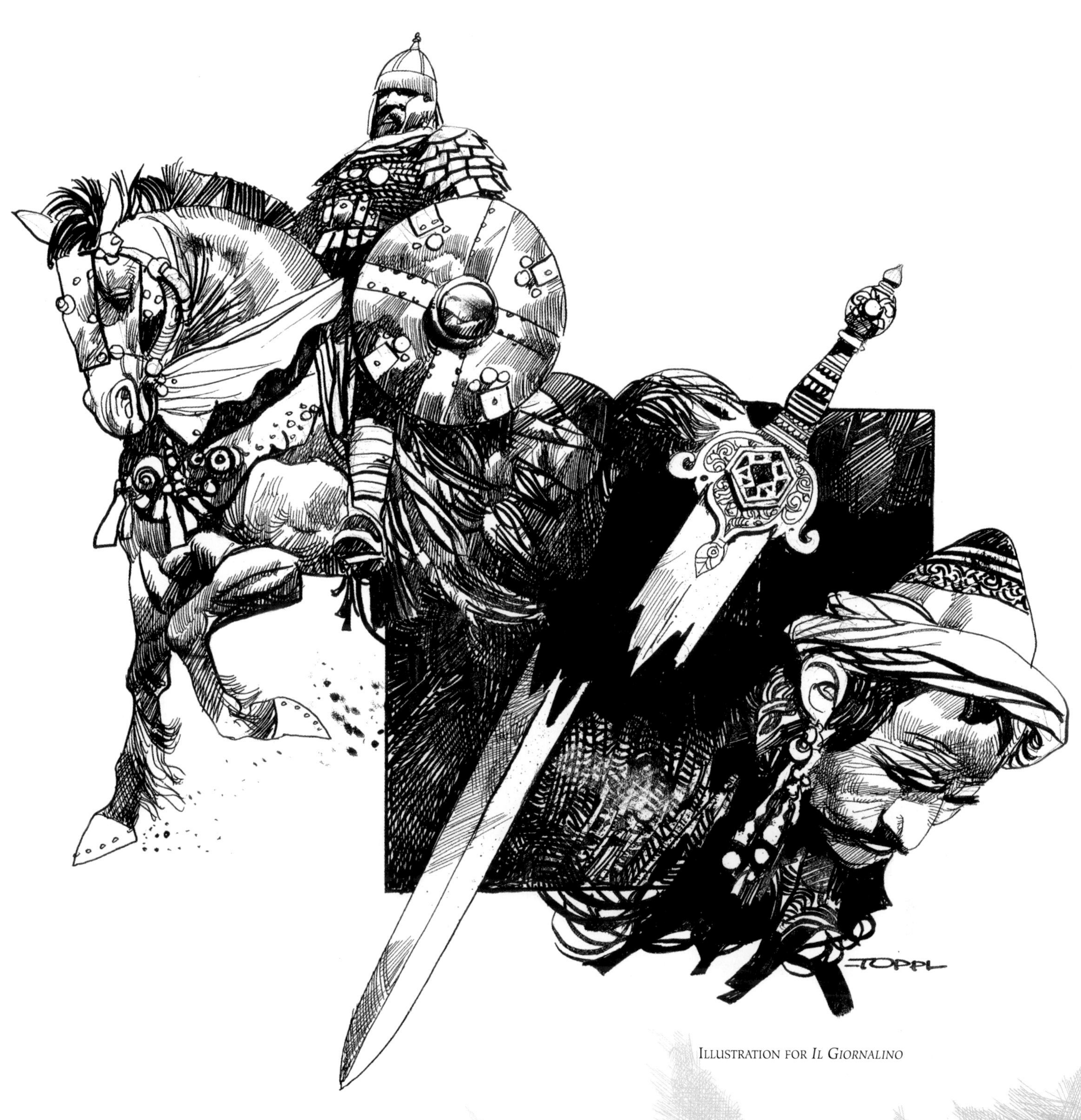

ILLUSTRATION FOR *IL GIORNALINO*

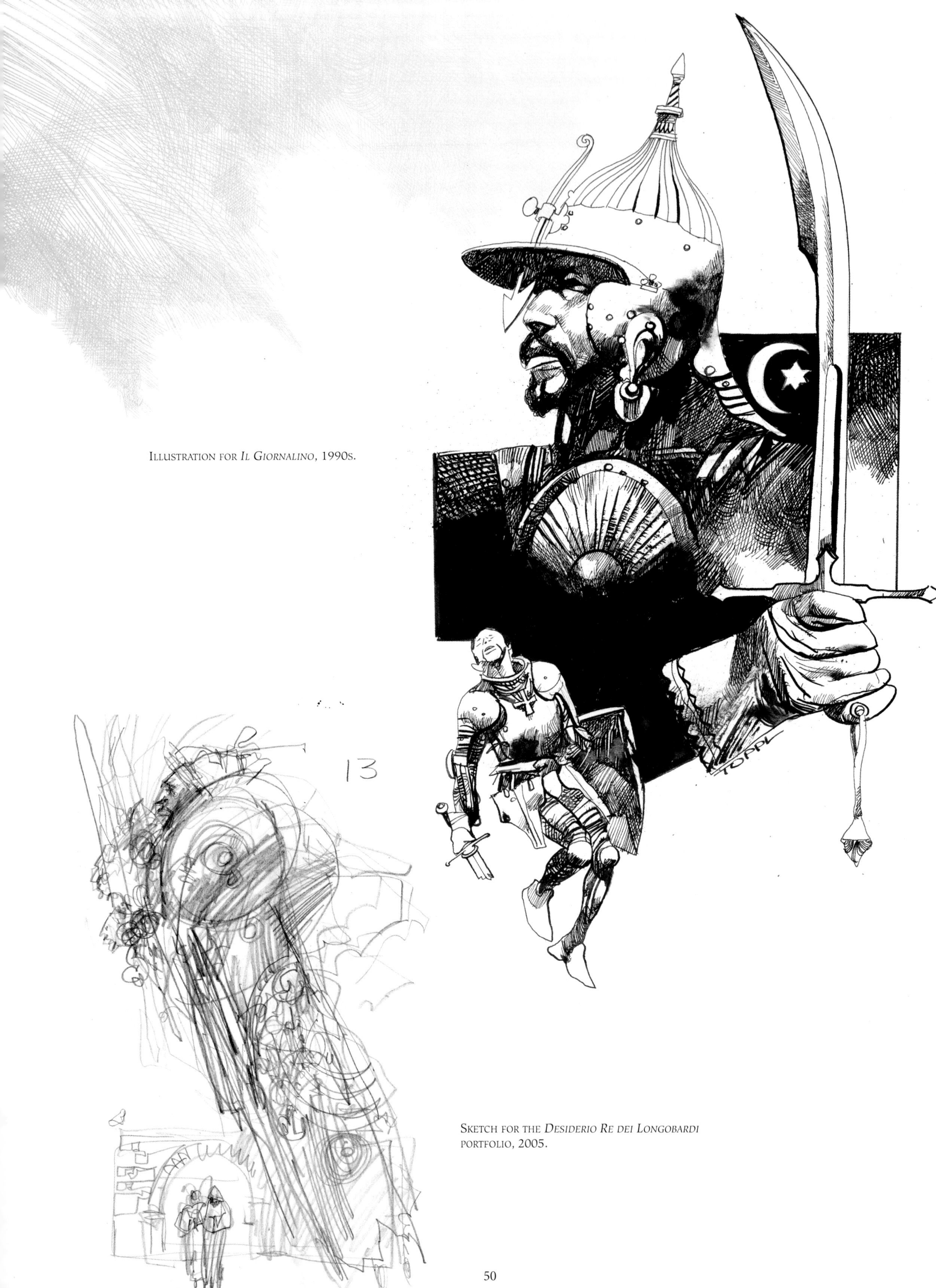

ILLUSTRATION FOR *IL GIORNALINO*, 1990S.

SKETCH FOR THE *DESIDERIO RE DEI LONGOBARDI*
PORTFOLIO, 2005.

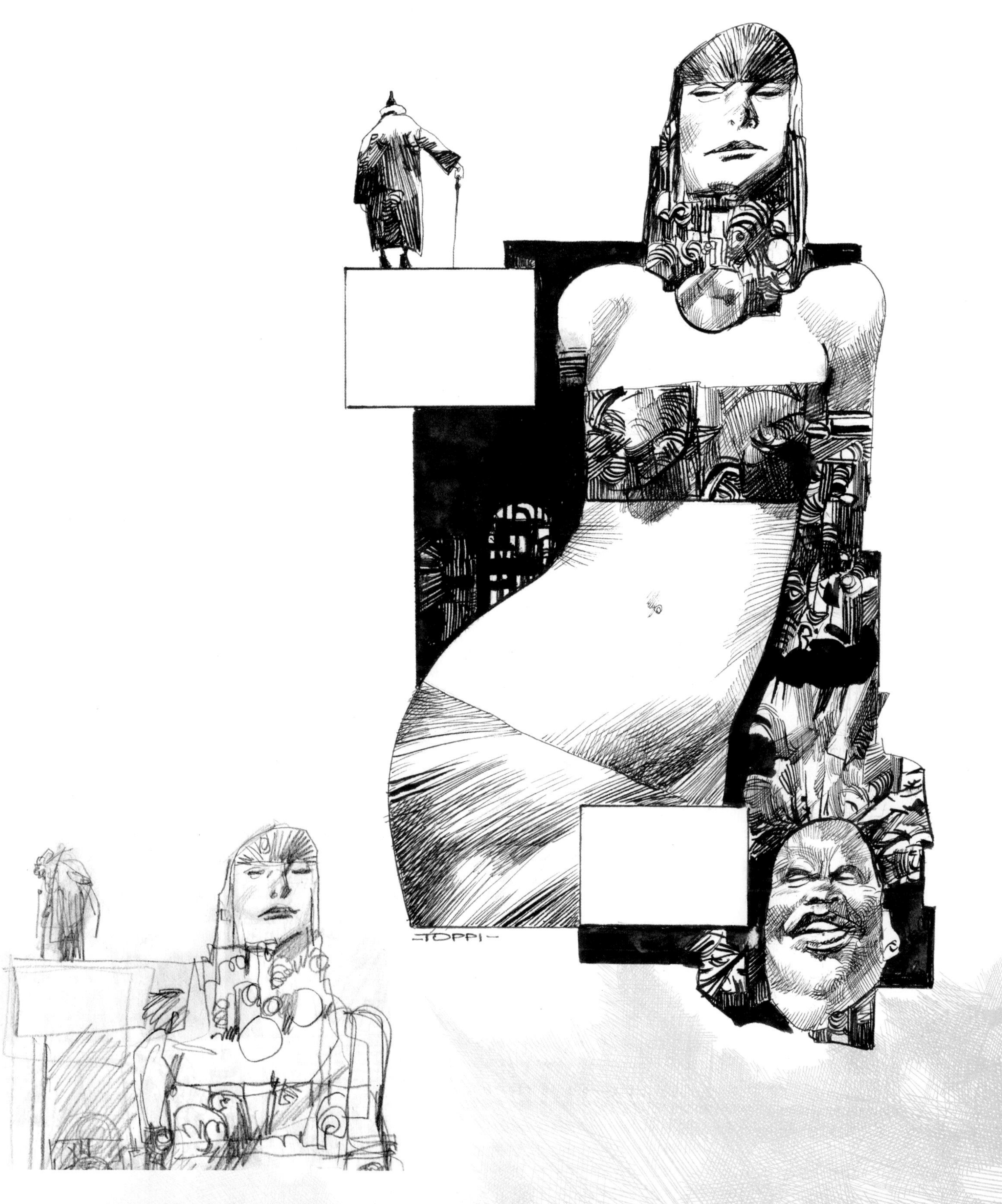

PAGES 51-54:
ILLUSTRATION FOR THE FRIEDRICH DÜRENMATT
NOVELLA *ABU CHANIFA E ANAN BEN DAVID* FOR
STUDIO MICHELANGELO, 2003.

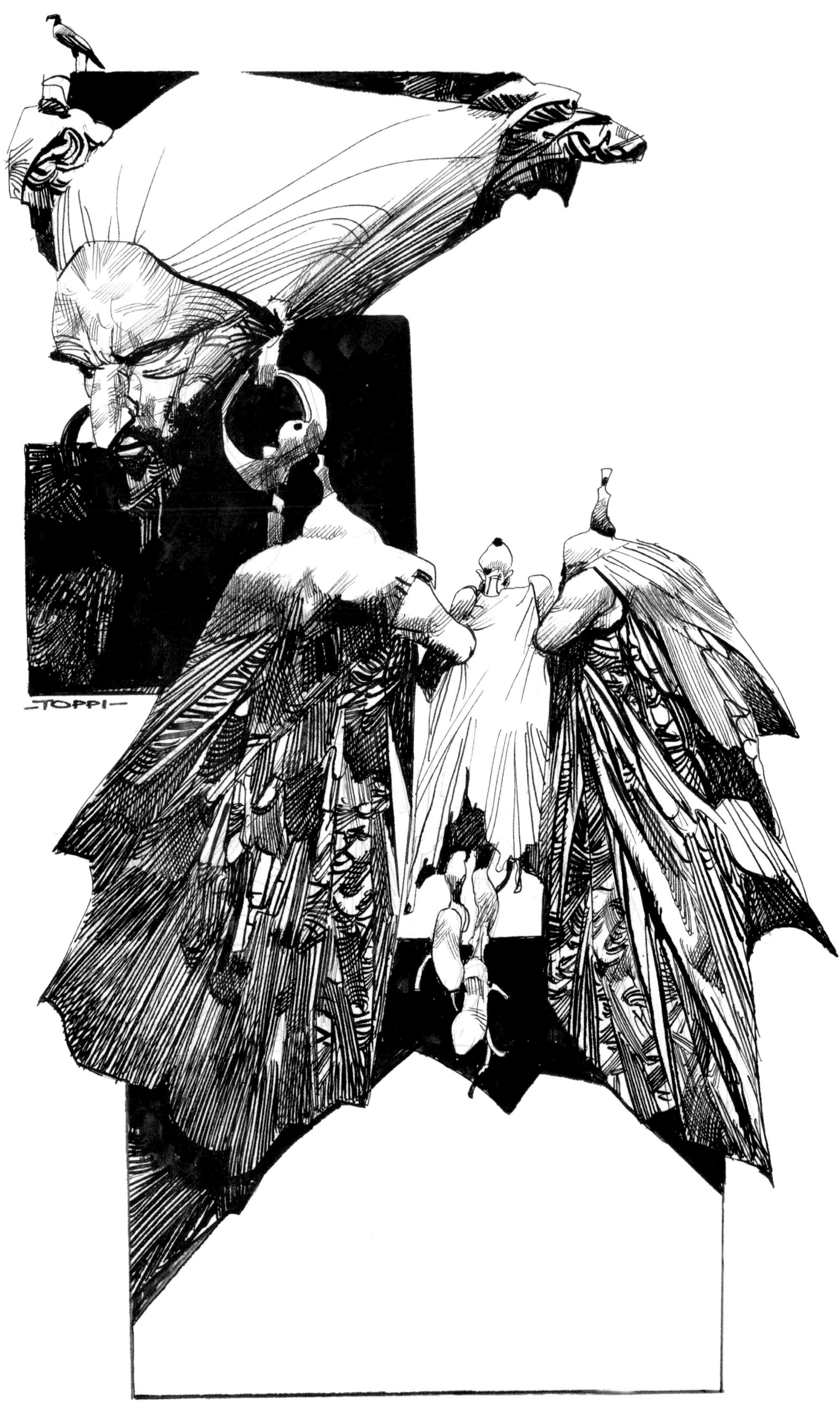

TOPPI

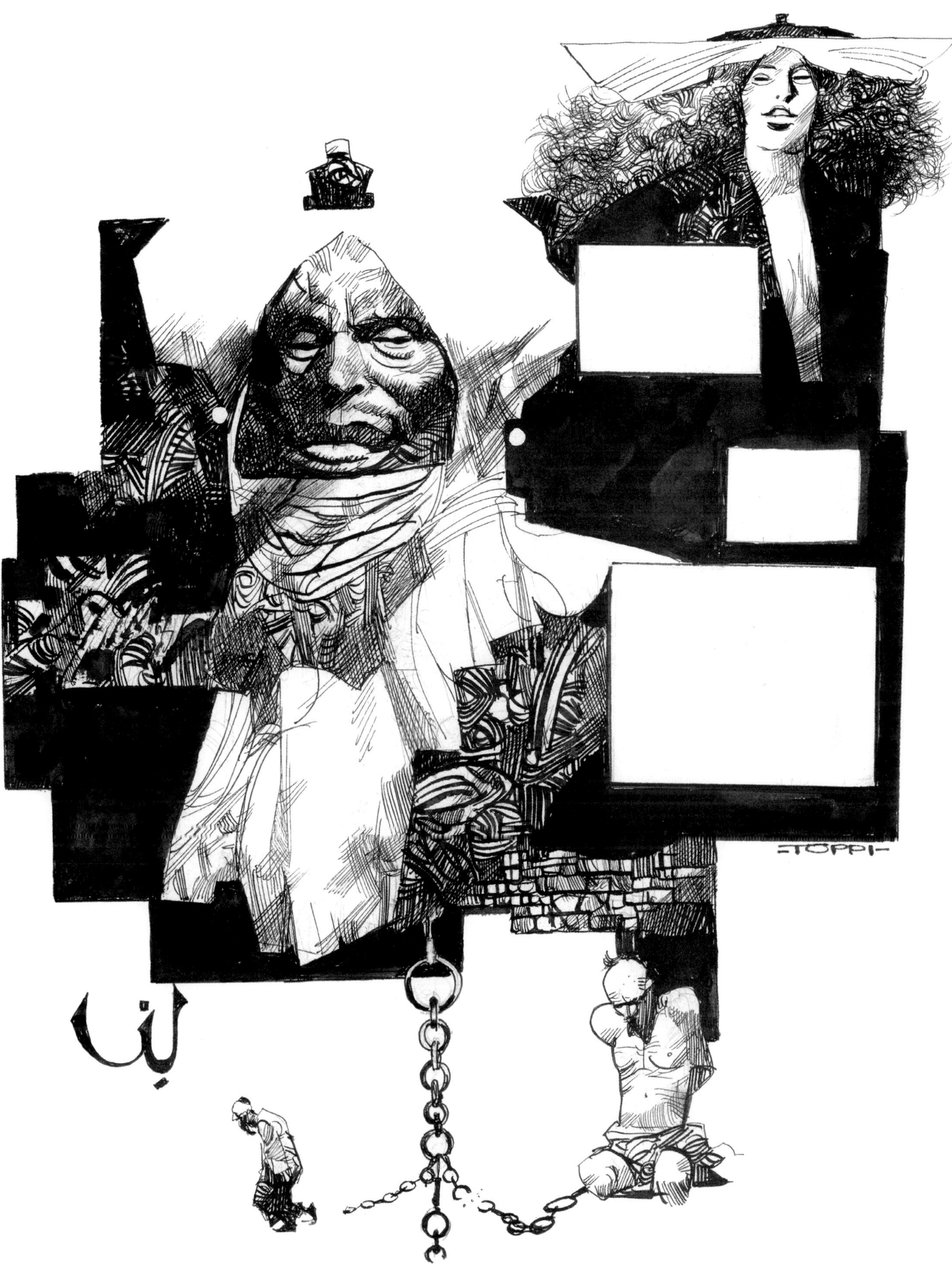

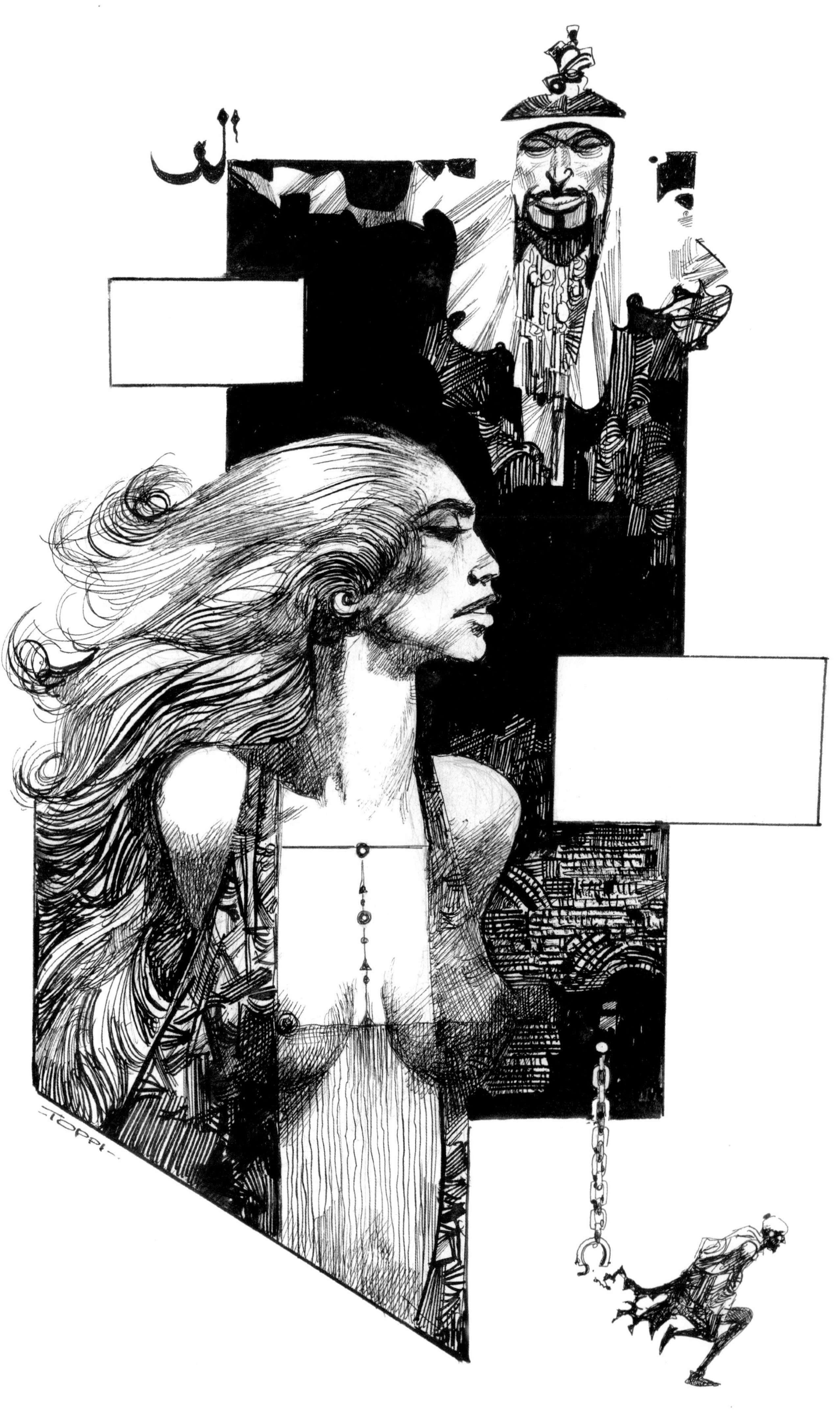

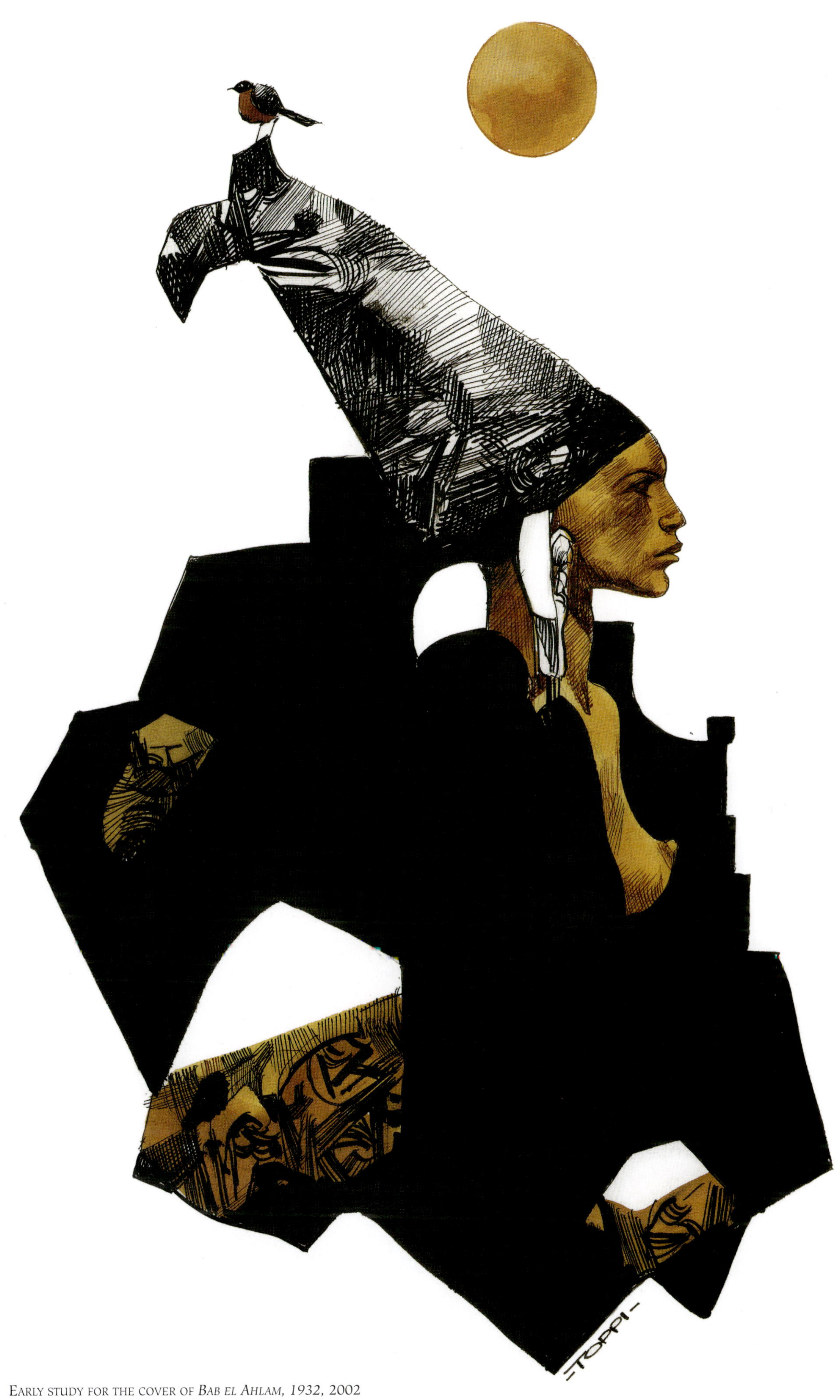

Early study for the cover of *Bab el Ahlam*, 1932, 2002

Whenever they could no longer stand each other, which occurred quite often, they would call each other poor devils, Beelzebub, or demons. This allowed them to let off steam, and strengthened their bond of brotherhood. Furthermore, they were moneylenders, who were hardly lenient with their delinquent debtors. And whenever they deemed themselves unpaid, they would become diabolical and demonic indeed. One with a pair of pliers, the other with a whip, they would claim their pound of flesh, which more often than not would cost their unfortunate victim his life. Little by little, they had taken on a diabolical appearance. All that was missing was the horns.

And yet… it was said that their respective spouses strived most diligently to make them wear the horns of the cuckold.

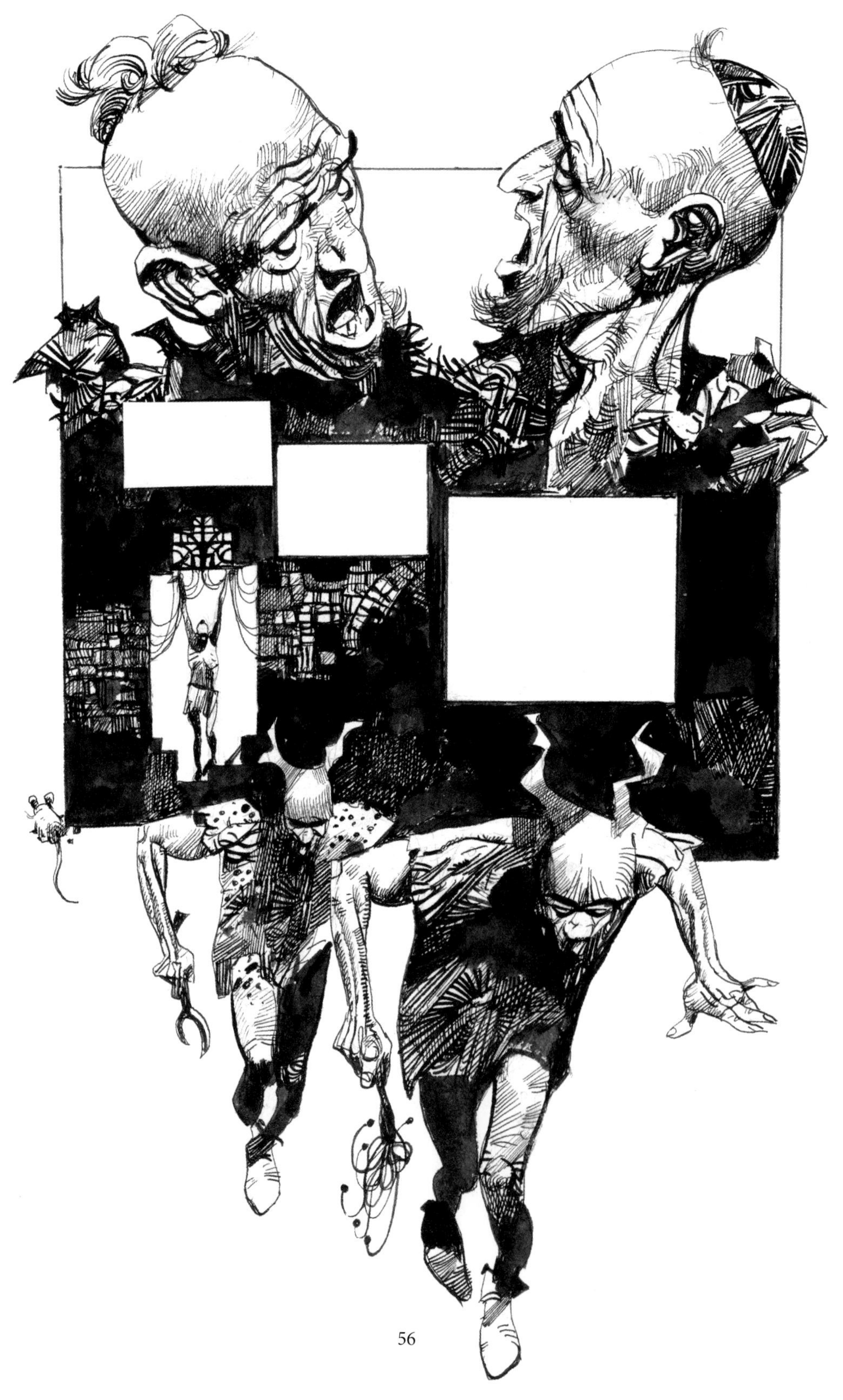

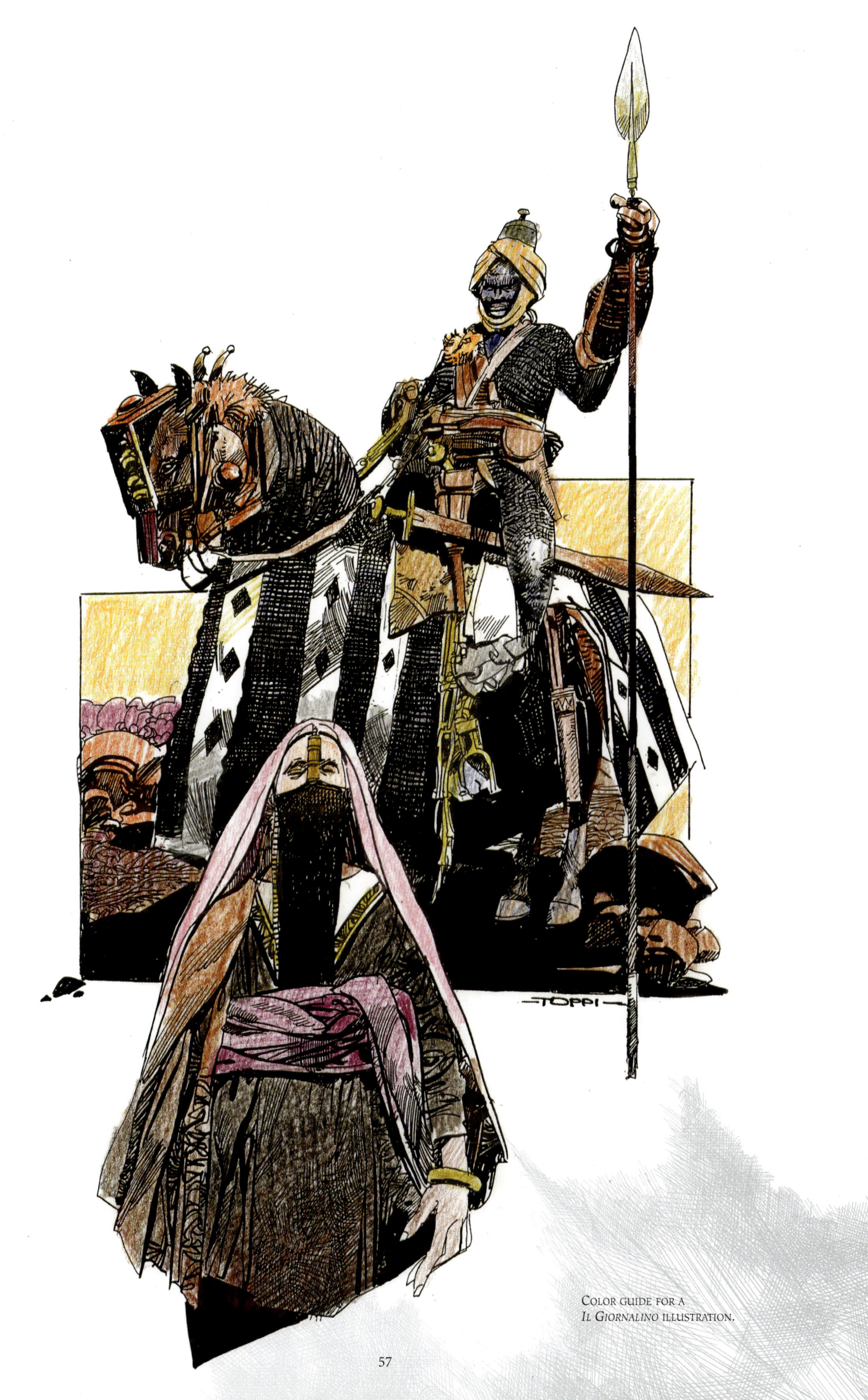

Color guide for a
Il Giornalino illustration.

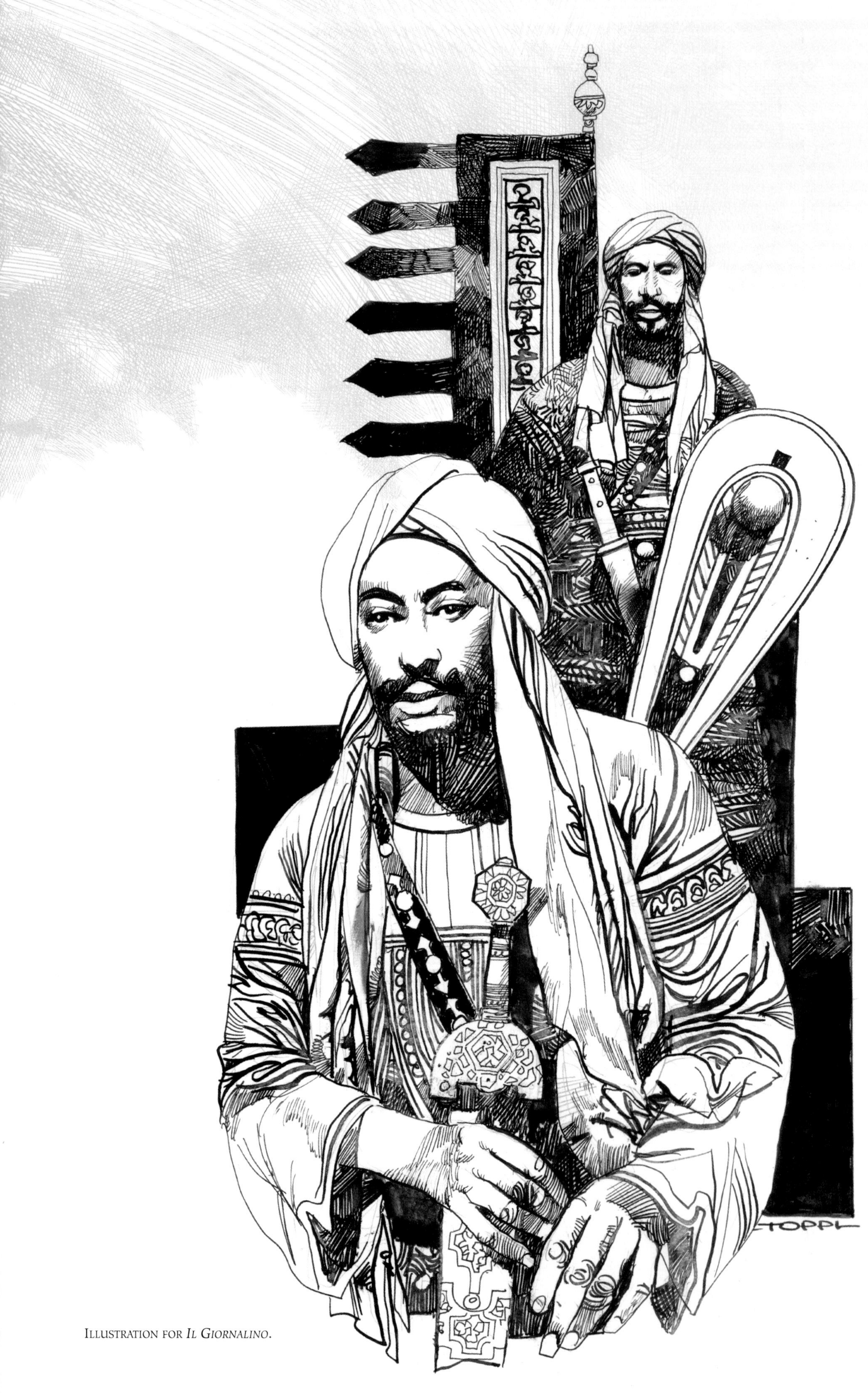

Illustration for *Il Giornalino*.

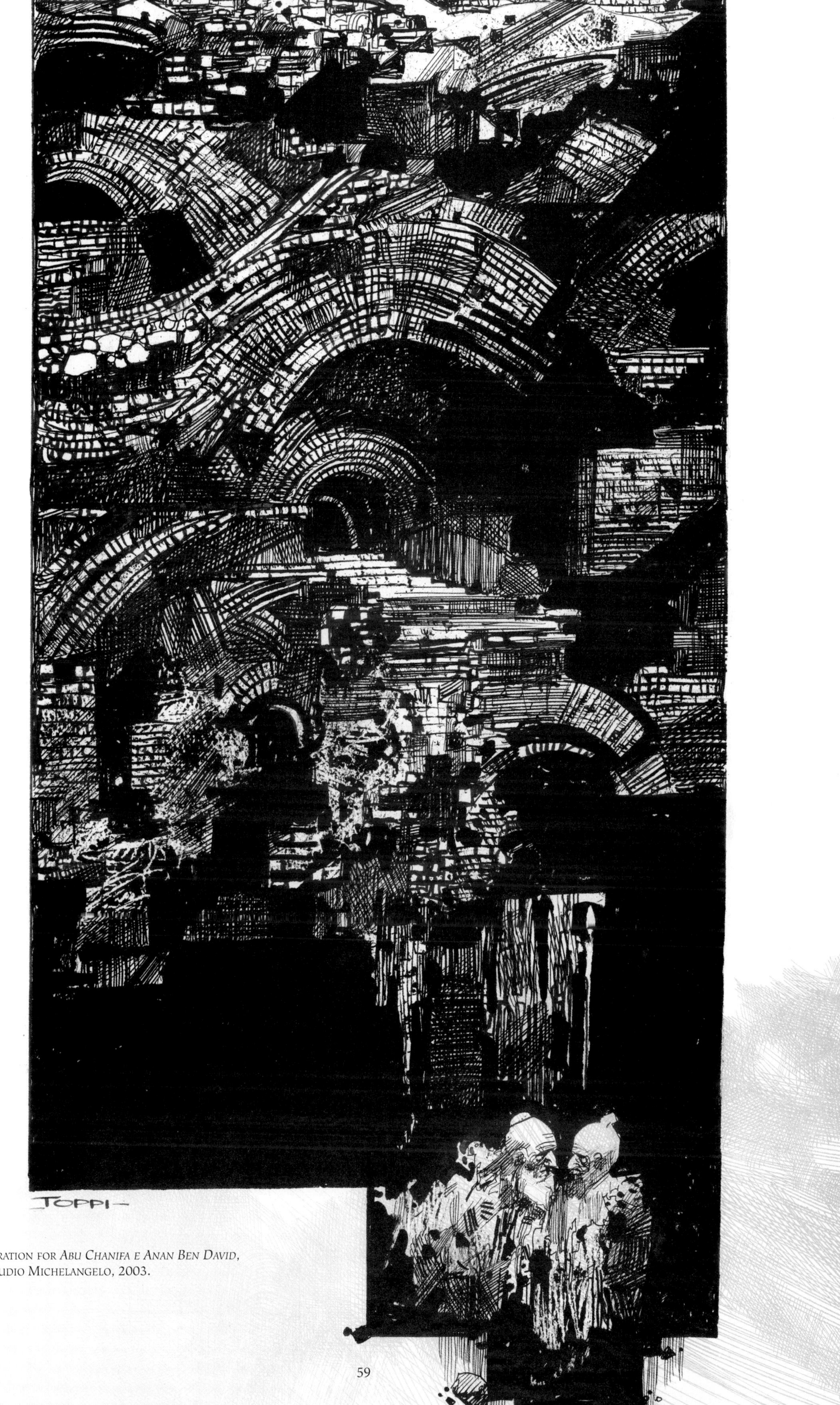

Illustration for *Abu Chanifa e Anan Ben David*,
for Studio Michelangelo, 2003.

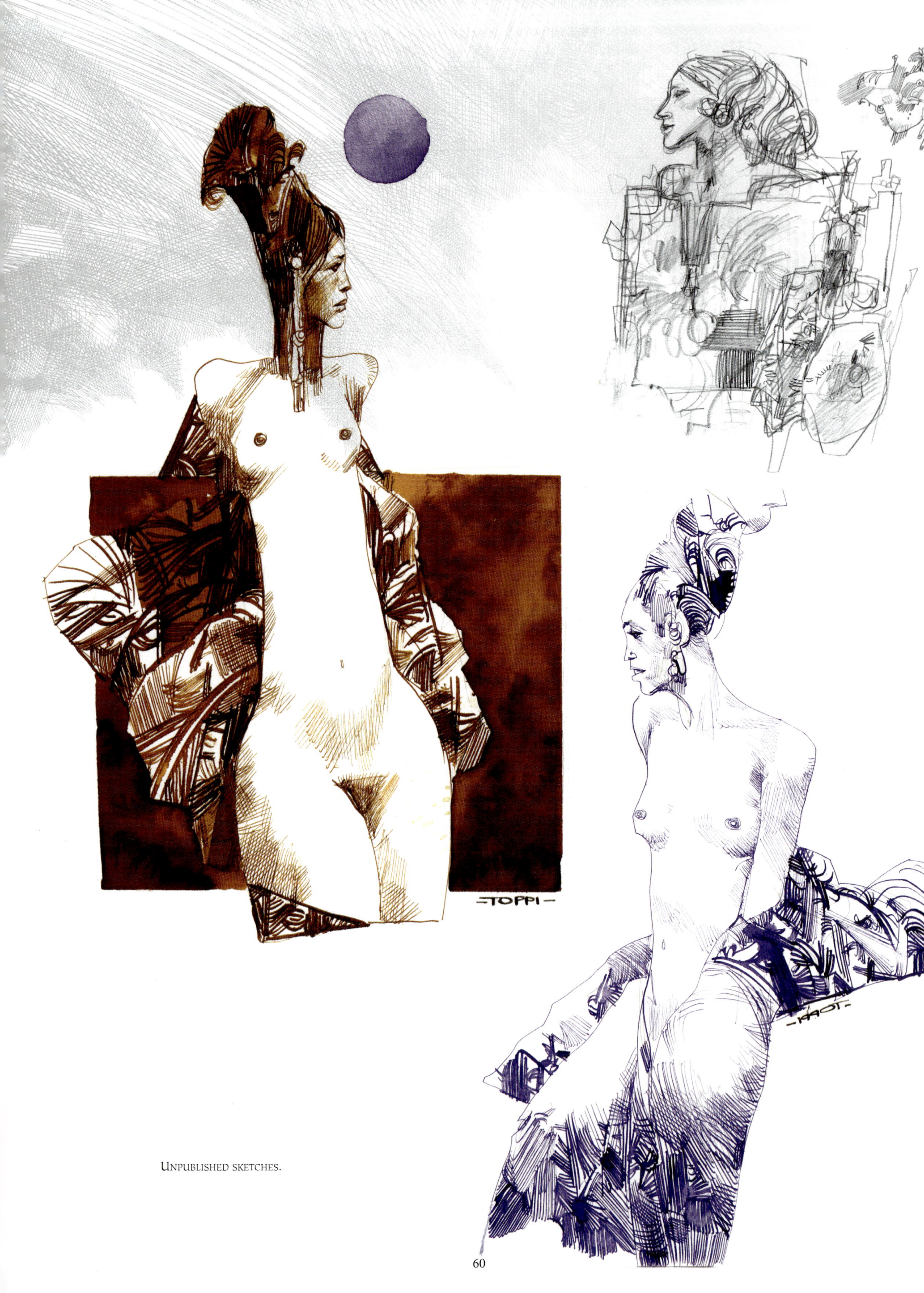

UNPUBLISHED SKETCHES.

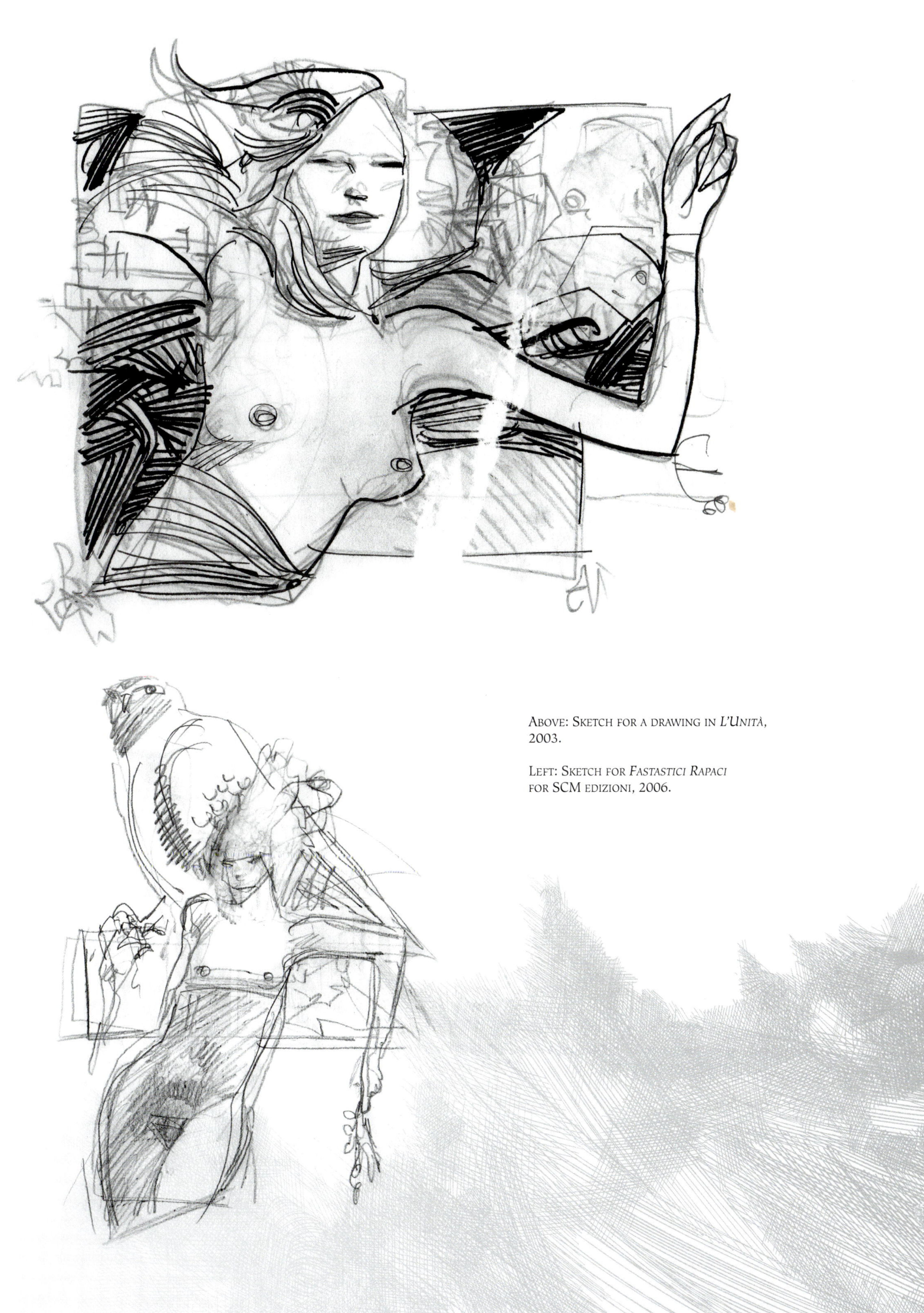

Above: Sketch for a drawing in *L'Unità*, 2003.

Left: Sketch for *Fastastici Rapaci* for SCM edizioni, 2006.

Lansquenets, 1527

A history lesson… In 1527, the Catholic Charles V, sworn enemy of the Lutherans, sent 12,000 Lansquenets (Lutherans) to take Rome, a Catholic state if ever there was one. 20,000 Roman Catholics perished at the swords of these Lutheran soldiers, on the orders of a Catholic emperor who despised Lutherans. How splendid!

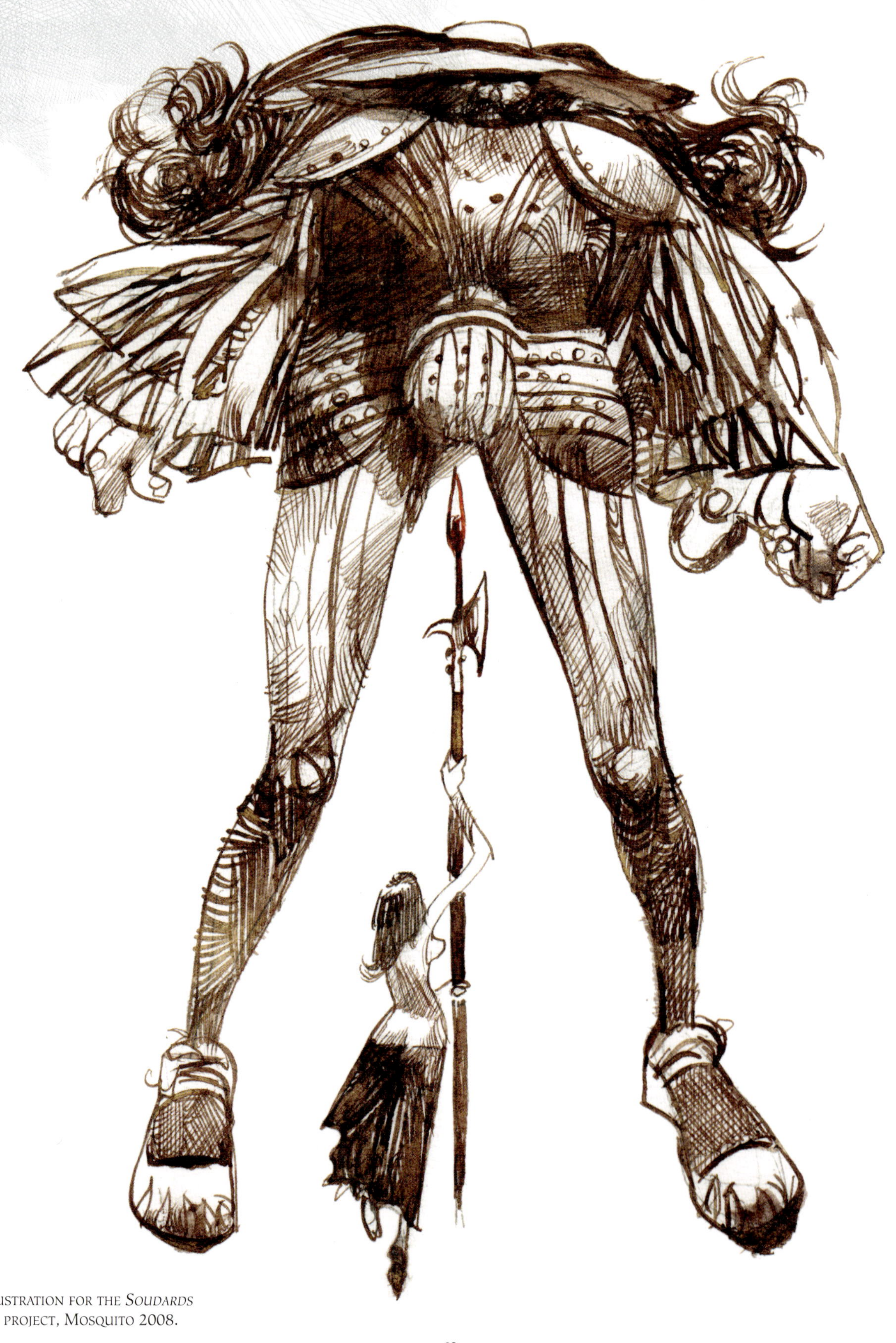

Unpublished illustration for the *Soudards et Belles Garces* project, Mosquito 2008.

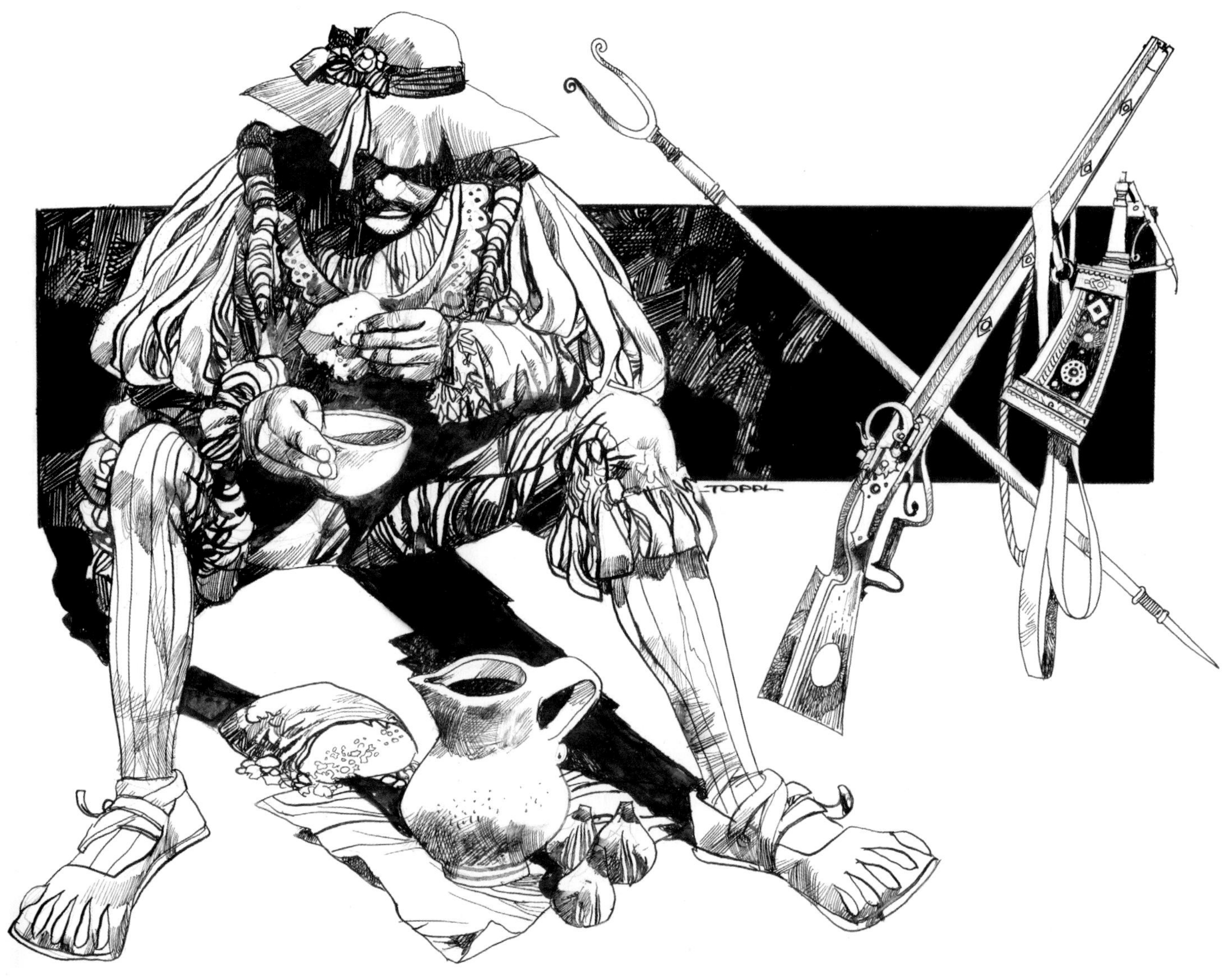

"They say I am a "Lansquenet." This means "servant of the country."
The country I serve is the one that gives me food to eat. I am godless and
lawless. I sell myself to the highest bidder. My employers gave me a uniform
and a rifle. As for the rifle, I live up to the expectations of the kingdom that
pays me. For the uniform, I couldn't really say. A bowl of gruel, a few figs, a
piece of bread, a jug of wine: I don't cost much, after all. I am far from my
homeland, I don't know anyone, and I have no friends. I spend my pay in
the first brothel that comes along. I believe in nothing, I think of nothing.

I kill, I eat, and I sleep."

ILLUSTRATION FOR *IL GIORNALINO*, 1980.

PAGES 86 AND 93
ILLUSTRATIONS FOR THE IL SACCO DI ROMA PORTFOLIO
PRODUCED BY ANGELO NENCETTI IN LUCCA, 2004.

"I, Carolus Quintus, Charles, fifth of the name, Emperor of the Holy Roman Germanic Empire, Prince of the Netherlands, King of Spain and King of Sicily, Son of Philip the Handsome and Joanna the Mad, was the most powerful ruler of my time, but I did not know how to reign.

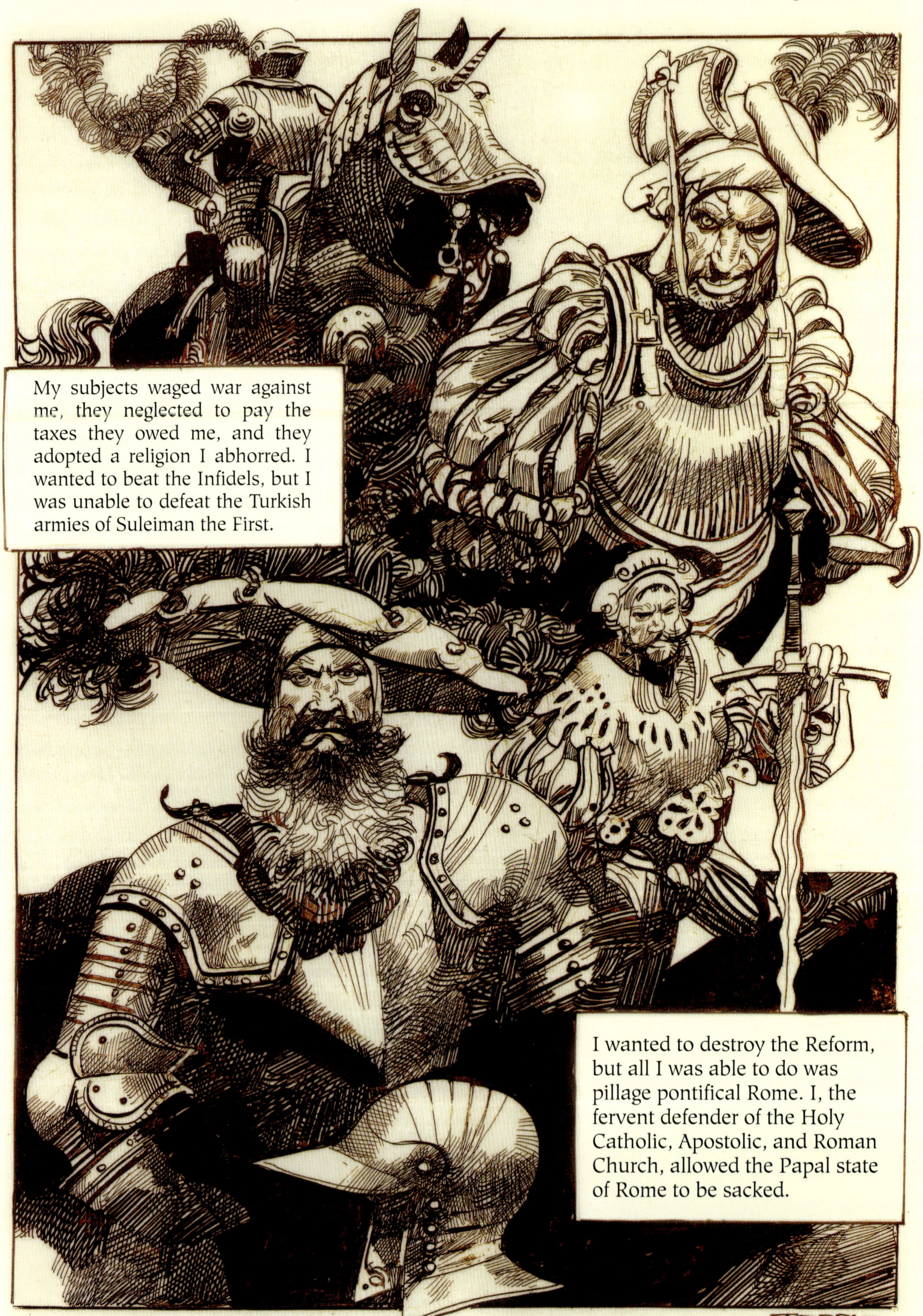

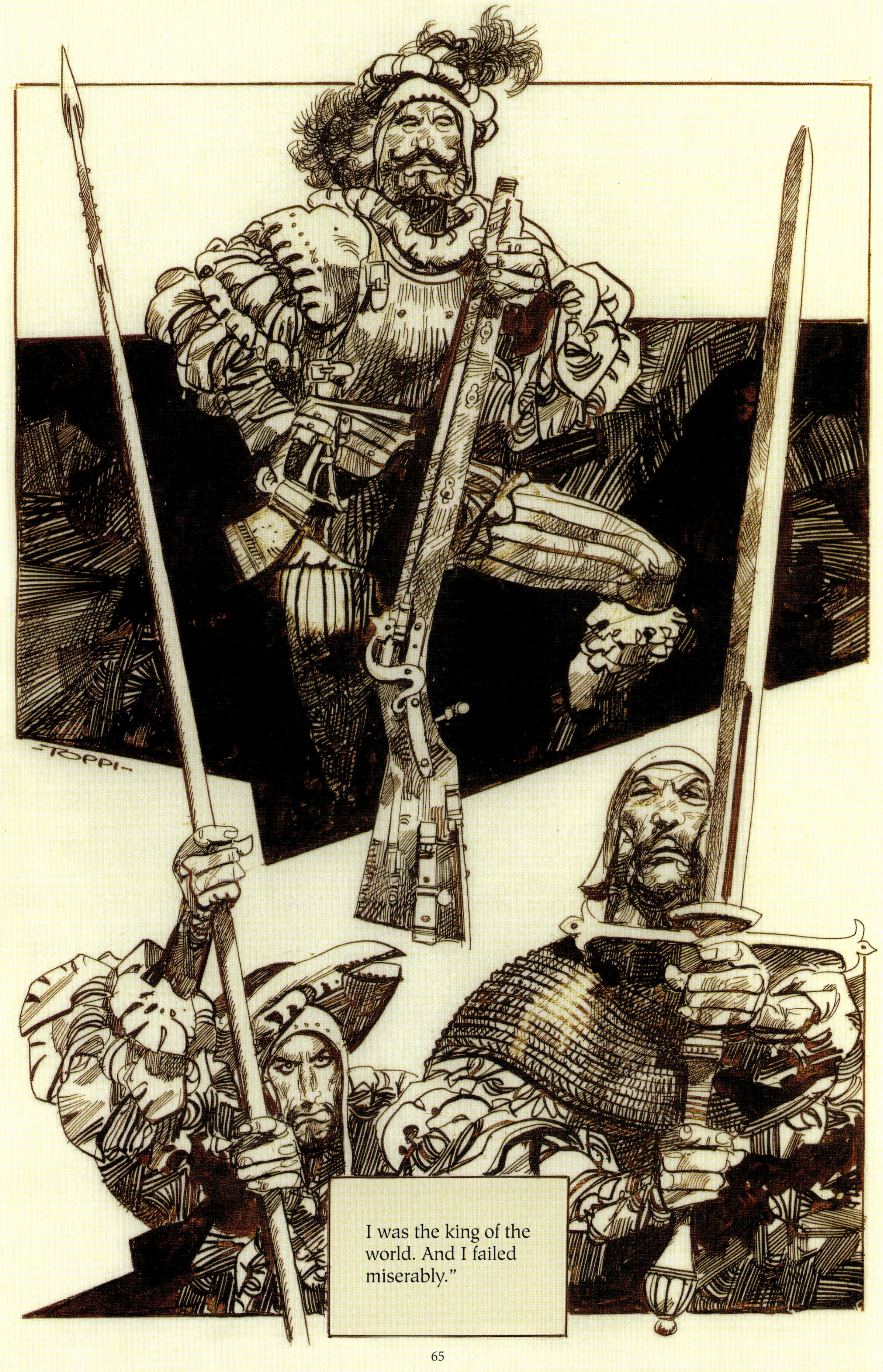
I was the king of the
world. And I failed
miserably."

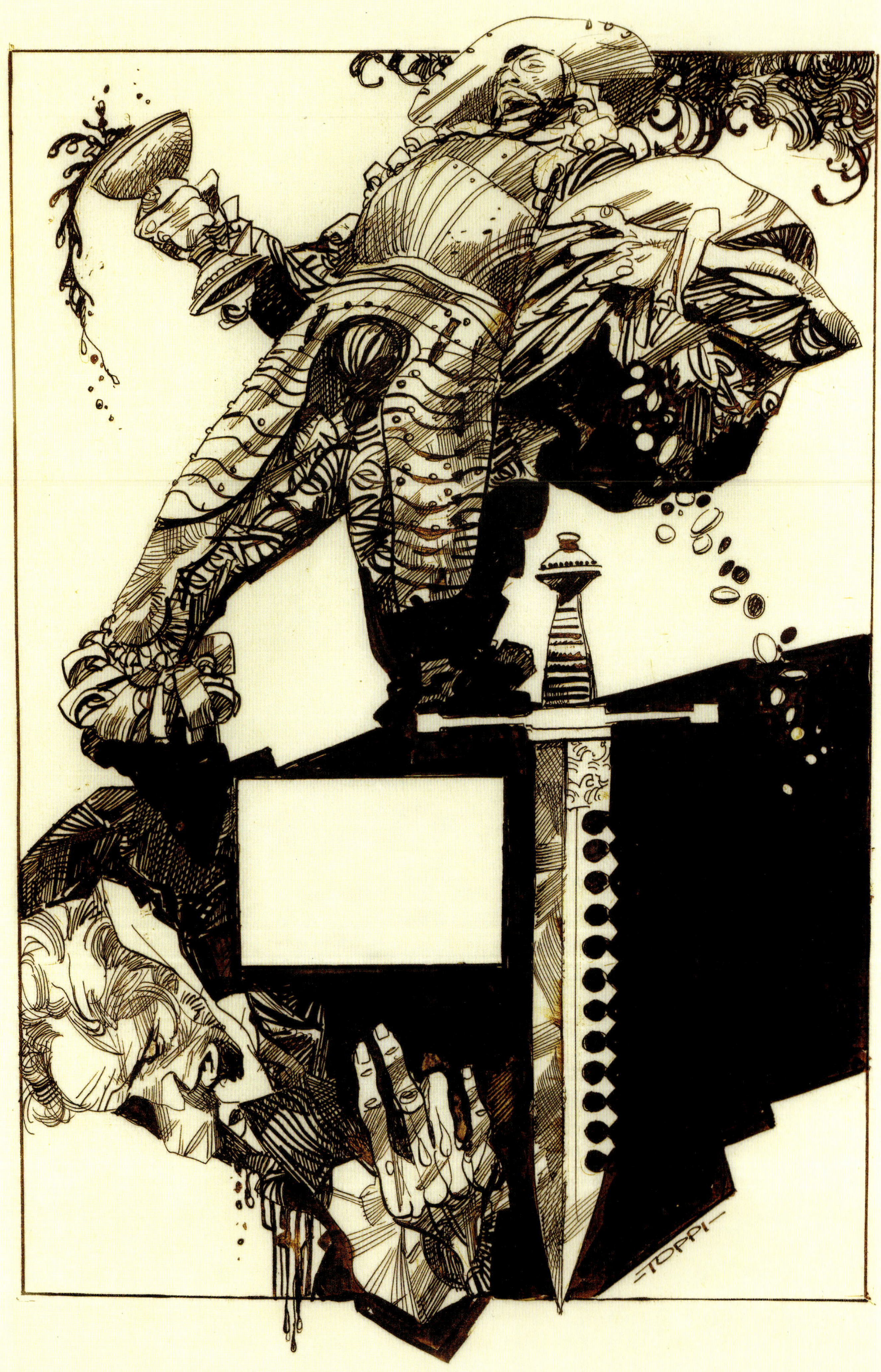

Le Padre was not, strictly speaking, what one might call a soft-hearted person. Imagining himself vested with the powers of Grand Inquisitor of his parish, he enthusiastically pursued the prosecution, conviction, and punishment of Reformists, Jews, actors, philosophers, poets, painters, and, needless to say, sodomites.

He suspected all women of sorcery. His sermons from the pulpit exhorted one and all to pray for Divine fury to be unleashed. He would have the world put to fire and the sword "in order to purify it," he would bellow. To hear him speak, Christ on the cross called out for vengeance, the apocalypse, and destruction.

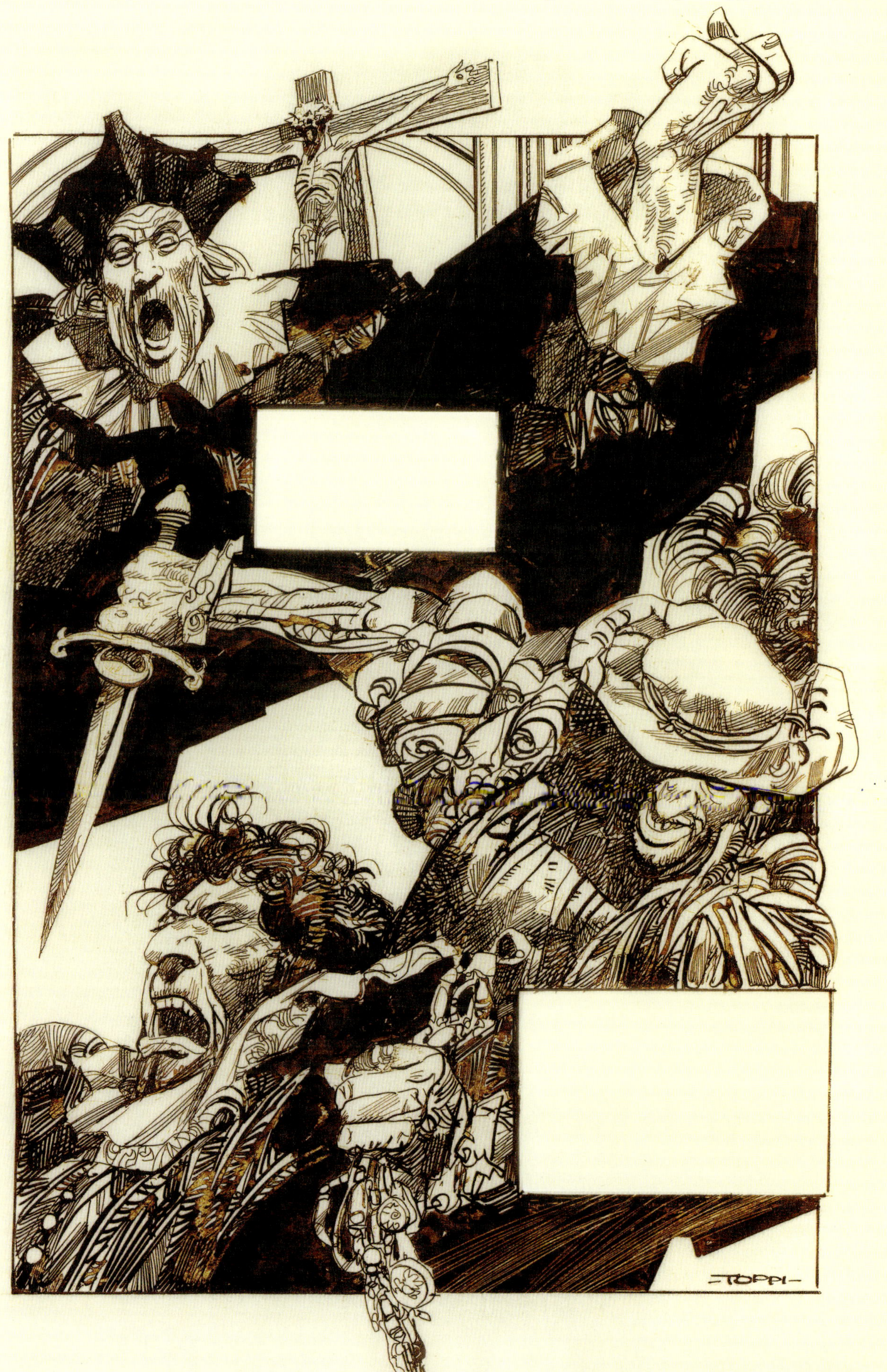

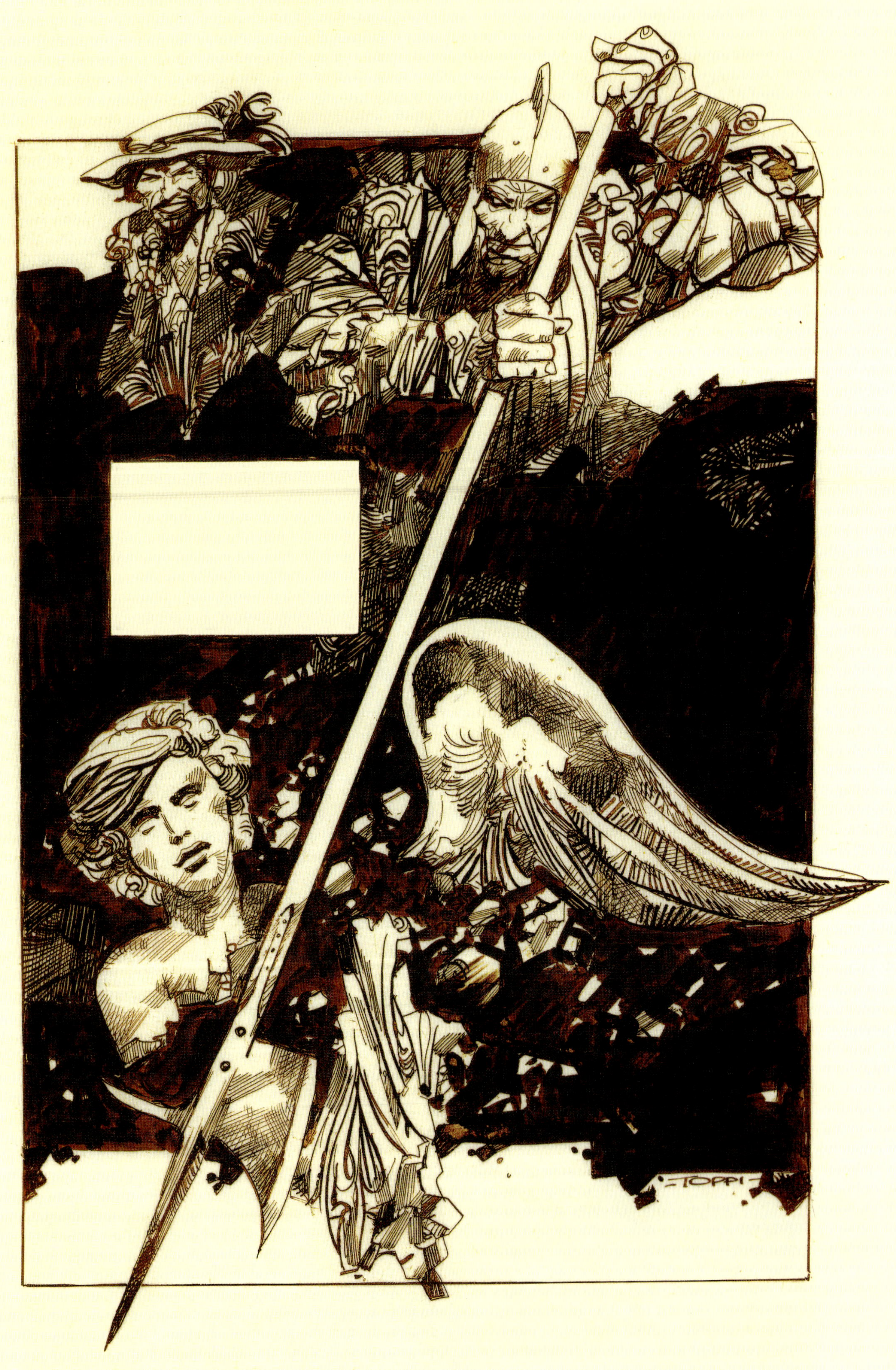

On May 6, 1527, Charles V's troops entered Rome. By nightfall, they stood before the presbytery of Le Padre. Indeed, the Apocalypse had come. For one who hoped for a world of fire and blood, his prayers had been answered. But he was not allowed the good fortune of seeing this for himself. Fulminating at the arrival of the Germanic soldiers, he was immediately put to the sword.

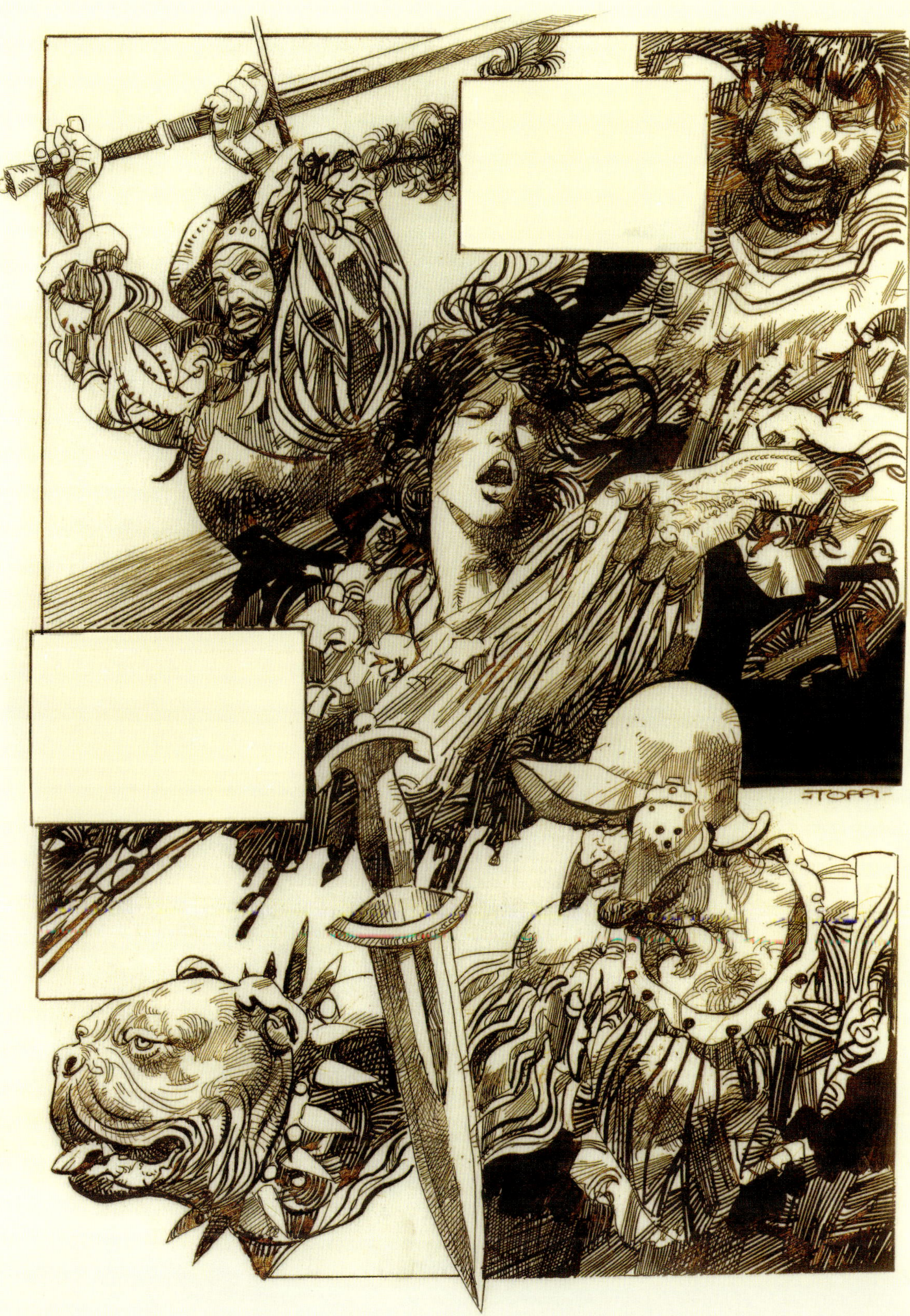

They were called dogs, so they therefore behaved like dogs. They entered the alley barking, so sure of their actions, so sure of their rights. They burst open the doors of homes and forced themselves on the women within. They were like savage beasts. They had a German Mastiff as their mascot; it was, in a matter of speaking, the only human in their entire regiment.

Why bother asking what one can take? This woman pleased him, so he took her. The idea, however, was not a good one. Conqueror, perhaps, but he was far from convincing. In vain, he ripped off her clothes, tore out her hair, covered her with a litany of insults, and forced her into the most indecent of postures. But nothing happened. The piece of skin between his legs did not even twitch. It hung there, limp and pathetic. He hated himself. He let go of the woman, suddenly losing interest in her, and was seized by overwhelming rage. He broke the windows, emptied the cupboards, stole the fine silverware, turned heel, and stormed outside. All powerful, if you say so; yet most definitely vanquished.

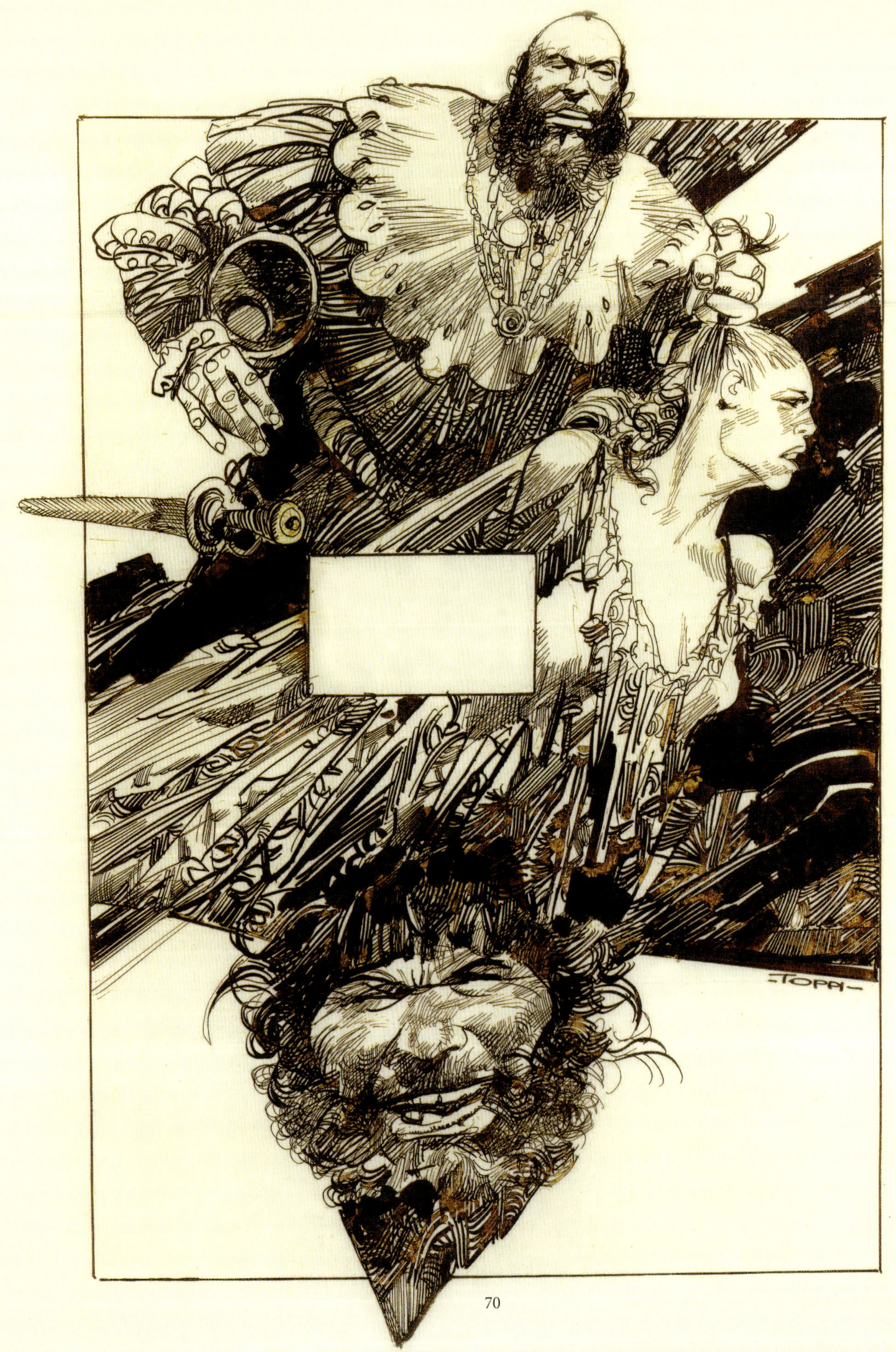

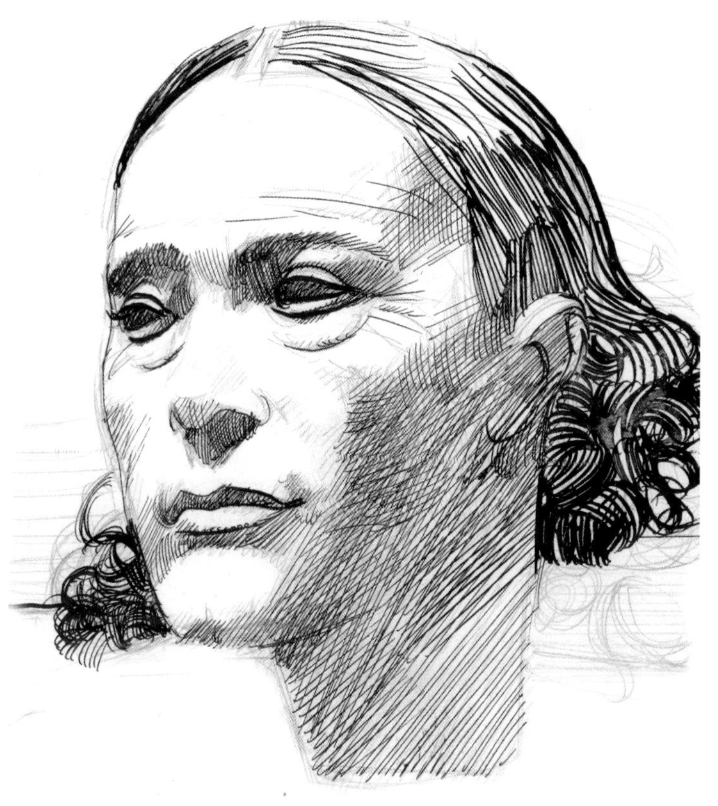

Study for an allegorical figure
representing Italy, 1990.

Vienna 1683

When the Ottomans failed their siege of Vienna in 1683, the city's bakers
were given the privilege of preparing a cake in the shape of a crescent moon
(the traditional symbol of the Ottoman Empire).

Ah, if only a pastry were enough to sweeten this world's wars!

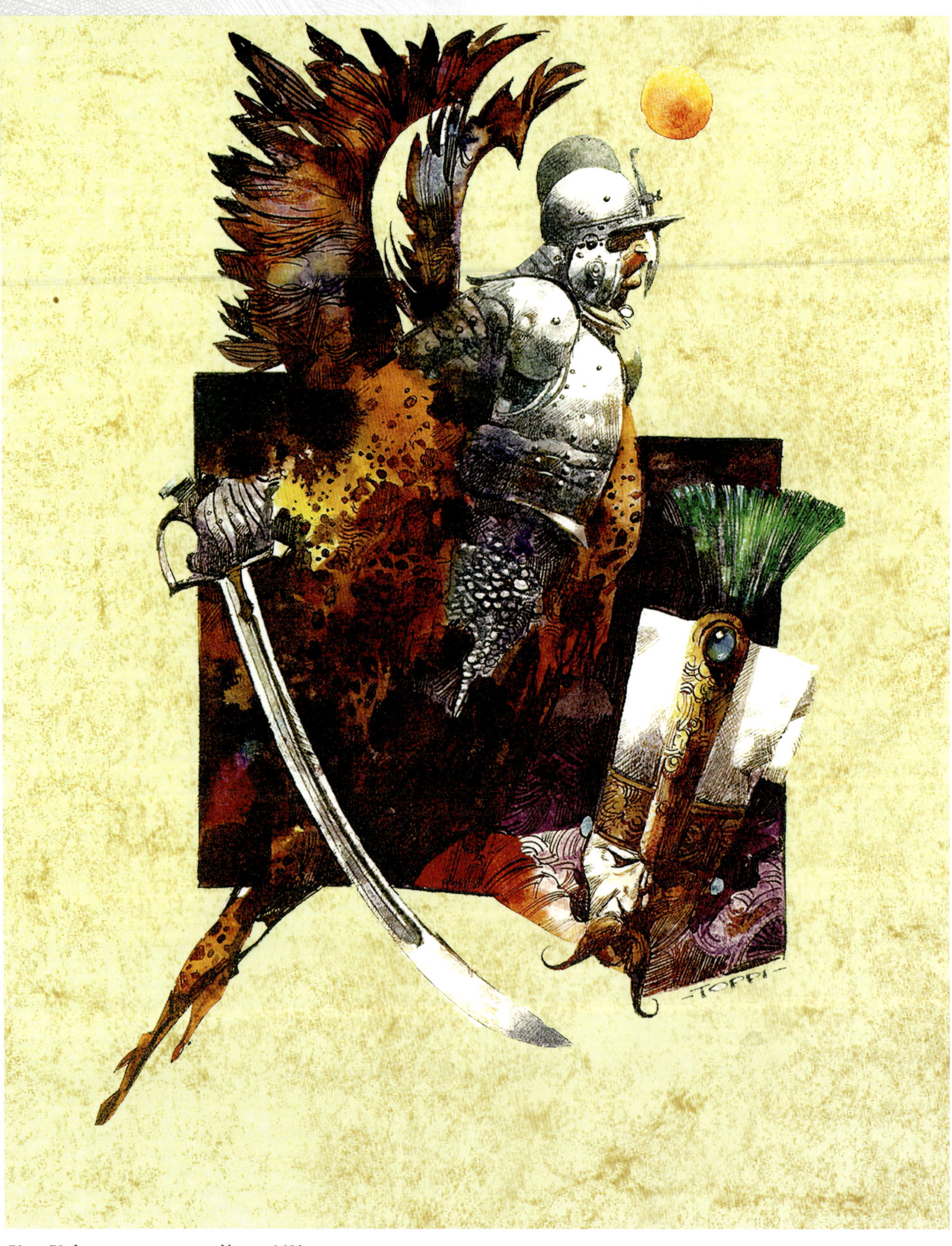

Pages 72 to 79: Illustrations for the *Vienna 1683* portfolio
Produced by Angelo Nencetti, Lucca 2002.

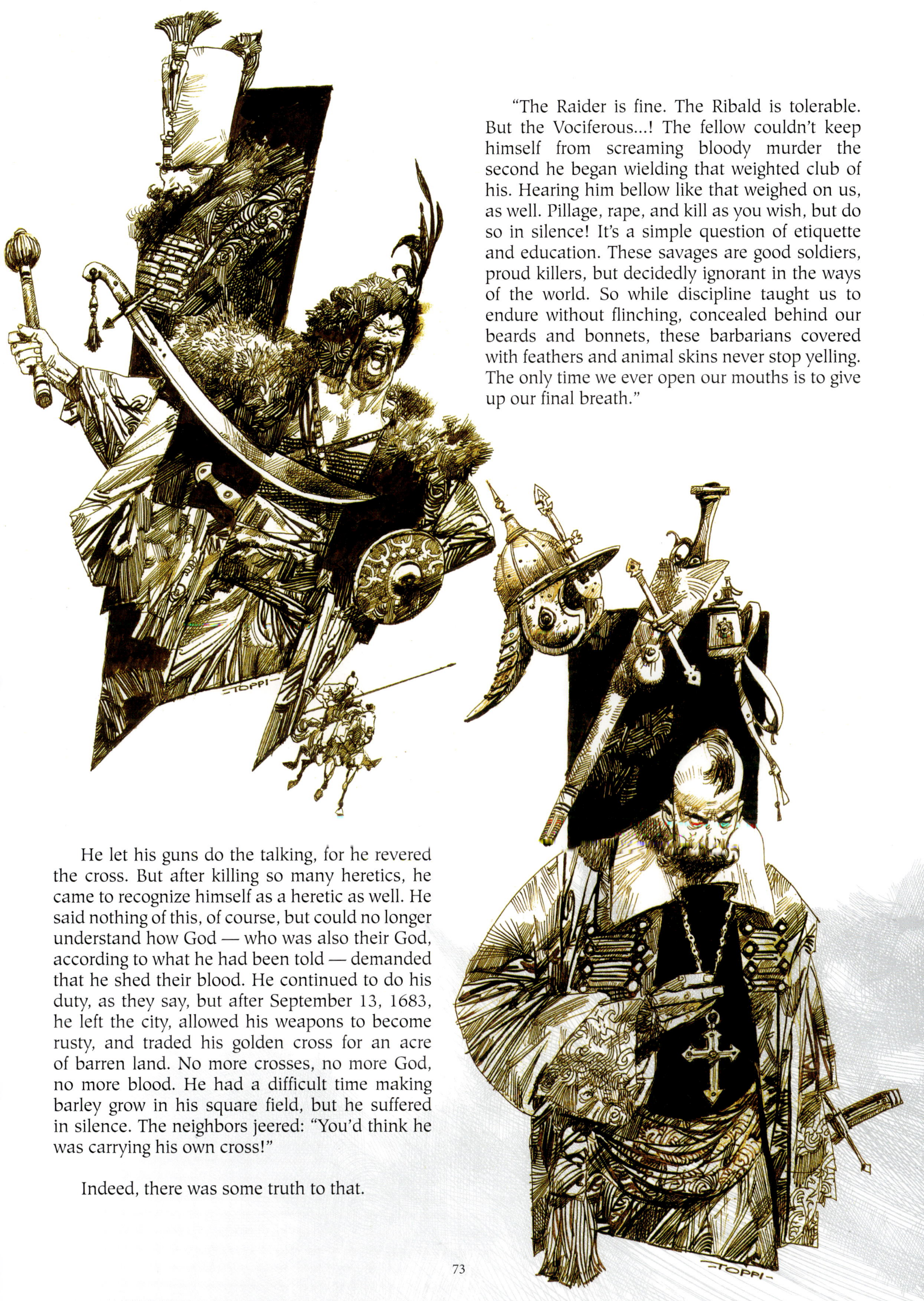

"The Raider is fine. The Ribald is tolerable. But the Vociferous...! The fellow couldn't keep himself from screaming bloody murder the second he began wielding that weighted club of his. Hearing him bellow like that weighed on us, as well. Pillage, rape, and kill as you wish, but do so in silence! It's a simple question of etiquette and education. These savages are good soldiers, proud killers, but decidedly ignorant in the ways of the world. So while discipline taught us to endure without flinching, concealed behind our beards and bonnets, these barbarians covered with feathers and animal skins never stop yelling. The only time we ever open our mouths is to give up our final breath."

He let his guns do the talking, for he revered the cross. But after killing so many heretics, he came to recognize himself as a heretic as well. He said nothing of this, of course, but could no longer understand how God — who was also their God, according to what he had been told — demanded that he shed their blood. He continued to do his duty, as they say, but after September 13, 1683, he left the city, allowed his weapons to become rusty, and traded his golden cross for an acre of barren land. No more crosses, no more God, no more blood. He had a difficult time making barley grow in his square field, but he suffered in silence. The neighbors jeered: "You'd think he was carrying his own cross!"

Indeed, there was some truth to that.

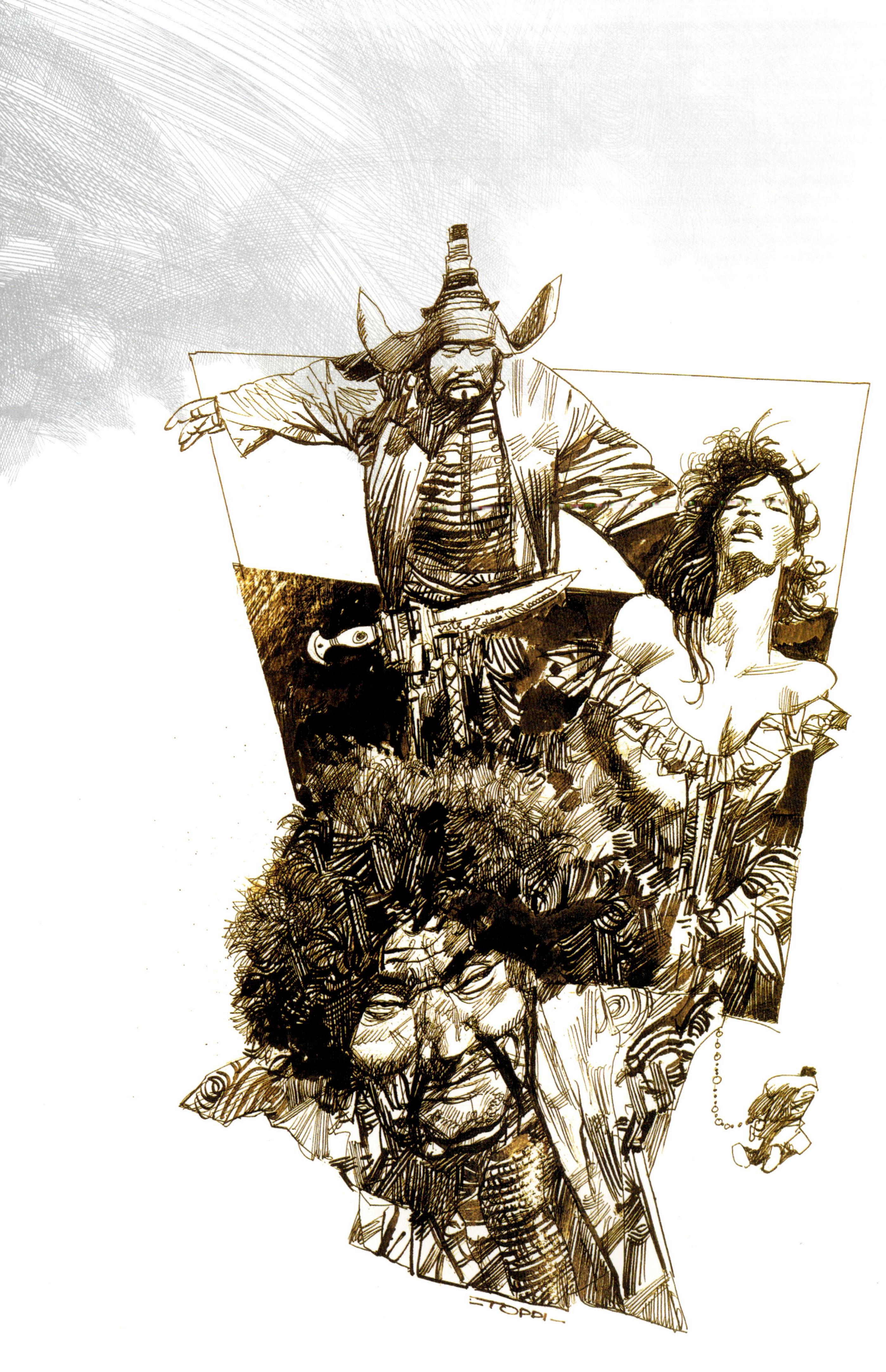

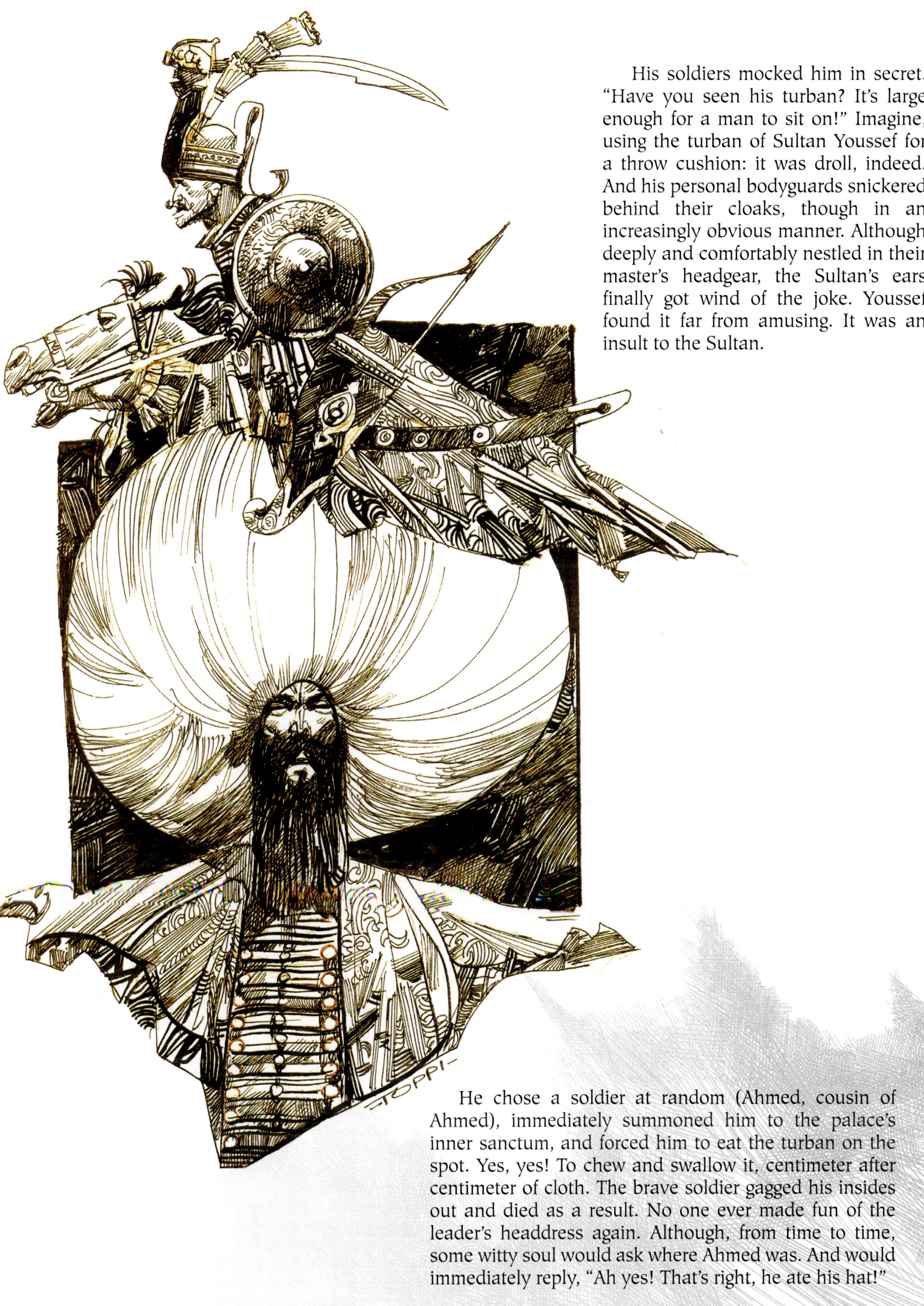

His soldiers mocked him in secret. "Have you seen his turban? It's large enough for a man to sit on!" Imagine, using the turban of Sultan Youssef for a throw cushion: it was droll, indeed. And his personal bodyguards snickered behind their cloaks, though in an increasingly obvious manner. Although deeply and comfortably nestled in their master's headgear, the Sultan's ears finally got wind of the joke. Youssef found it far from amusing. It was an insult to the Sultan.

He chose a soldier at random (Ahmed, cousin of Ahmed), immediately summoned him to the palace's inner sanctum, and forced him to eat the turban on the spot. Yes, yes! To chew and swallow it, centimeter after centimeter of cloth. The brave soldier gagged his insides out and died as a result. No one ever made fun of the leader's headdress again. Although, from time to time, some witty soul would ask where Ahmed was. And would immediately reply, "Ah yes! That's right, he ate his hat!"

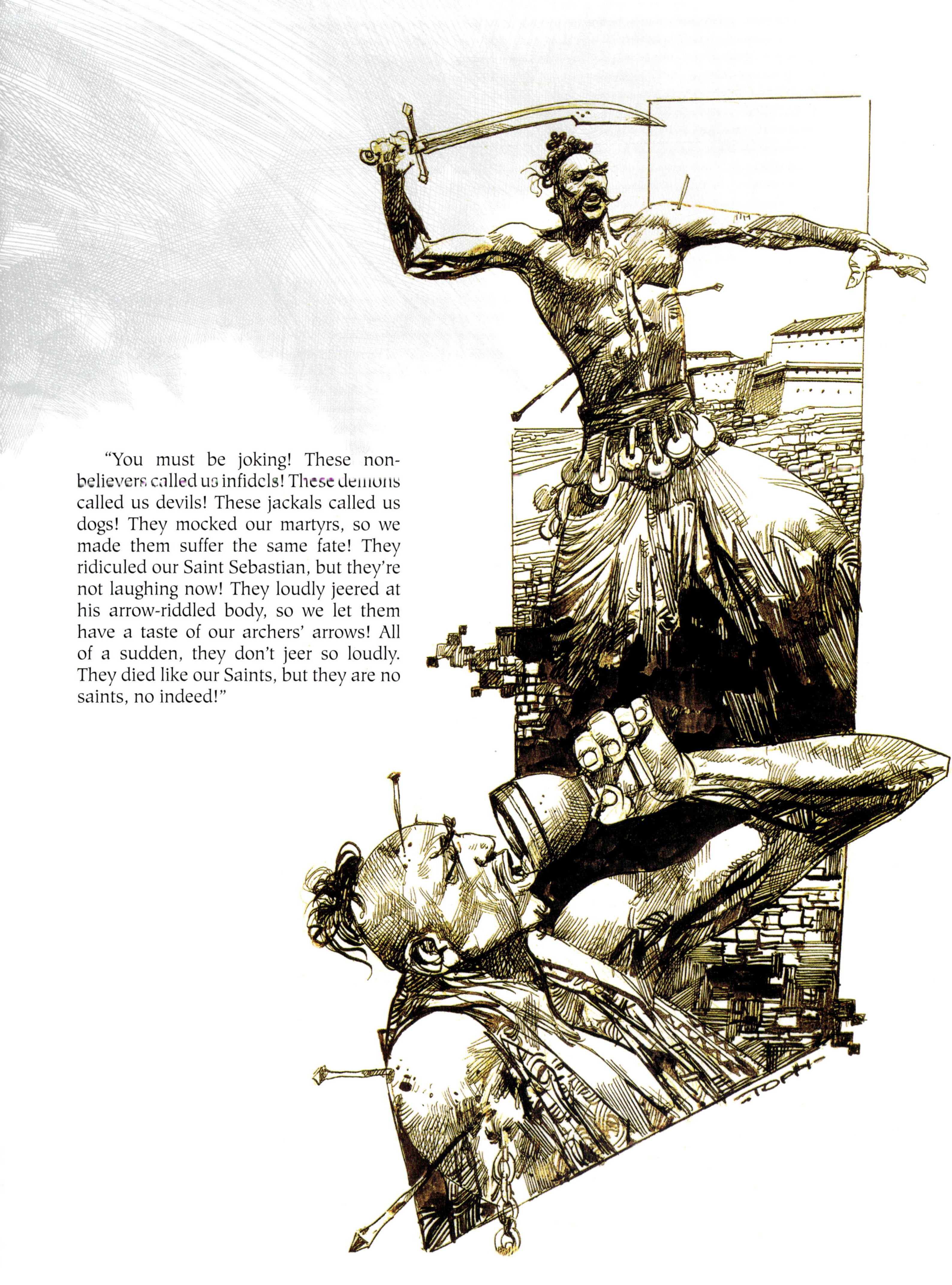

"You must be joking! These non-believers called us infidels! These demons called us devils! These jackals called us dogs! They mocked our martyrs, so we made them suffer the same fate! They ridiculed our Saint Sebastian, but they're not laughing now! They loudly jeered at his arrow-riddled body, so we let them have a taste of our archers' arrows! All of a sudden, they don't jeer so loudly. They died like our Saints, but they are no saints, no indeed!"

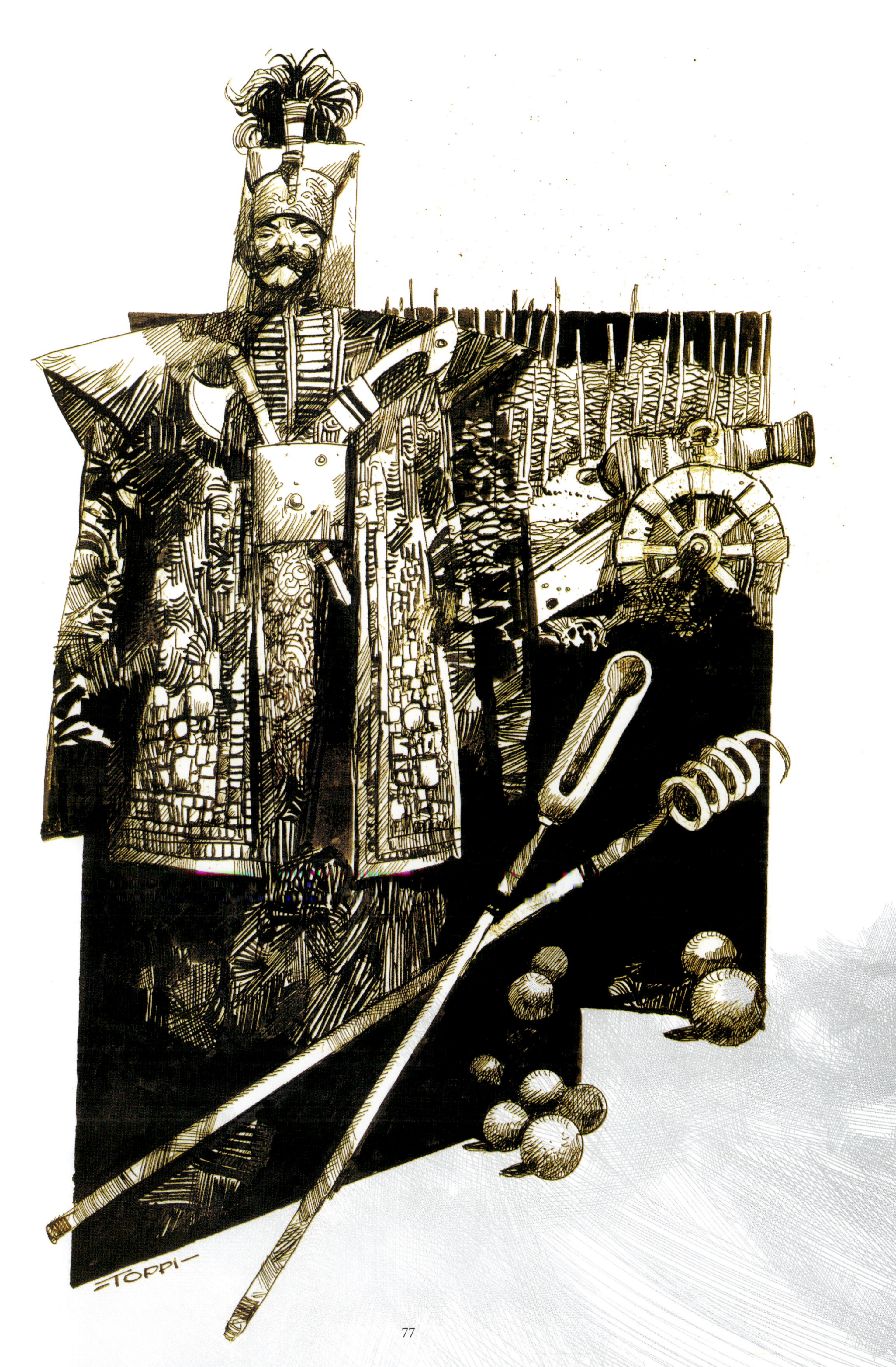

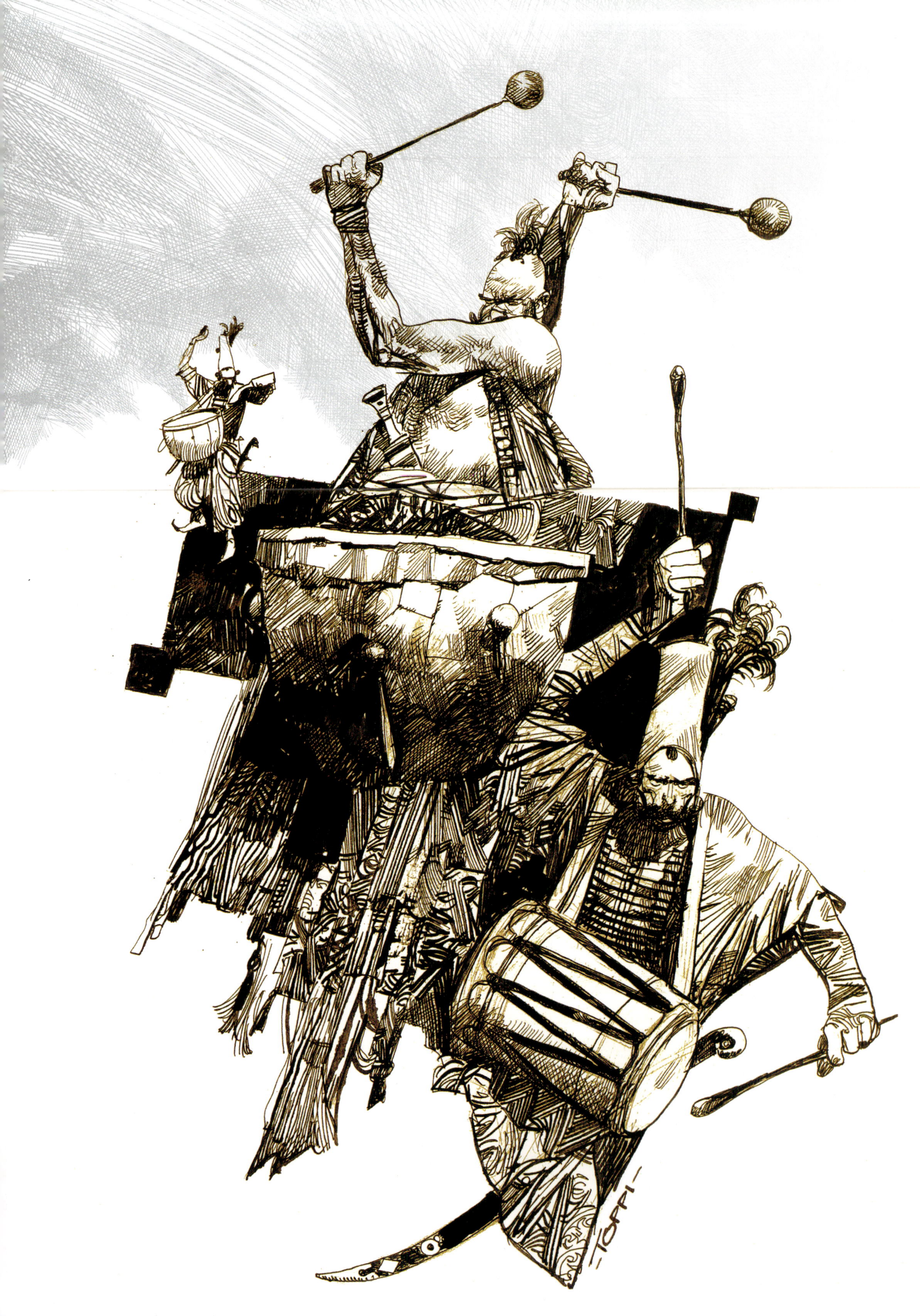
TOPPI

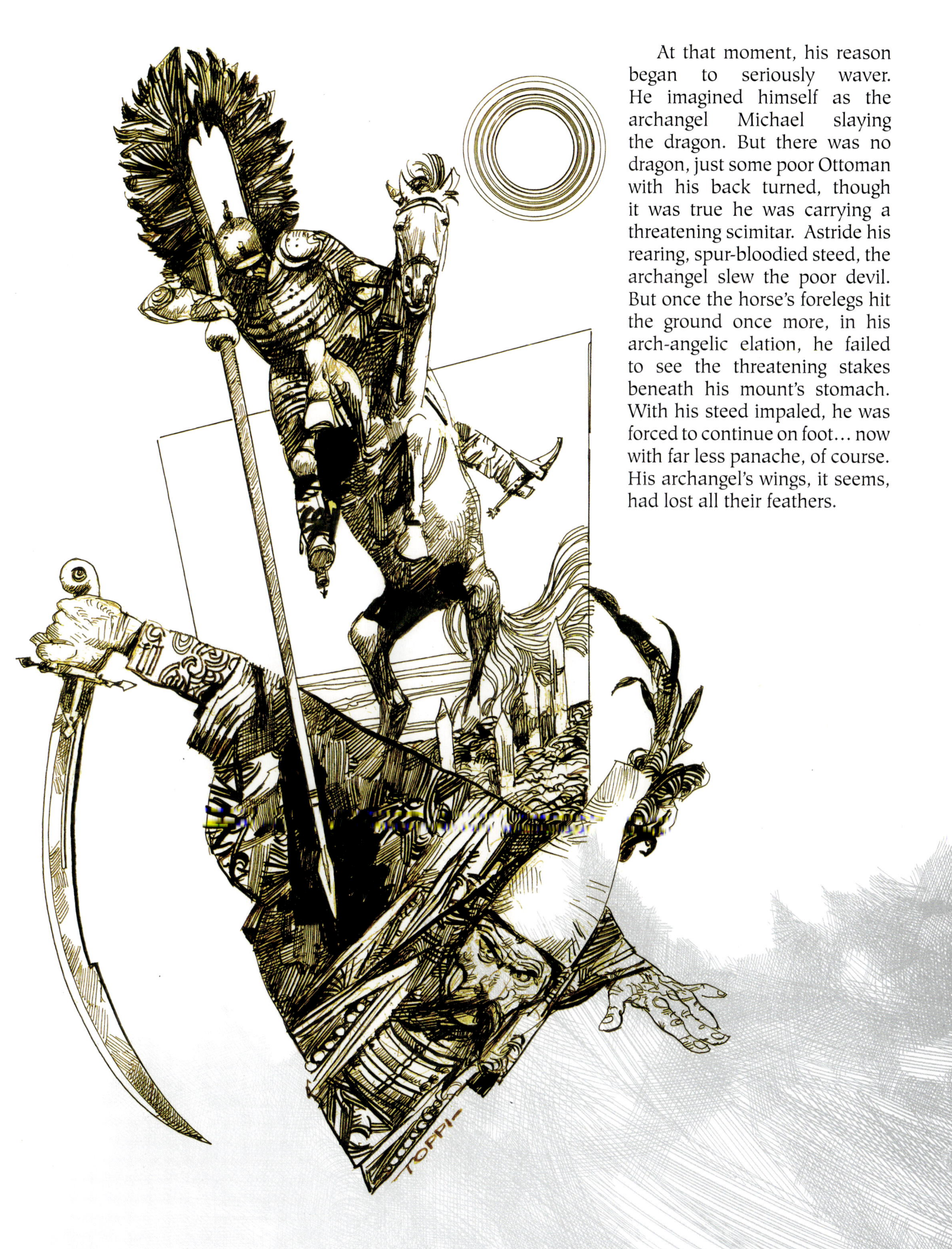

At that moment, his reason began to seriously waver. He imagined himself as the archangel Michael slaying the dragon. But there was no dragon, just some poor Ottoman with his back turned, though it was true he was carrying a threatening scimitar. Astride his rearing, spur-bloodied steed, the archangel slew the poor devil. But once the horse's forelegs hit the ground once more, in his arch-angelic elation, he failed to see the threatening stakes beneath his mount's stomach. With his steed impaled, he was forced to continue on foot… now with far less panache, of course. His archangel's wings, it seems, had lost all their feathers.

The Katana's blade

What is elsewhere is obviously better, since it isn't where we are.

Japan is what dreams are made of, because it is far away — far from our lands, far from our customs. The samurai wielding his katana with both hands, the geisha graciously performing the tea ceremony...

Japan is no country, it's a Western fantasy.

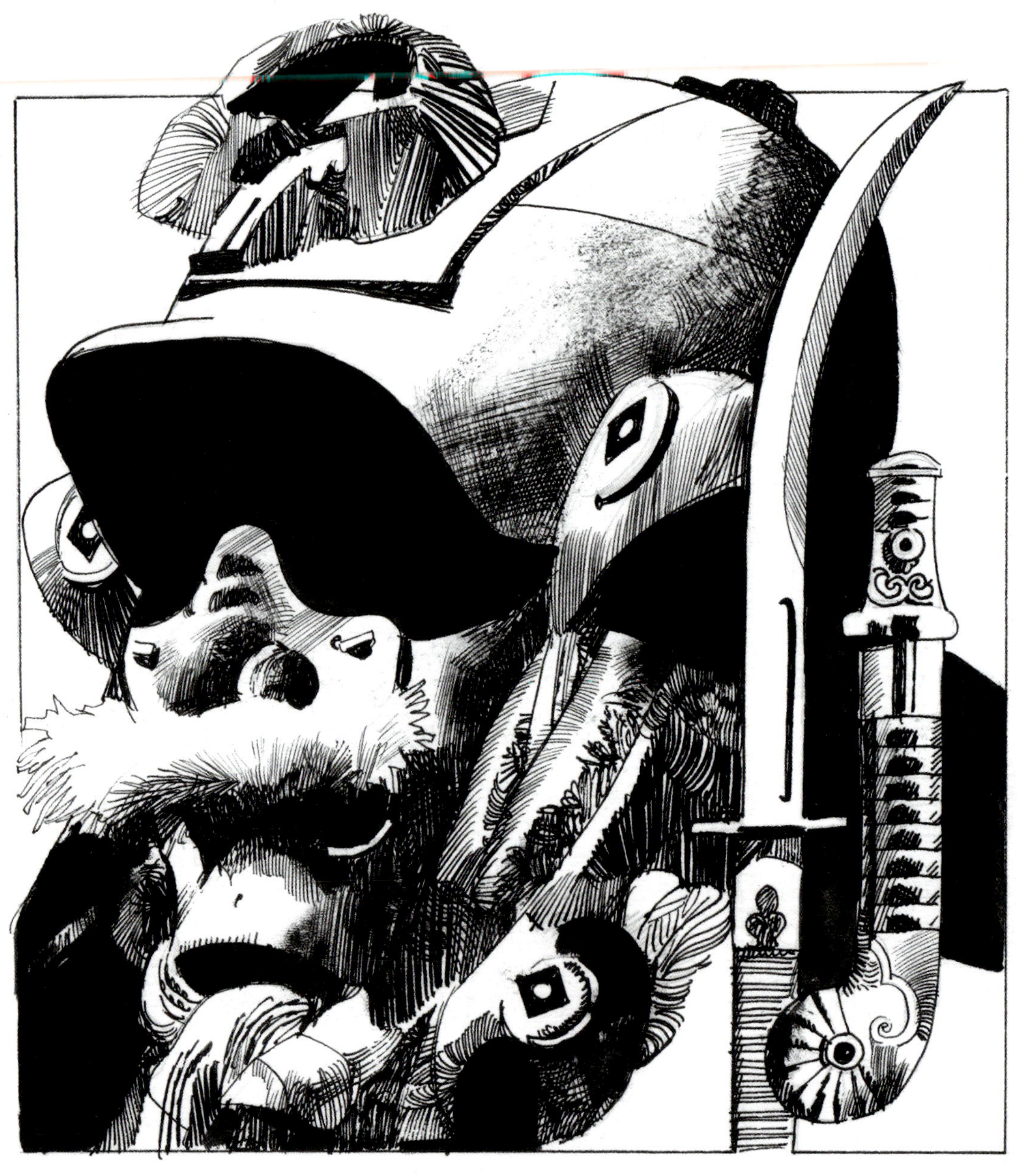

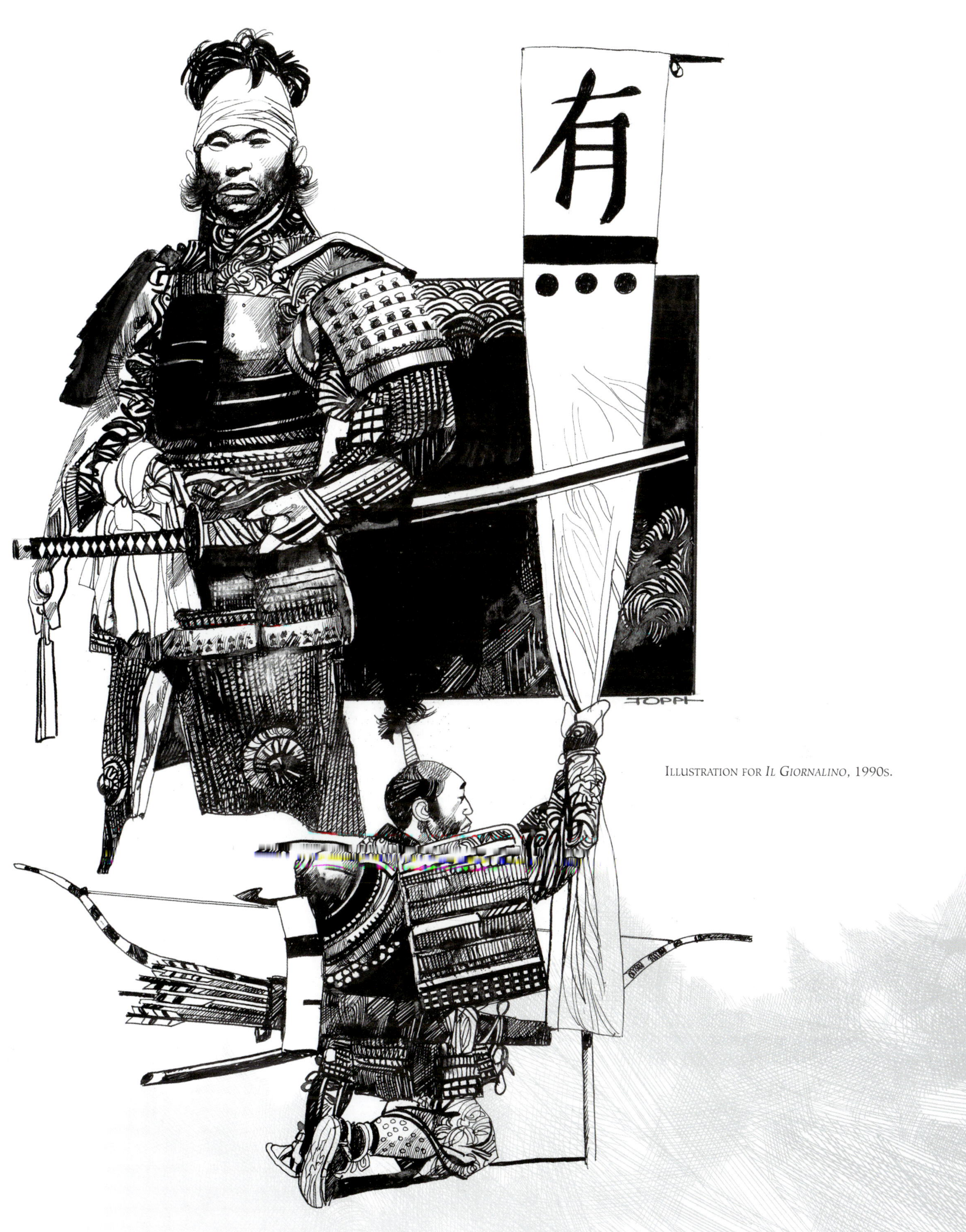

ILLUSTRATION FOR *IL GIORNALINO*, 1990s.

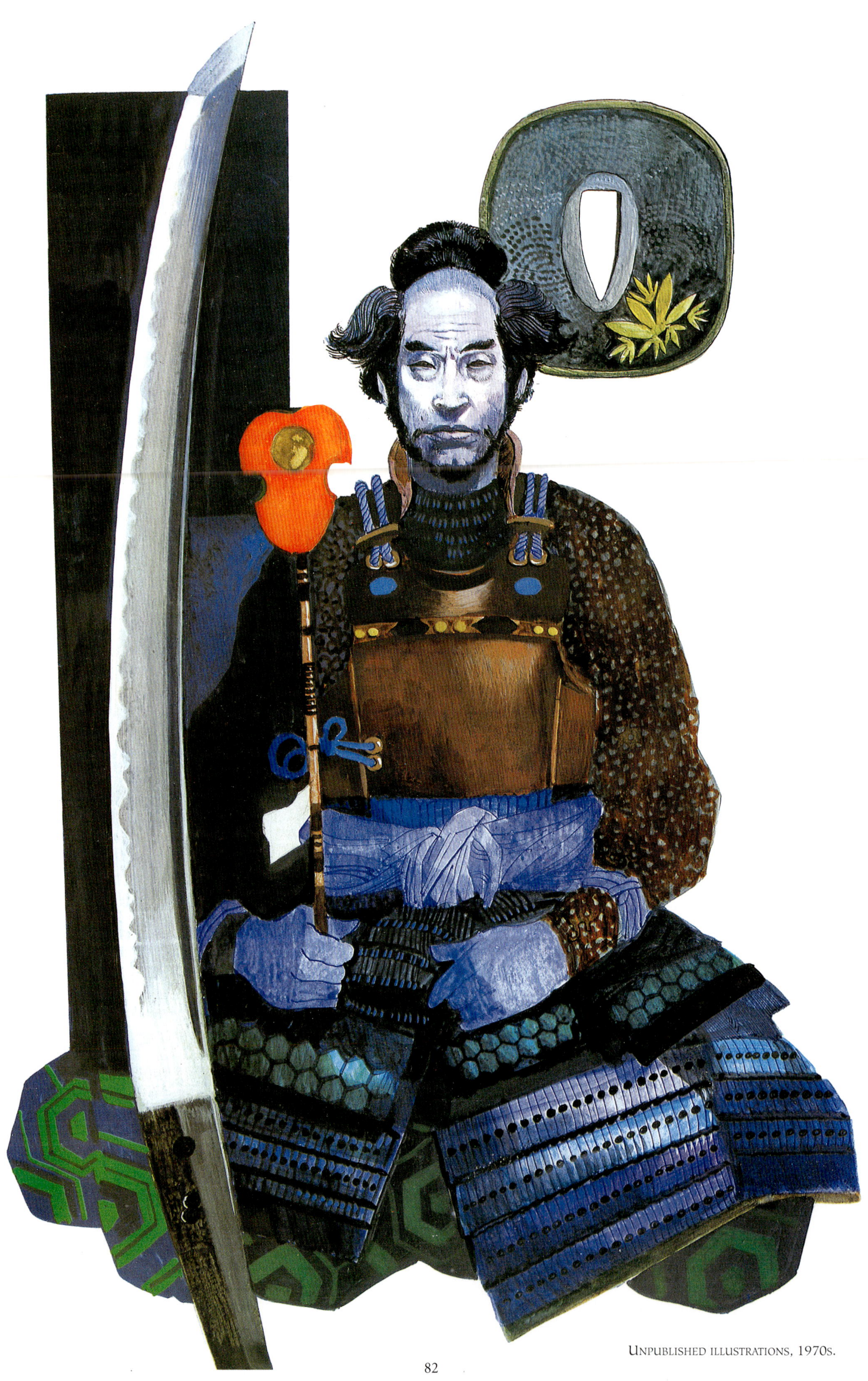

Unpublished illustrations, 1970s.

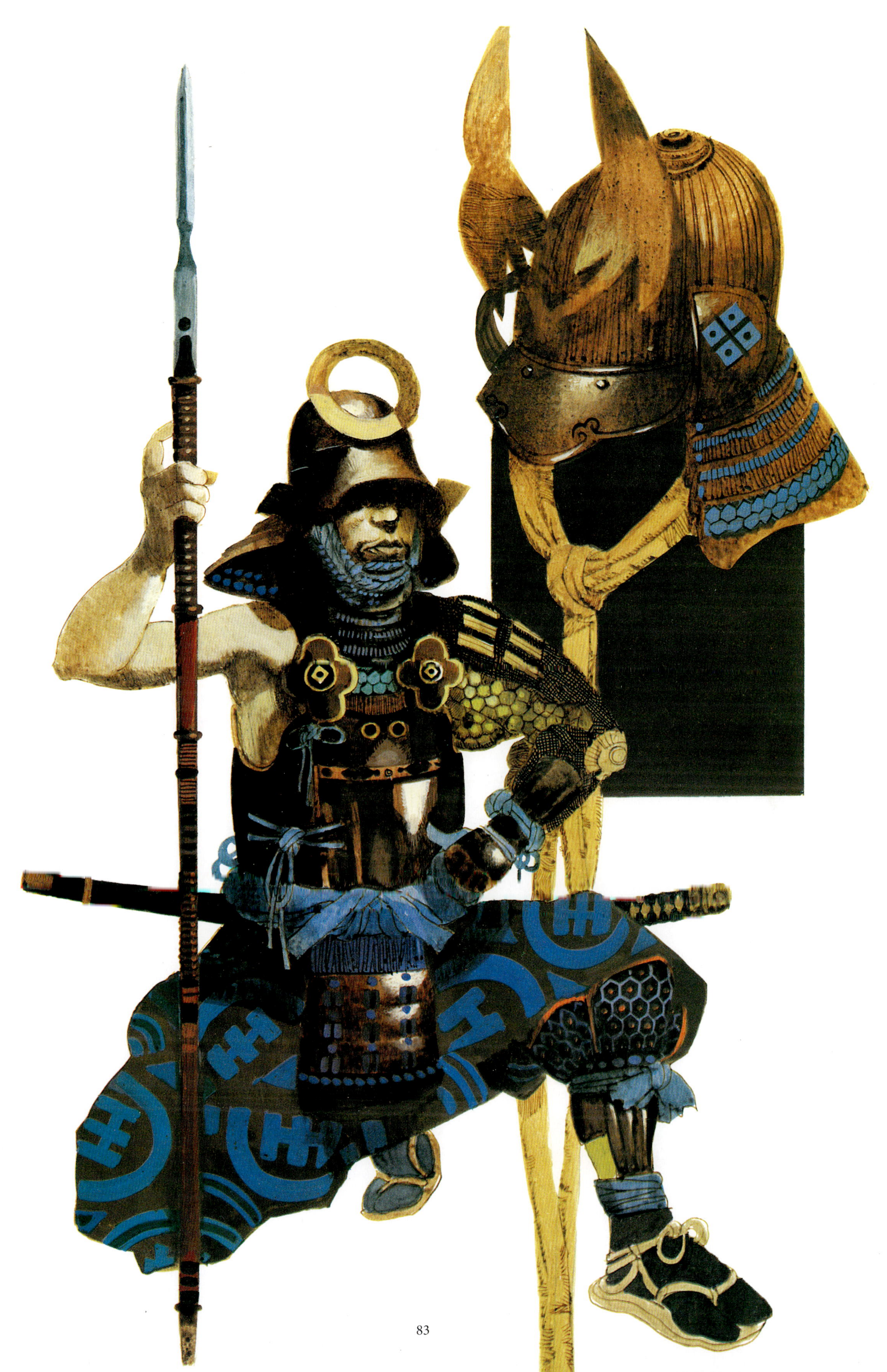

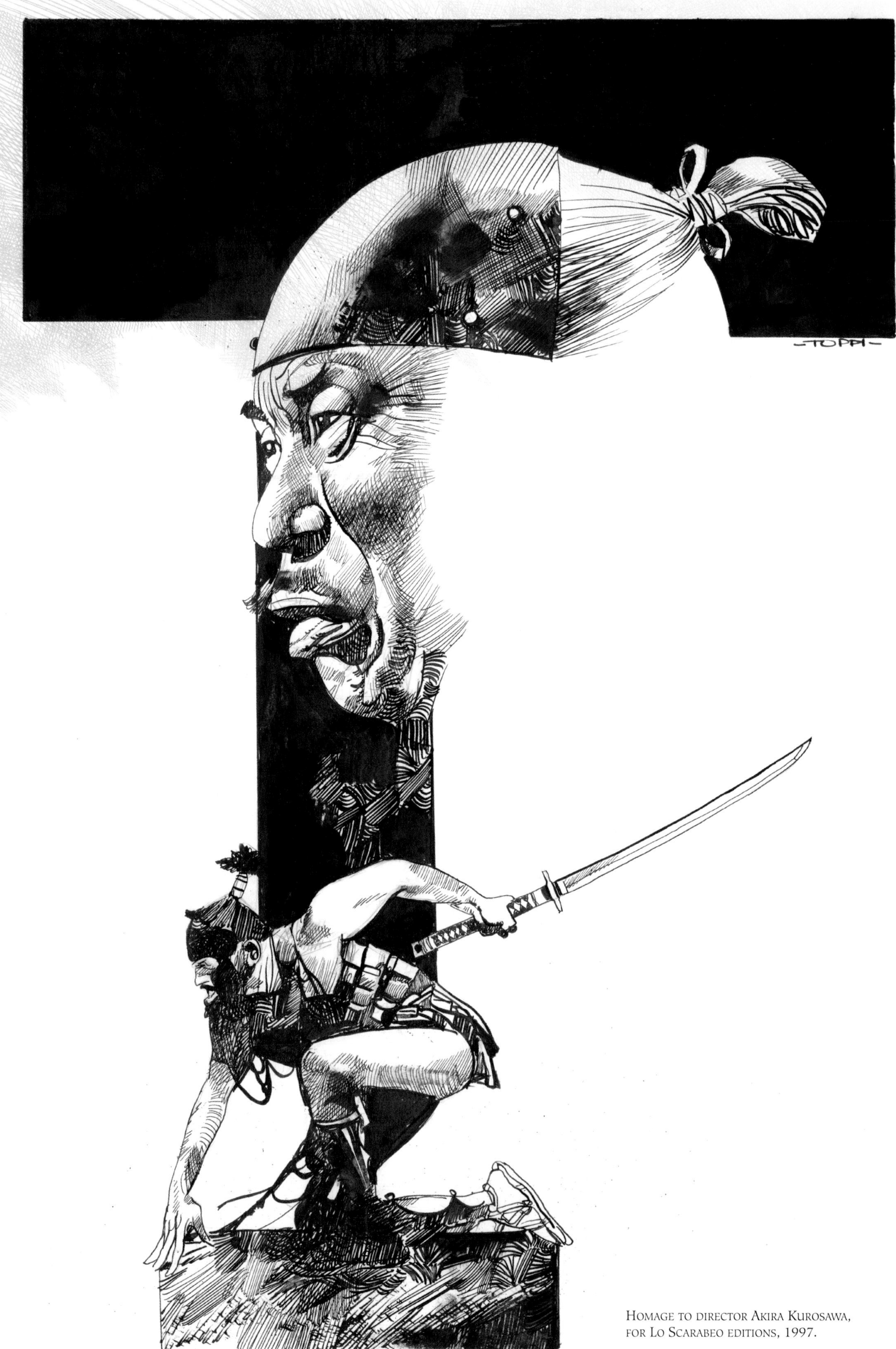

HOMAGE TO DIRECTOR AKIRA KUROSAWA,
FOR LO SCARABEO EDITIONS, 1997.

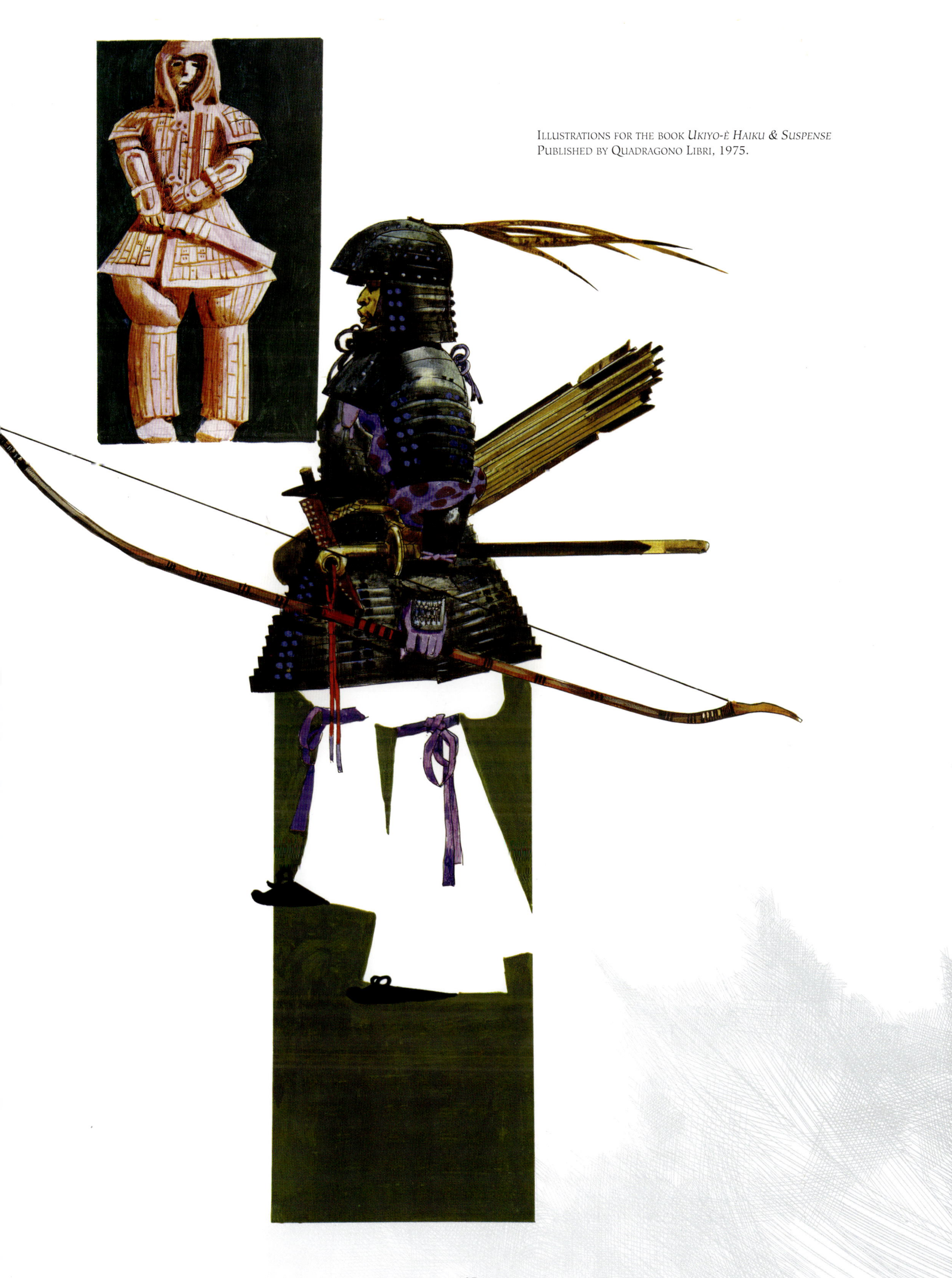

ILLUSTRATIONS FOR THE BOOK Ukiyo-è Haiku & Suspense
PUBLISHED BY QUADRAGONO LIBRI, 1975.

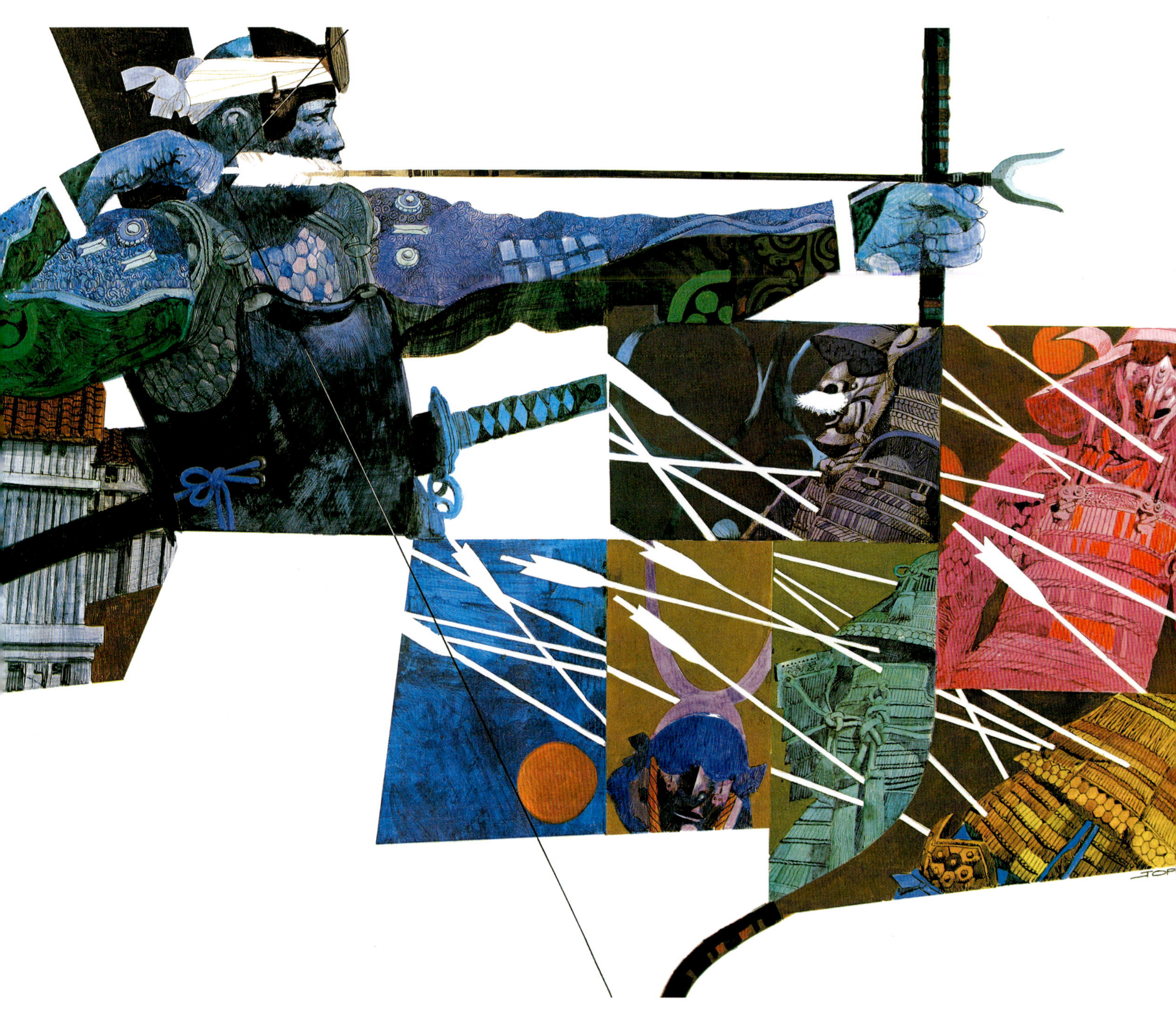

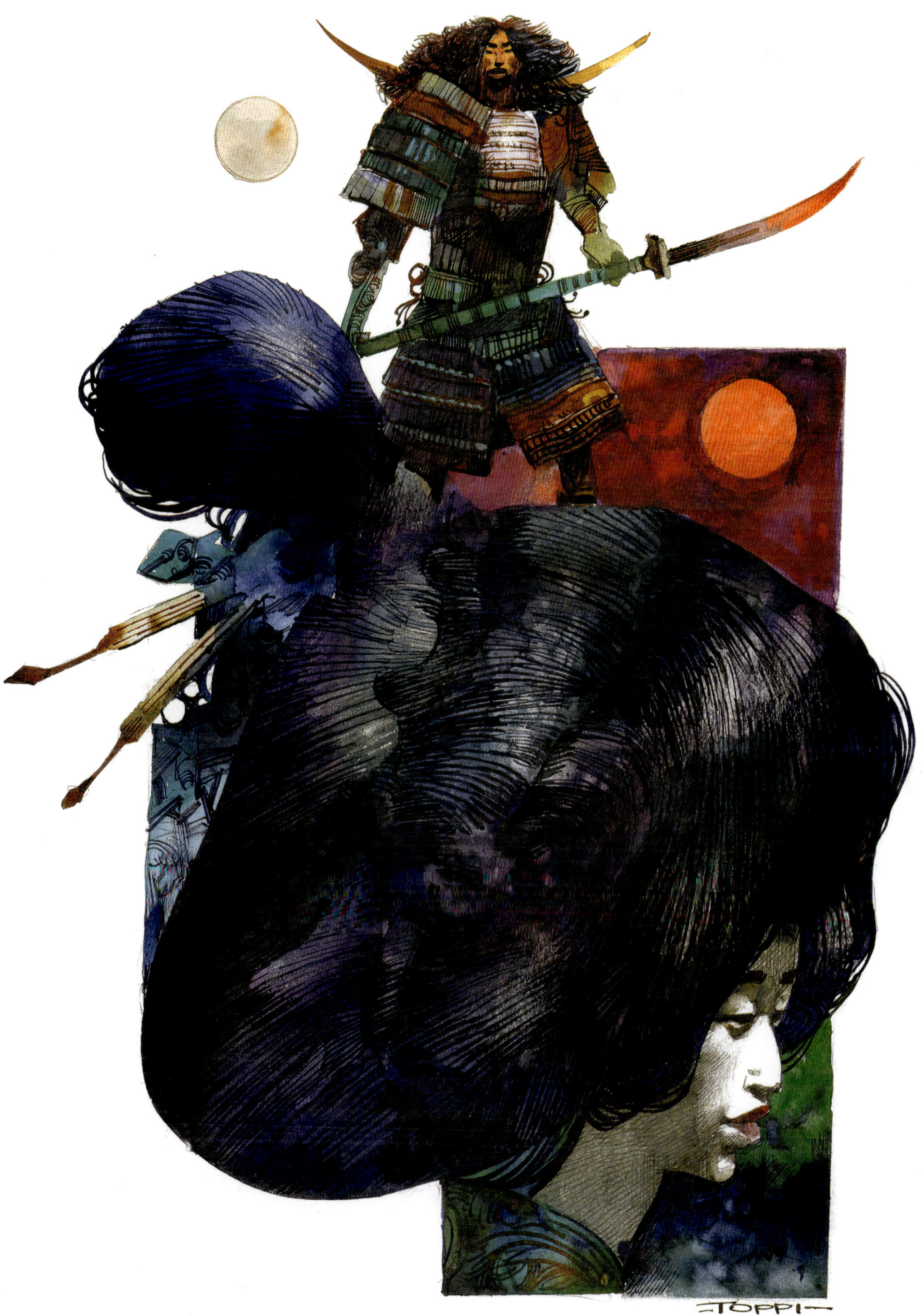

ILLUSTRATION FOR THE *Leggende senza tempo* PORTFOLIO
PUBLISHED BY CRAPAPELADA, MILAN, 2003.

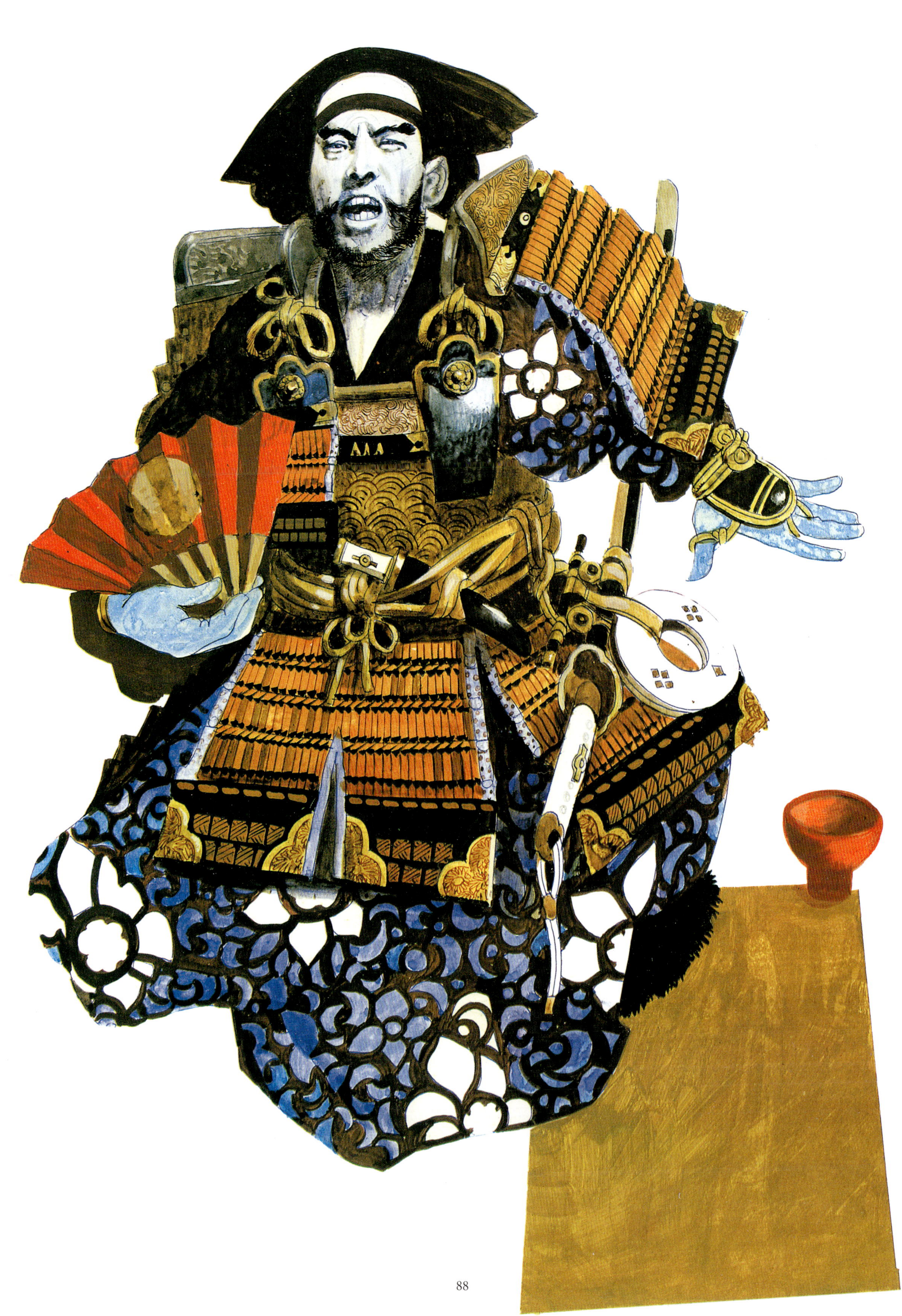

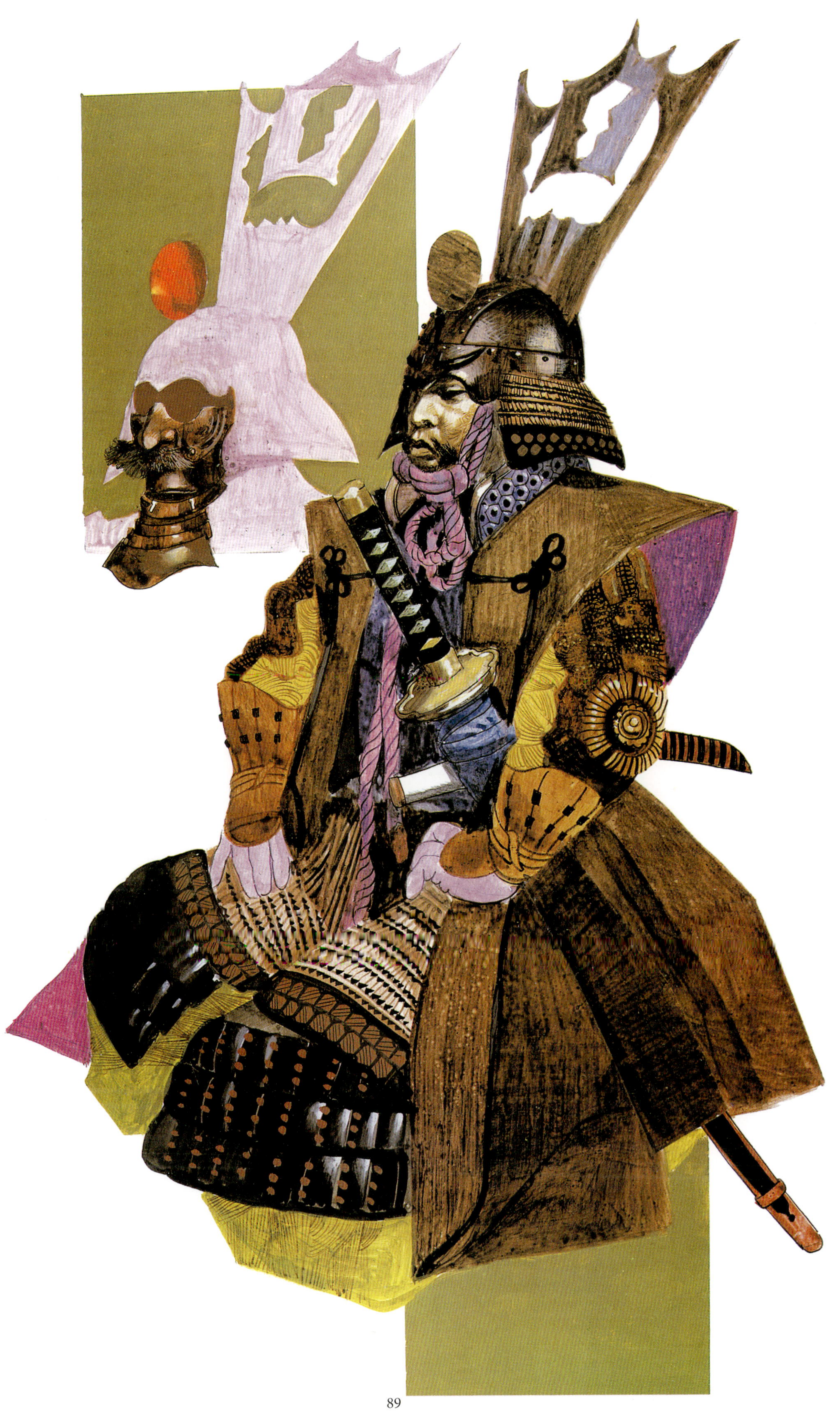

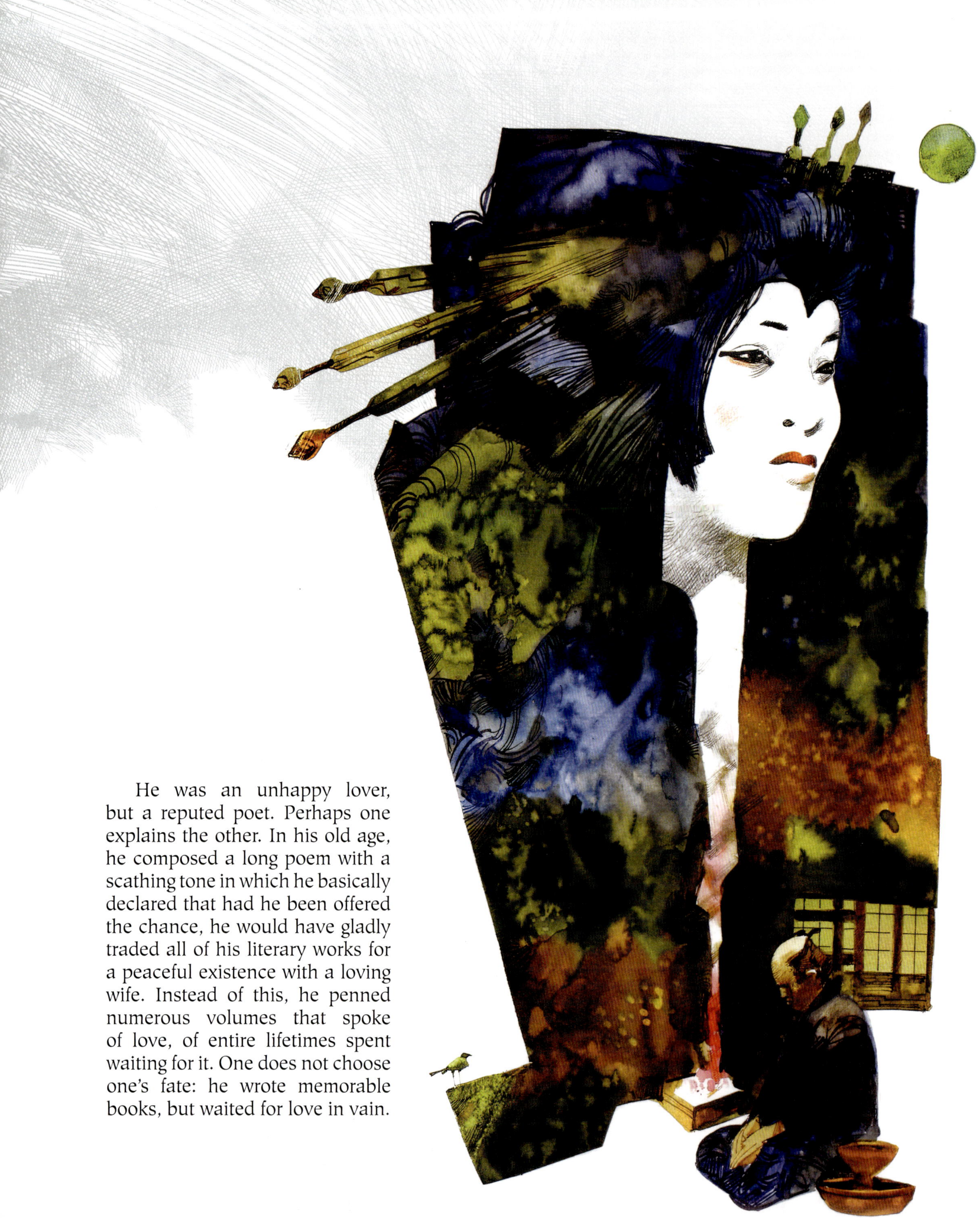

He was an unhappy lover, but a reputed poet. Perhaps one explains the other. In his old age, he composed a long poem with a scathing tone in which he basically declared that had he been offered the chance, he would have gladly traded all of his literary works for a peaceful existence with a loving wife. Instead of this, he penned numerous volumes that spoke of love, of entire lifetimes spent waiting for it. One does not choose one's fate: he wrote memorable books, but waited for love in vain.

Illustration for the *Hayku* portfolio
Published by the Crapapela gallery,
Milan, 2005.

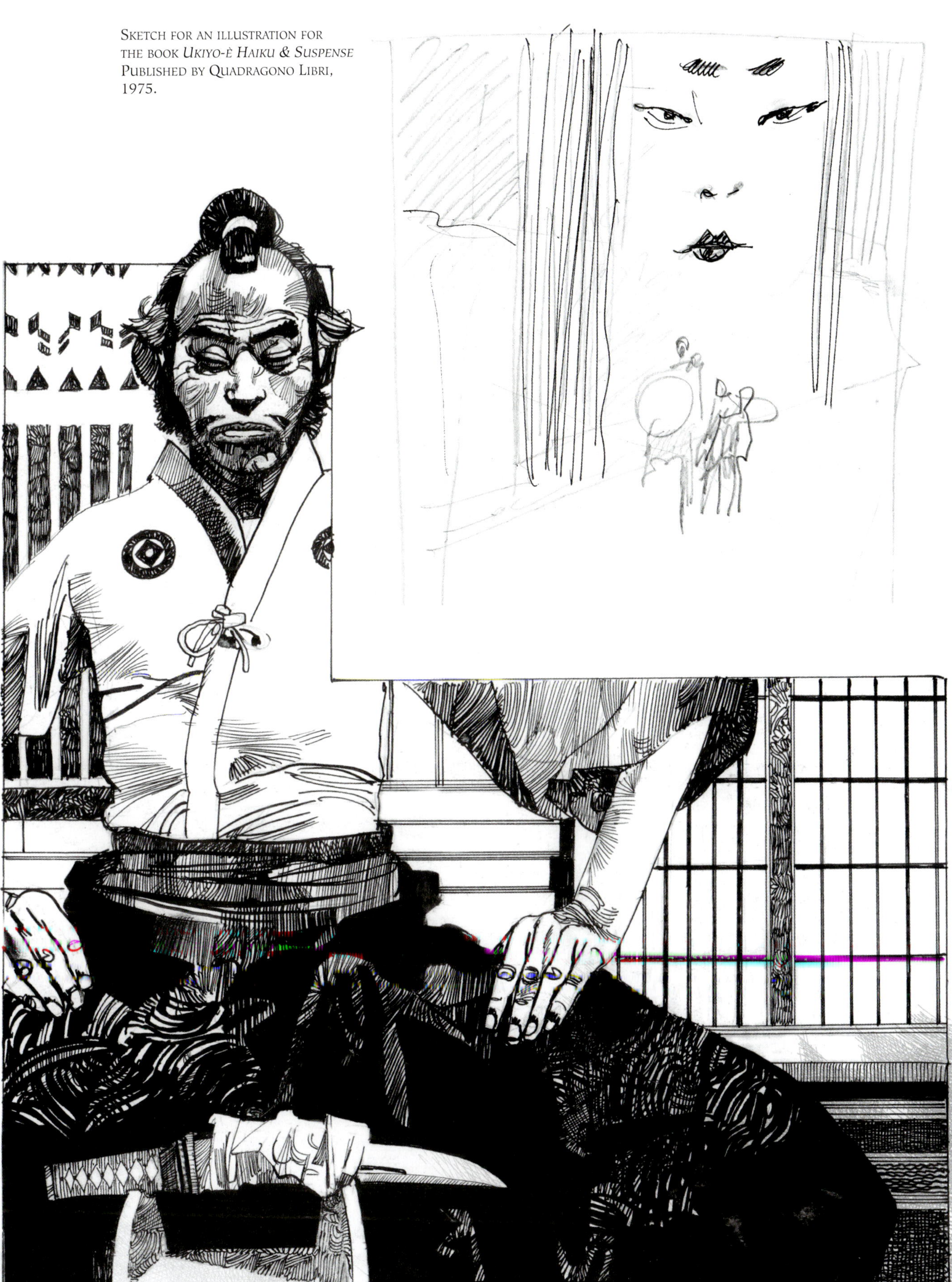

Seppuku, illustration for *Il Giornalino*, 1970s.

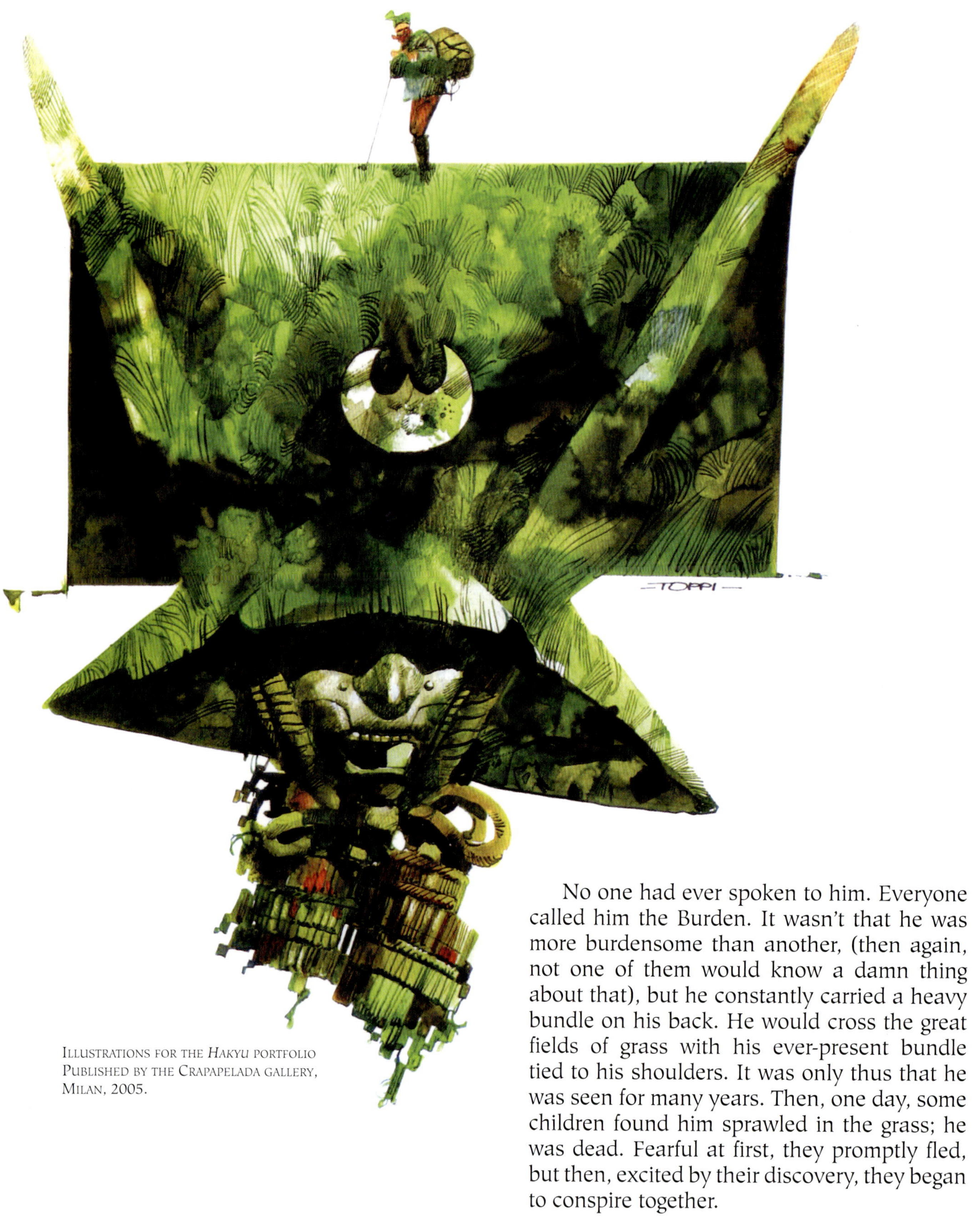

Illustrations for the *Hakyu* portfolio
Published by the Crapapelada gallery,
Milan, 2005.

No one had ever spoken to him. Everyone called him the Burden. It wasn't that he was more burdensome than another, (then again, not one of them would know a damn thing about that), but he constantly carried a heavy bundle on his back. He would cross the great fields of grass with his ever-present bundle tied to his shoulders. It was only thus that he was seen for many years. Then, one day, some children found him sprawled in the grass; he was dead. Fearful at first, they promptly fled, but then, excited by their discovery, they began to conspire together.

They convinced themselves that the time had now come to discover what was in the Burden's famous bundle. They went back and found it. Rolled up in filthy rags, there was a trophy. A human trophy. A head still wearing a hat held in place by a strange combination of blades, bamboo, and rope. An instrument of torture. Who was this torture victim? What wrong had he committed? And why had the Burden compelled himself to bear this trophy the way one might impose mortification upon oneself? The way one might atone for a crime...

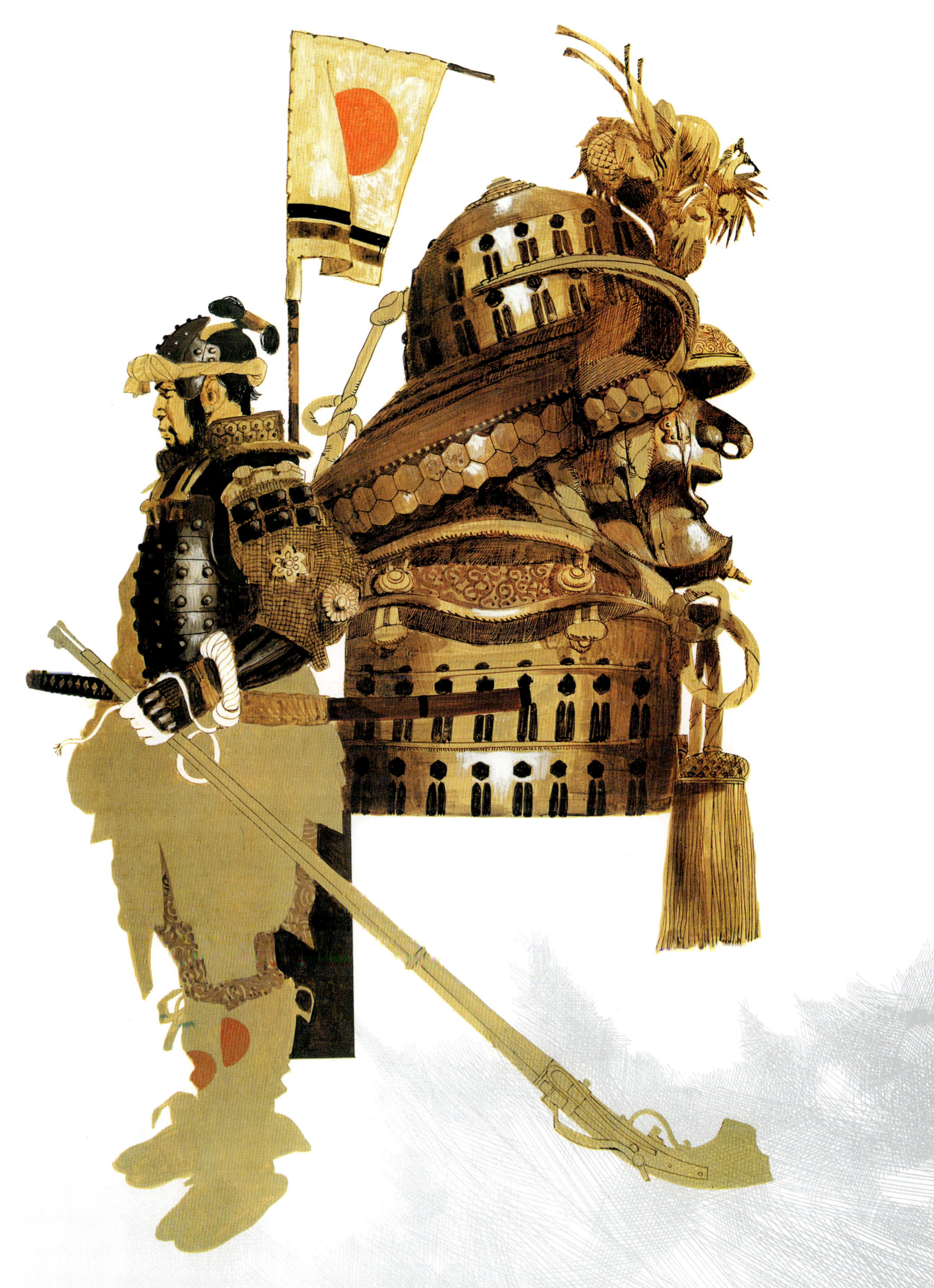

ILLUSTRATION FOR THE BOOK *UKIYO-È HAIKU & SUSPENSE*
PUBLISHED BY QUADRAGONO LIBRI, 1975.

I saw this: the left hand of the fierce samurai, armored and heavily armed, lightly touched the right hand of the young child, fresh from his mother's bosom. I saw this and could not decide which of the two was more powerful: the knight, suddenly embarrassed by his clumsy gesture, or the little man with his fearless and greedy candor. I now saw an unarmed warrior, despite his array of weapons. I could not say who warmed the other's heart the most.

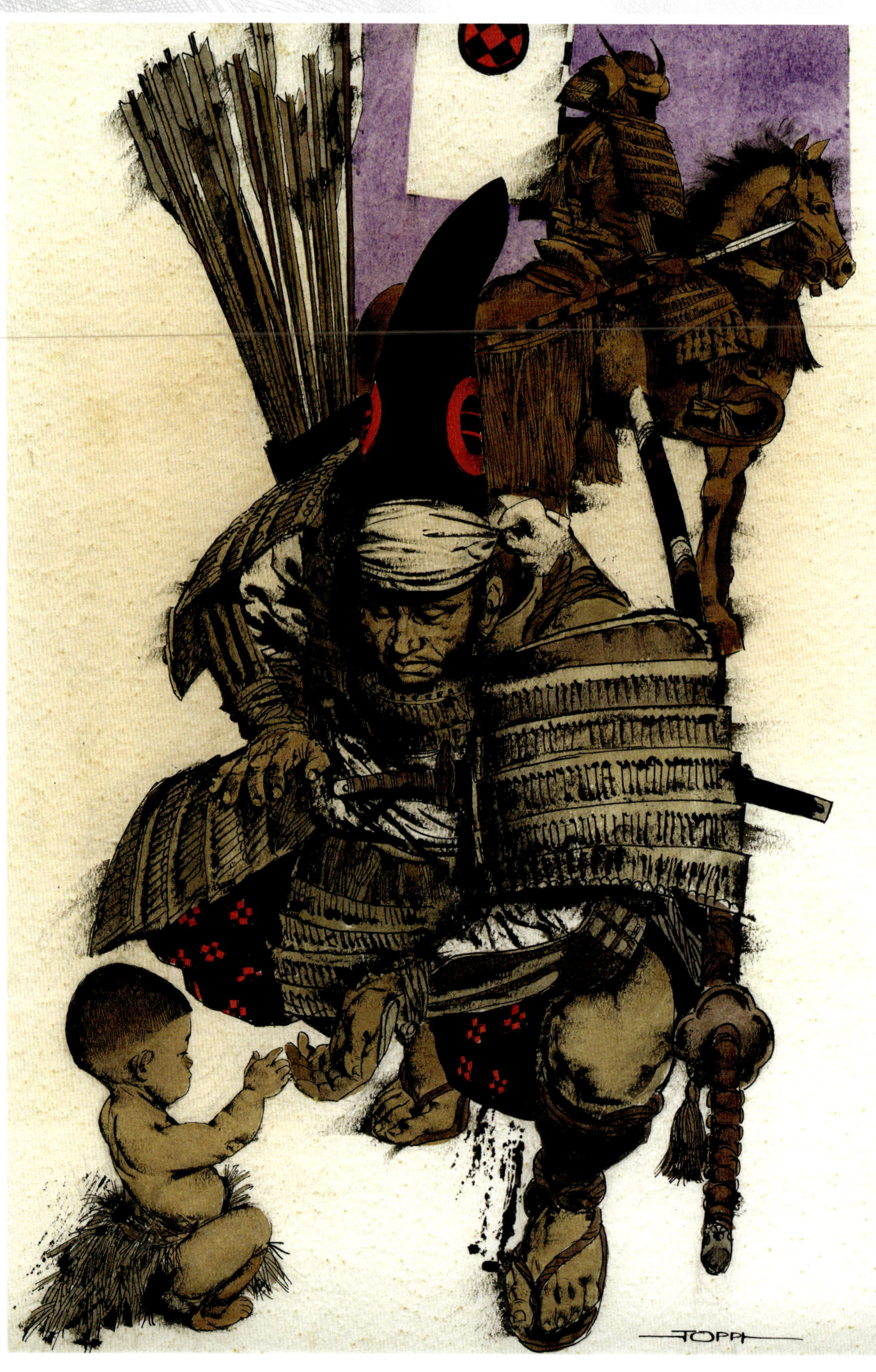

Black As Ebony

Here is a world where, it would seem, the sun always shines and the people live half-naked; an Eden, a Paradise Lost. Furthermore, archaeologists pretend that it is the cradle of humanity. Which suggests that the land of our distant ancestors would undoubtedly have a great many things to show us, if by mistake we were ever to listen to it...

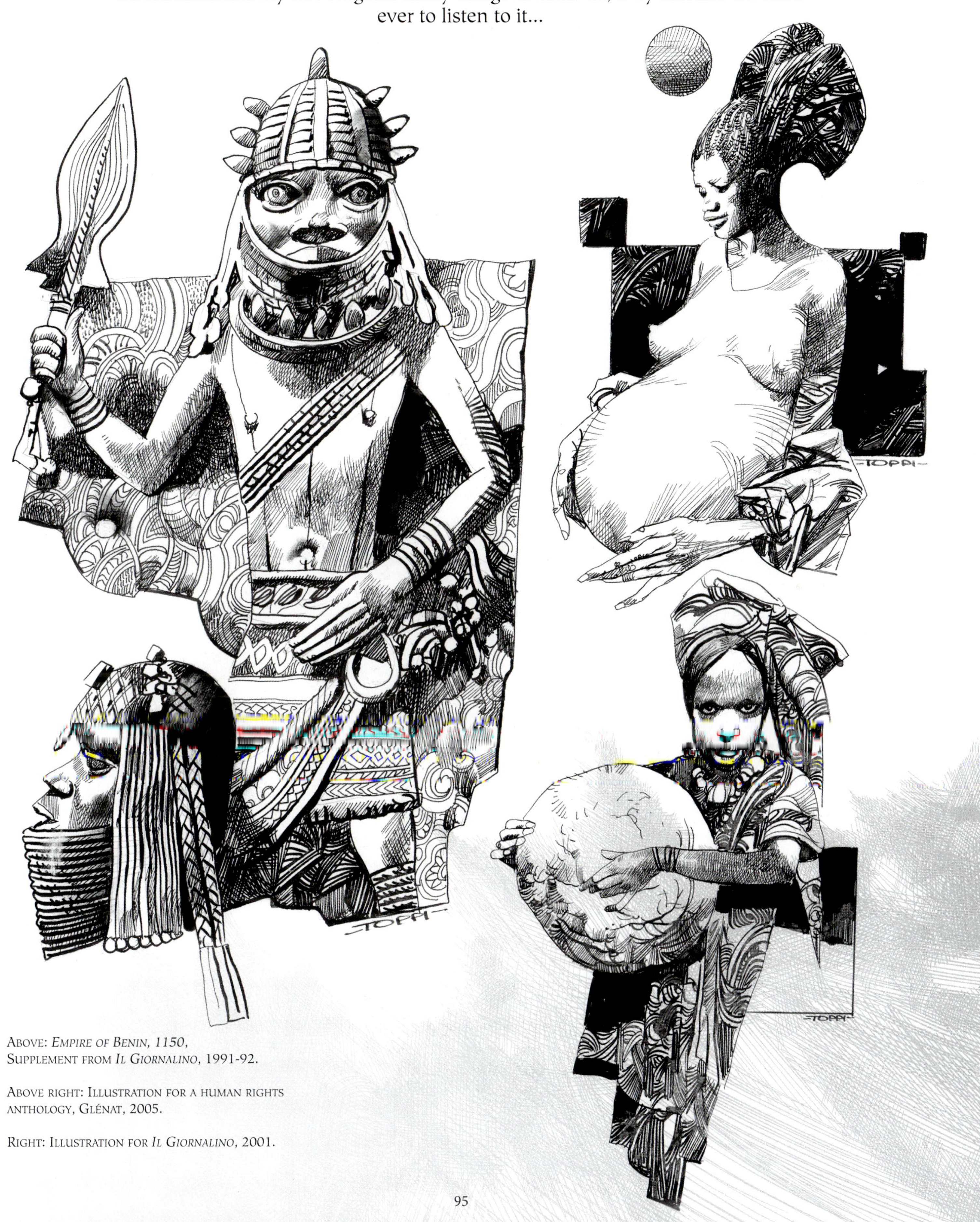

ABOVE: *EMPIRE OF BENIN, 1150*,
SUPPLEMENT FROM *IL GIORNALINO*, 1991-92.

ABOVE RIGHT: ILLUSTRATION FOR A HUMAN RIGHTS
ANTHOLOGY, GLÉNAT, 2005.

RIGHT: ILLUSTRATION FOR *IL GIORNALINO*, 2001.

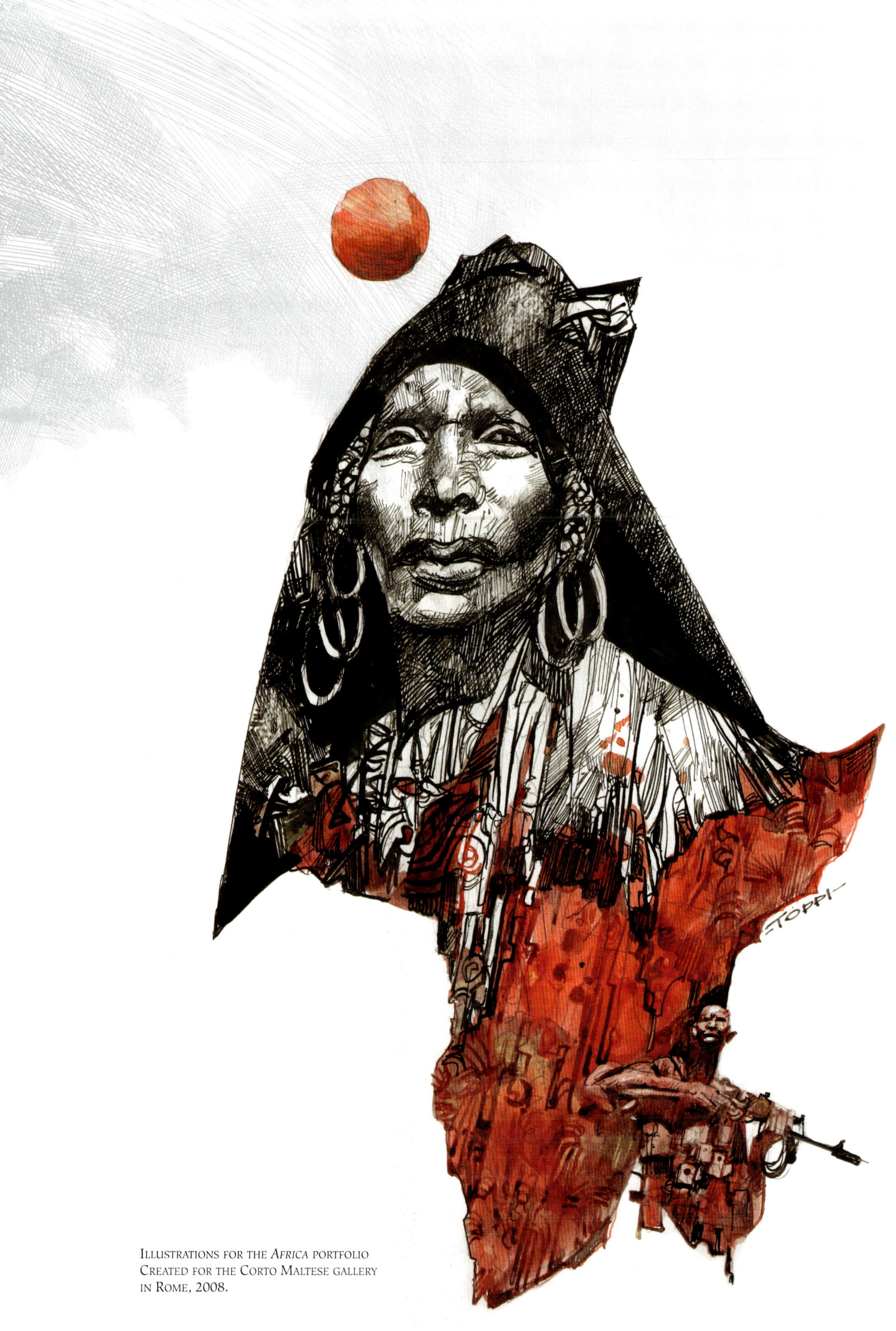

Illustrations for the *Africa* portfolio
Created for the Corto Maltese gallery
in Rome, 2008.

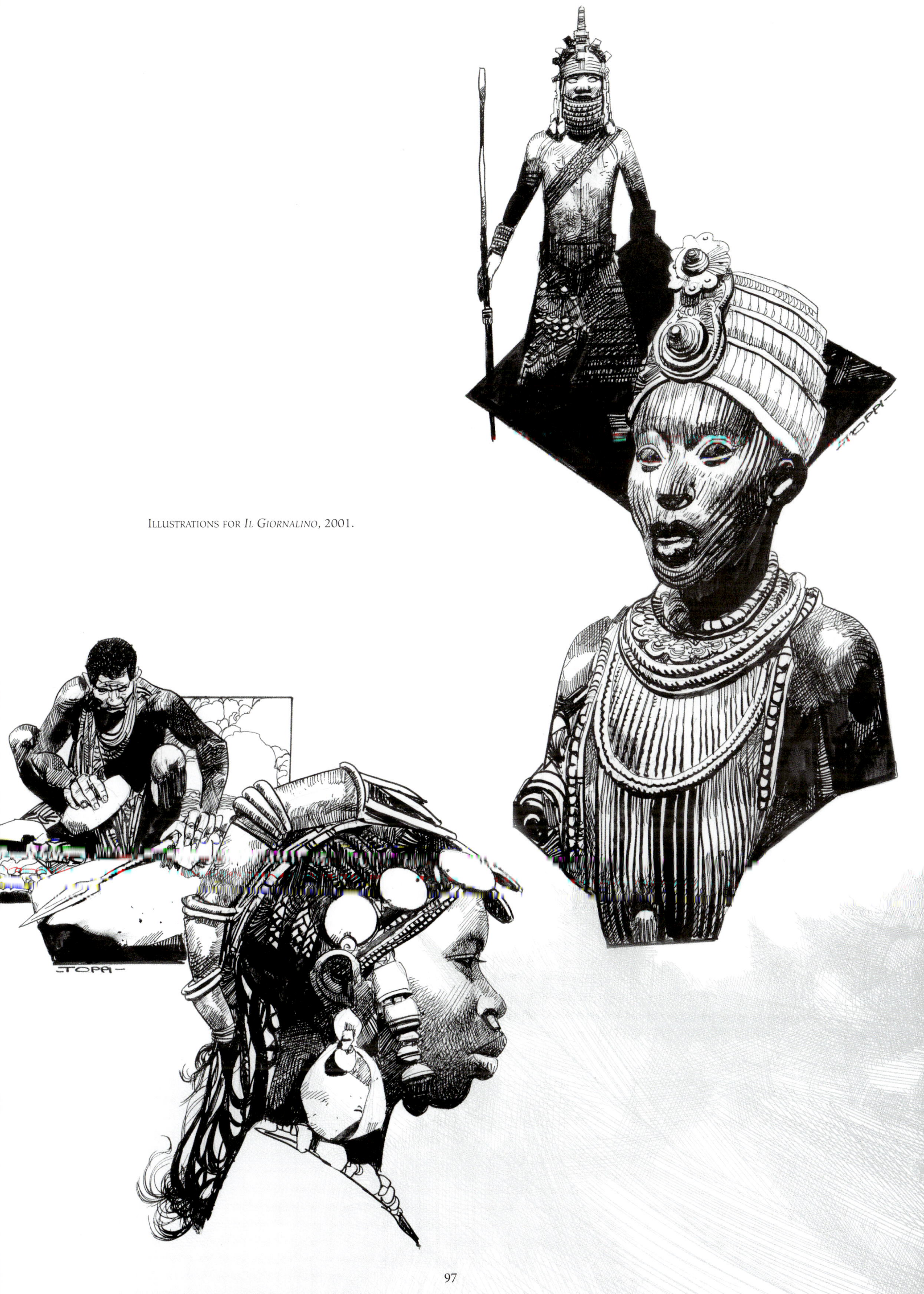

ILLUSTRATIONS FOR *IL GIORNALINO*, 2001.

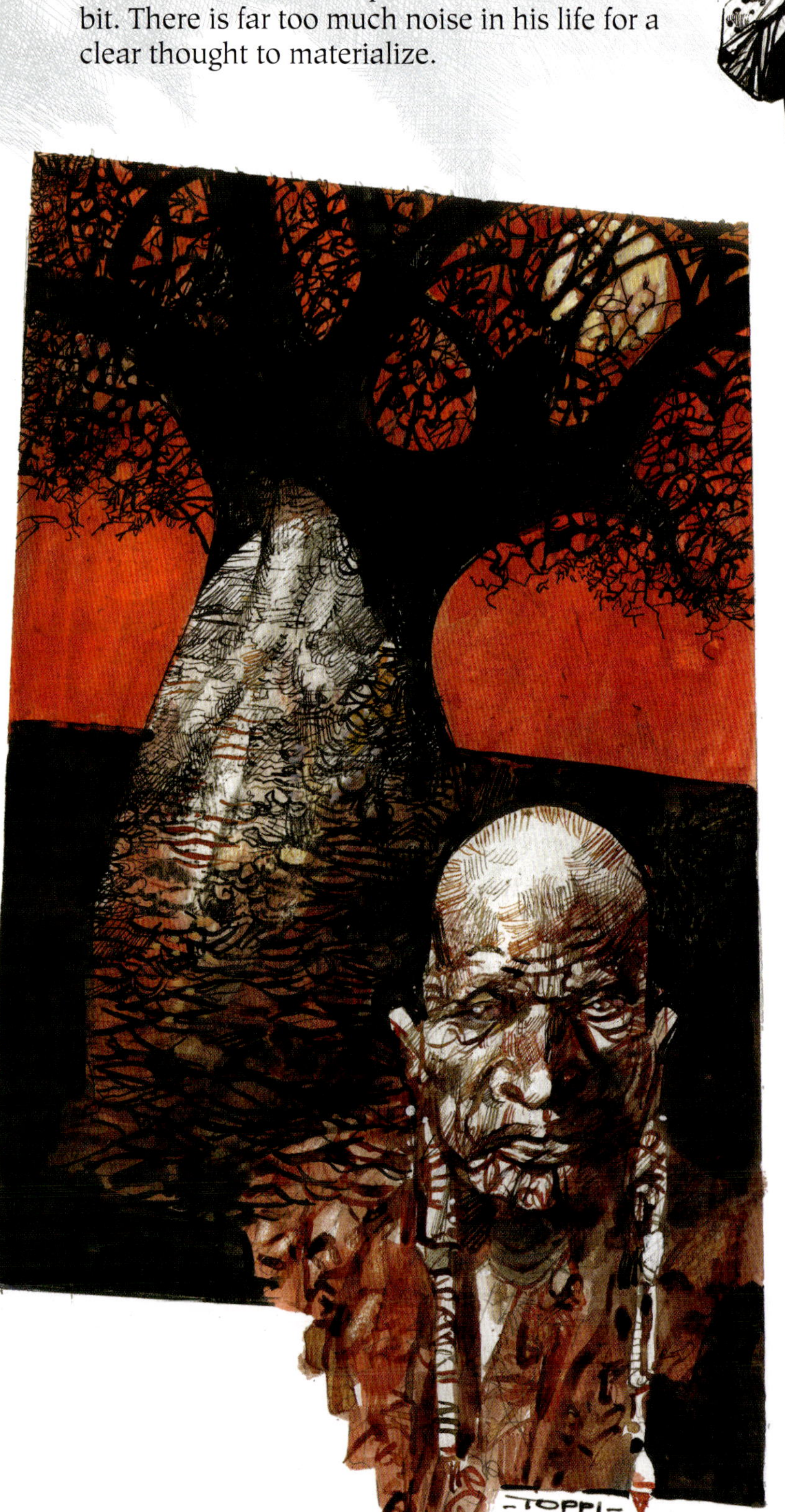

His father and his father's father hunted the gazelle for their own benefit. He, on the other hand, hunts diamonds for the benefit of another. His ancestors possessed the breath of the wind which whistled in their ears. He has but the deafening din of a compressor to accompany his dreams. His ancestors spoke endlessly in the light, he says nothing in the darkness. And yet, does he harbor any hatred towards those who exploit him? Not even a bit. There is far too much noise in his life for a clear thought to materialize.

The old man used to say that the baobab was the home of his ancestors. He would add that this was why the trunk of the sour gourd tree was so big: because he had so many ancestors. He would sit, in the evening, at the foot of the full trunk. He would say he could hear the whispers of the dead. He would say he didn't understand everything the dead whispered into his ear. He would say that their words were as dark as a moonless sky. He would never sit at the foot of the baobab on moonless nights. He said that he had tried it once, as a child; he heard terrifying secrets and had experienced the worst fright of his life.

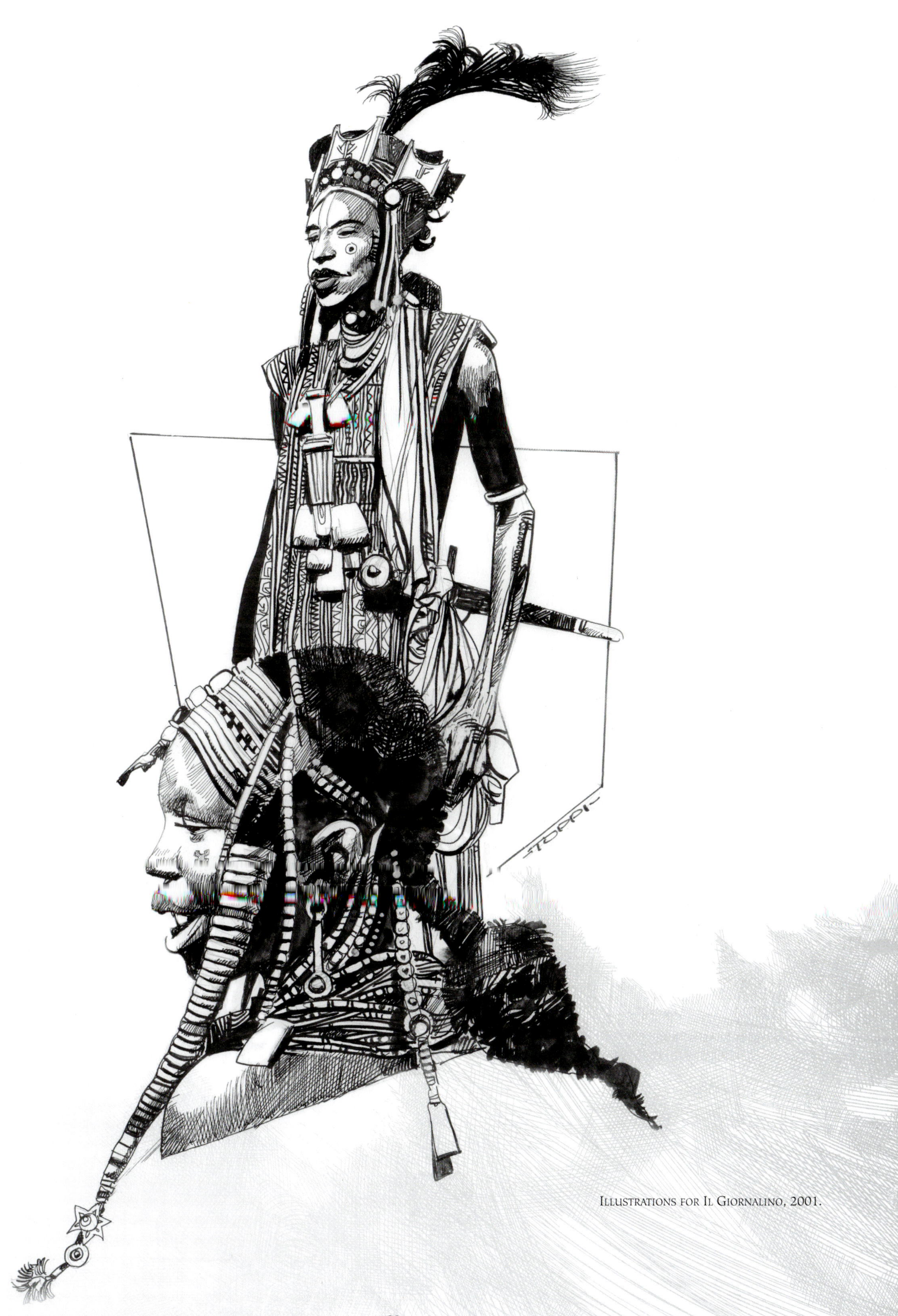

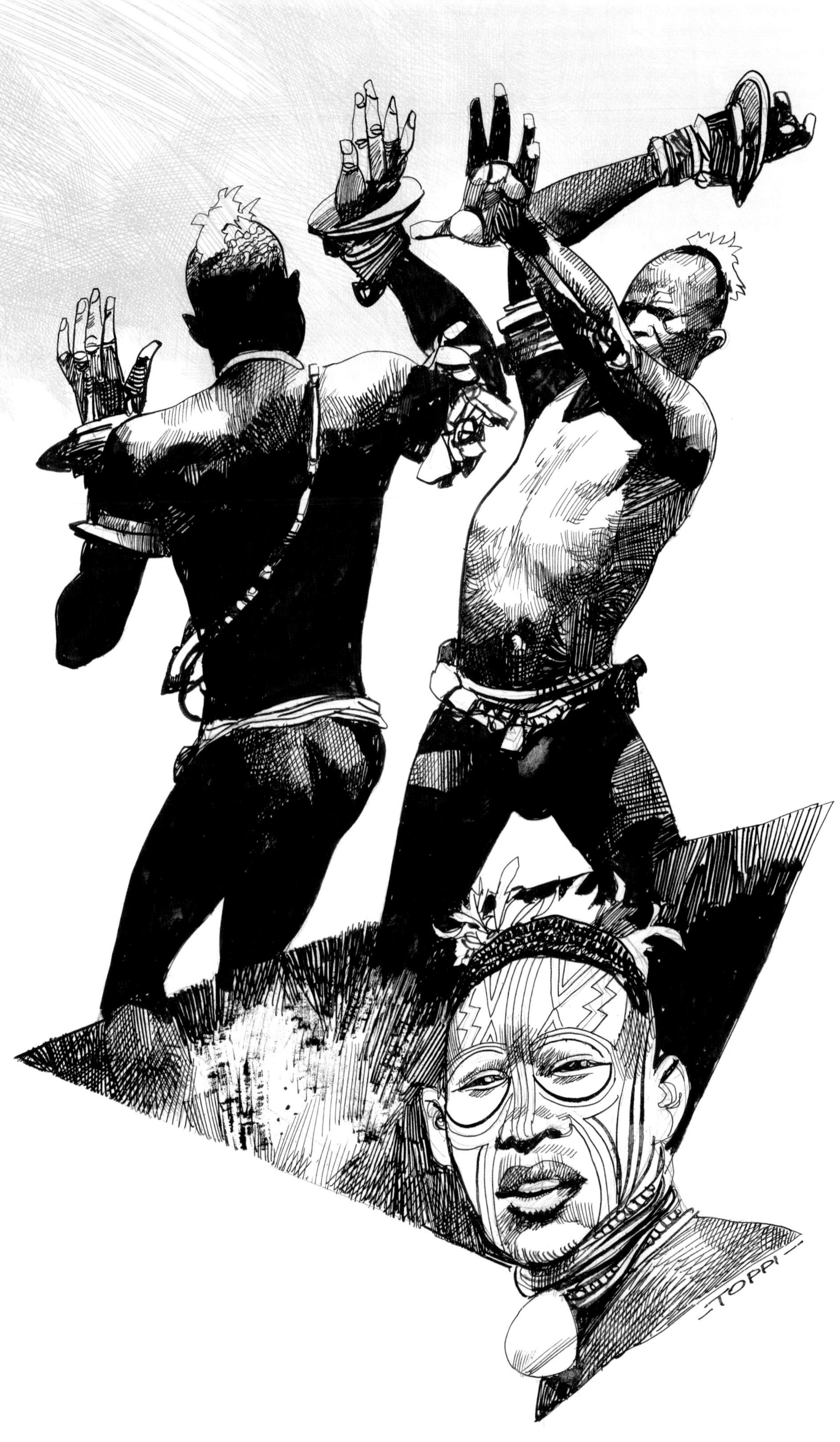

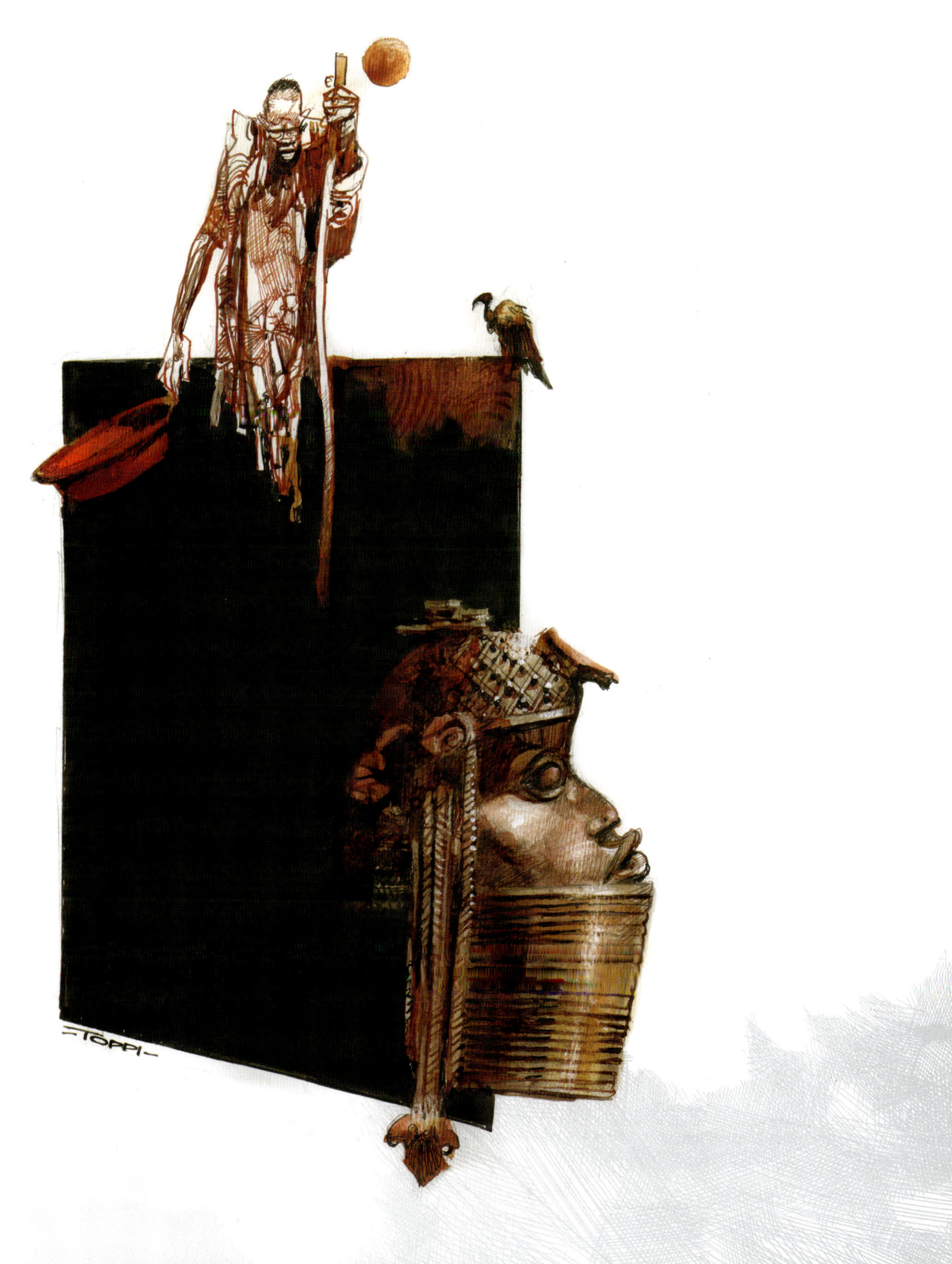

Illustrations for the *Africa* portfolio
Created for the Corto Maltese gallery in Rome, 2008.

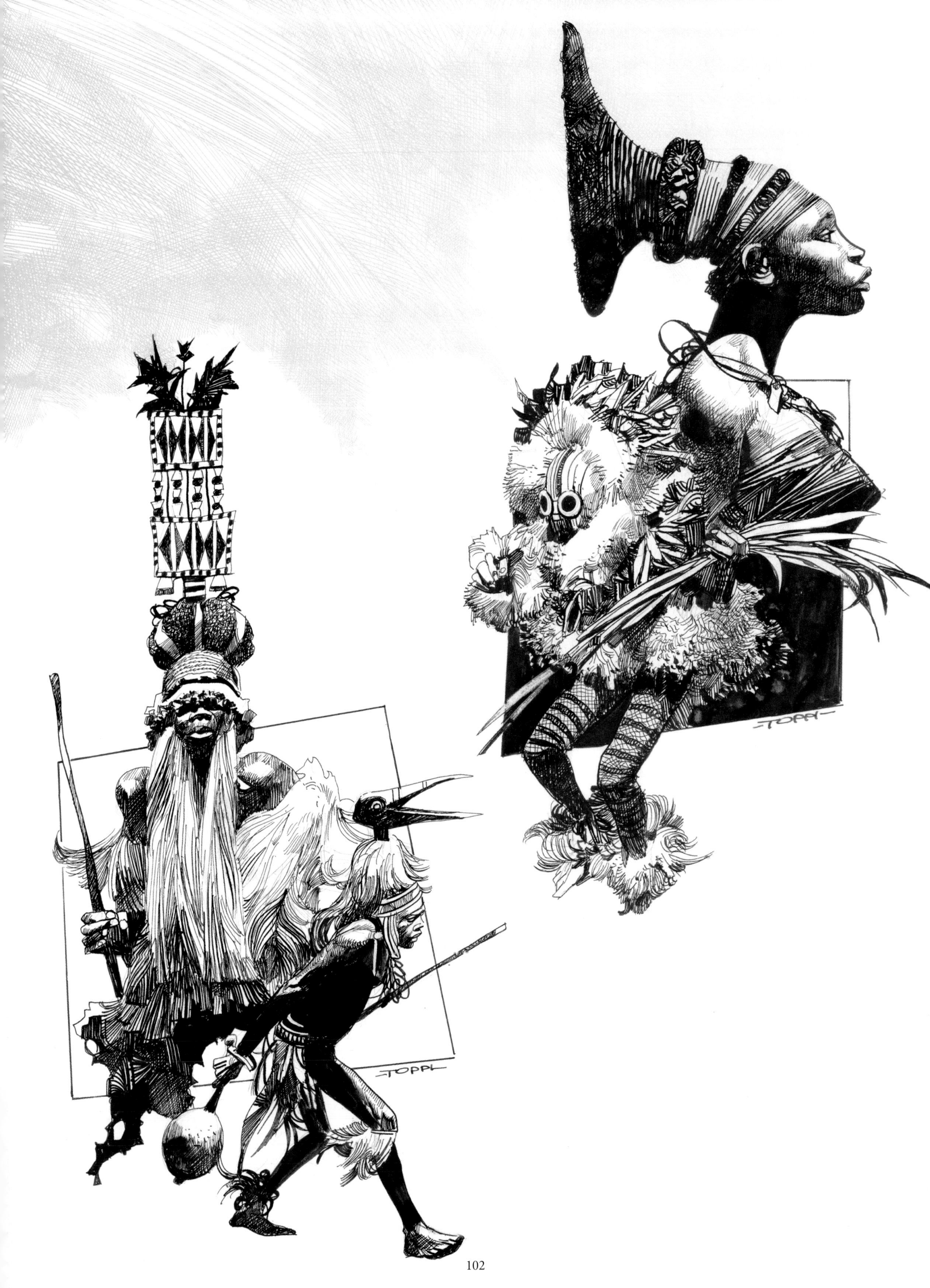

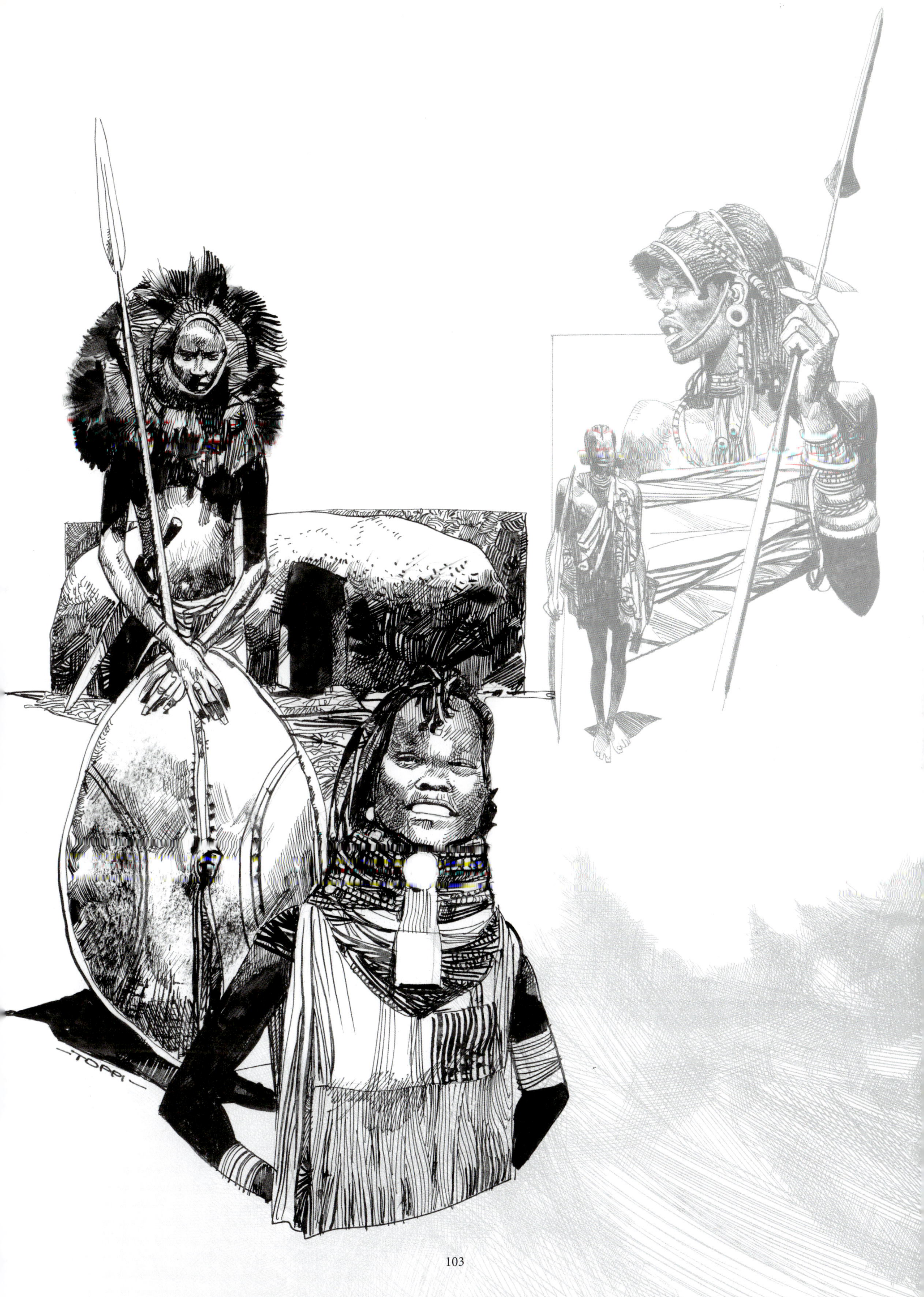

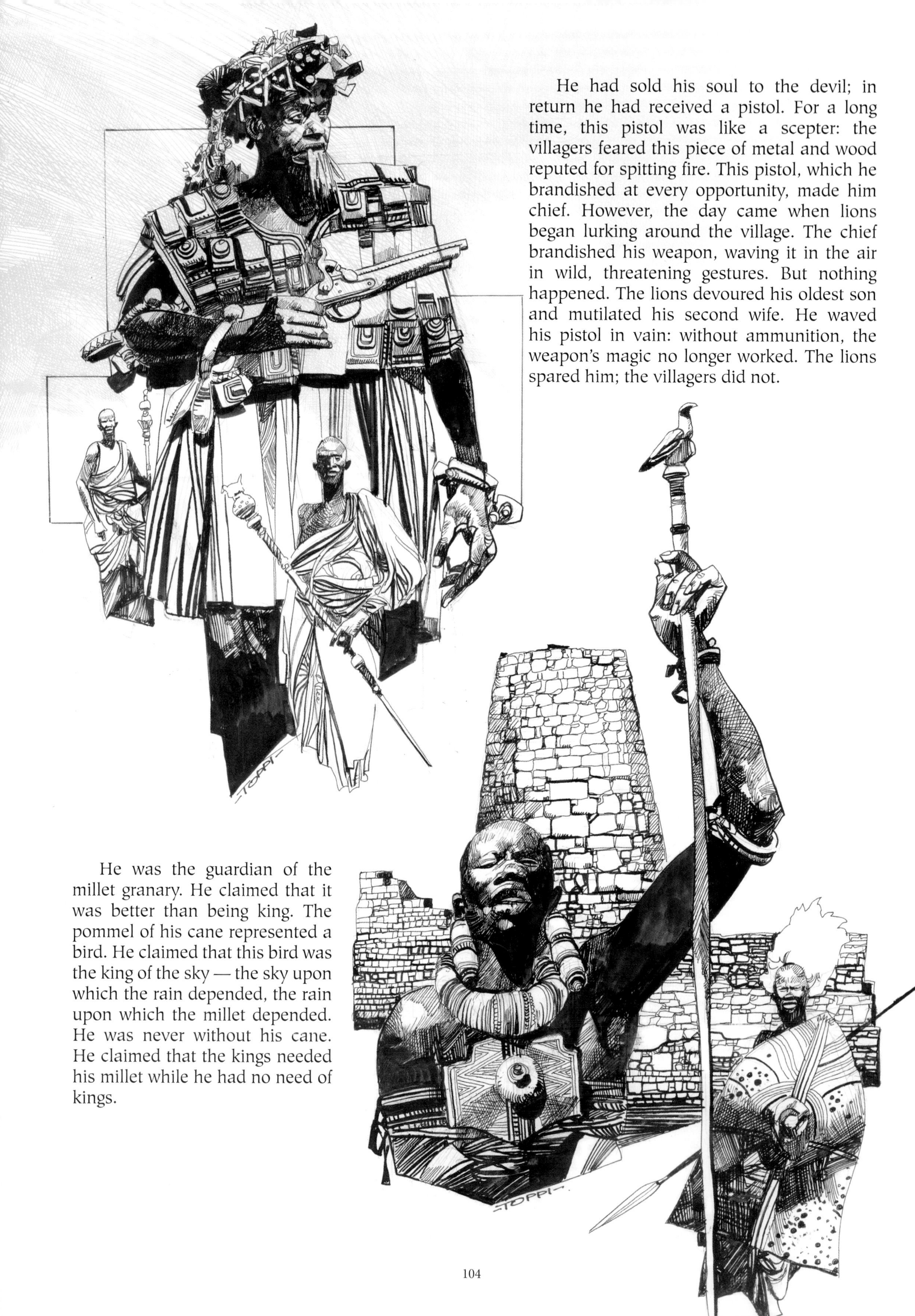

He had sold his soul to the devil; in return he had received a pistol. For a long time, this pistol was like a scepter: the villagers feared this piece of metal and wood reputed for spitting fire. This pistol, which he brandished at every opportunity, made him chief. However, the day came when lions began lurking around the village. The chief brandished his weapon, waving it in the air in wild, threatening gestures. But nothing happened. The lions devoured his oldest son and mutilated his second wife. He waved his pistol in vain: without ammunition, the weapon's magic no longer worked. The lions spared him; the villagers did not.

He was the guardian of the millet granary. He claimed that it was better than being king. The pommel of his cane represented a bird. He claimed that this bird was the king of the sky — the sky upon which the rain depended, the rain upon which the millet depended. He was never without his cane. He claimed that the kings needed his millet while he had no need of kings.

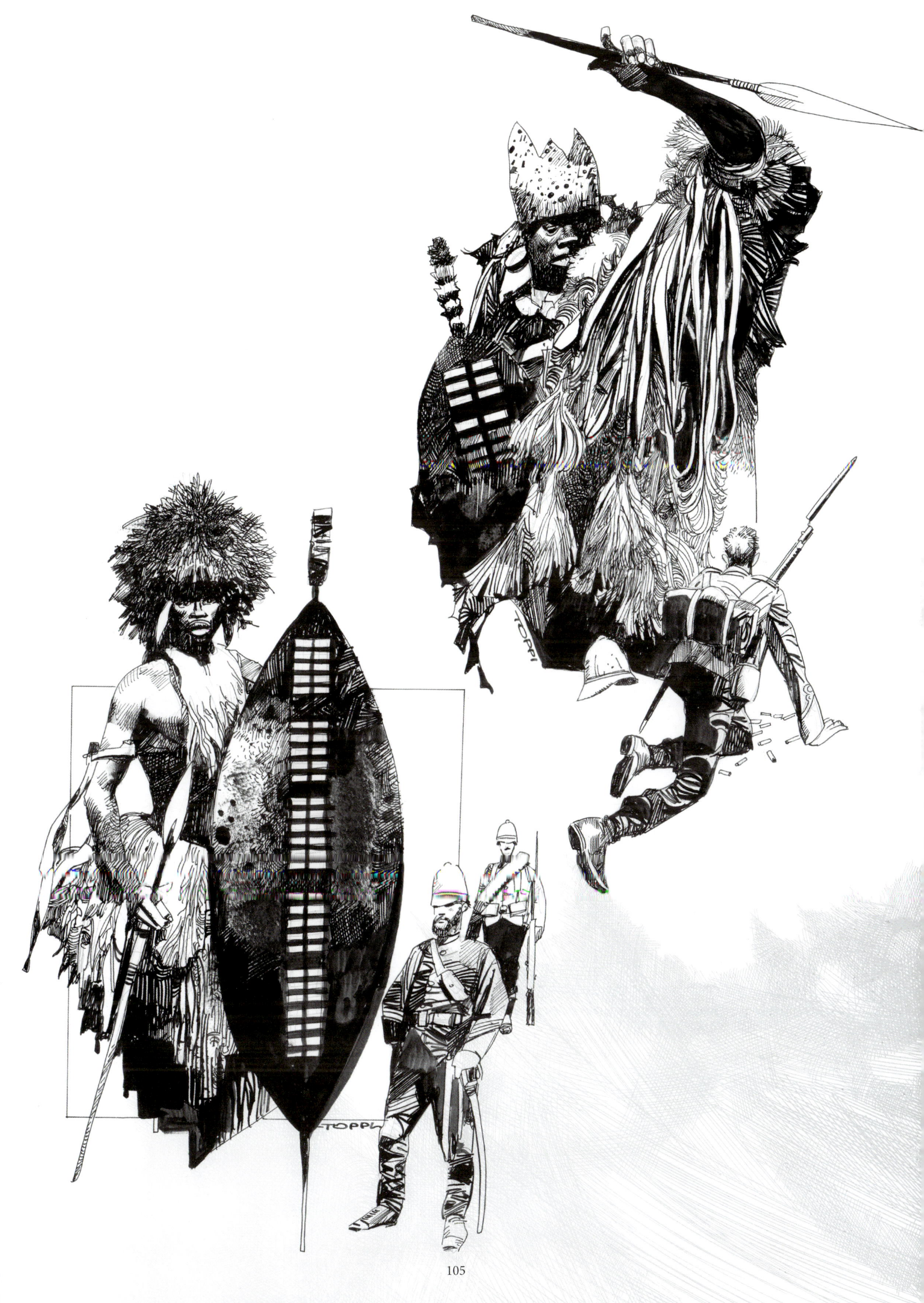

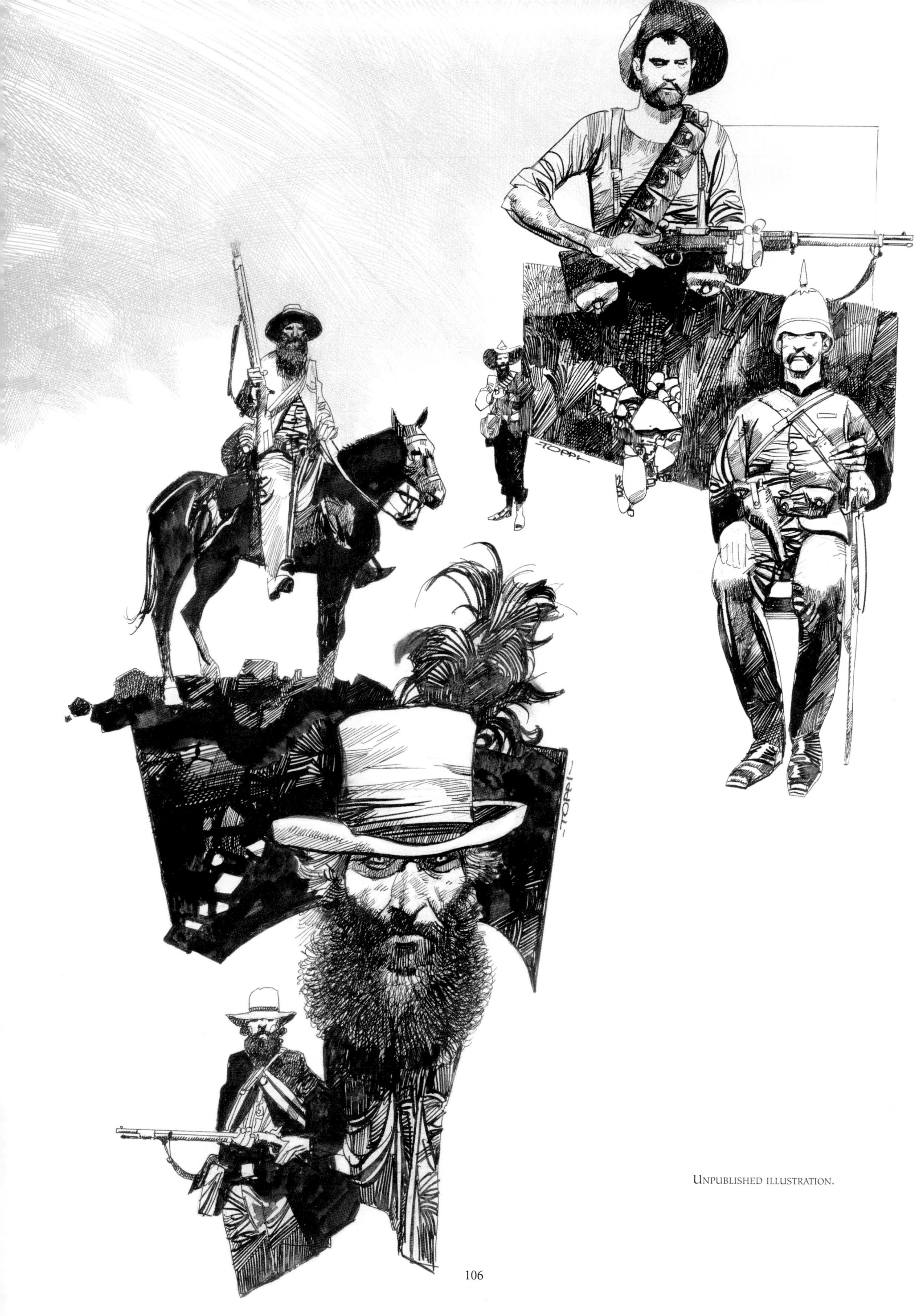

UNPUBLISHED ILLUSTRATION.

106

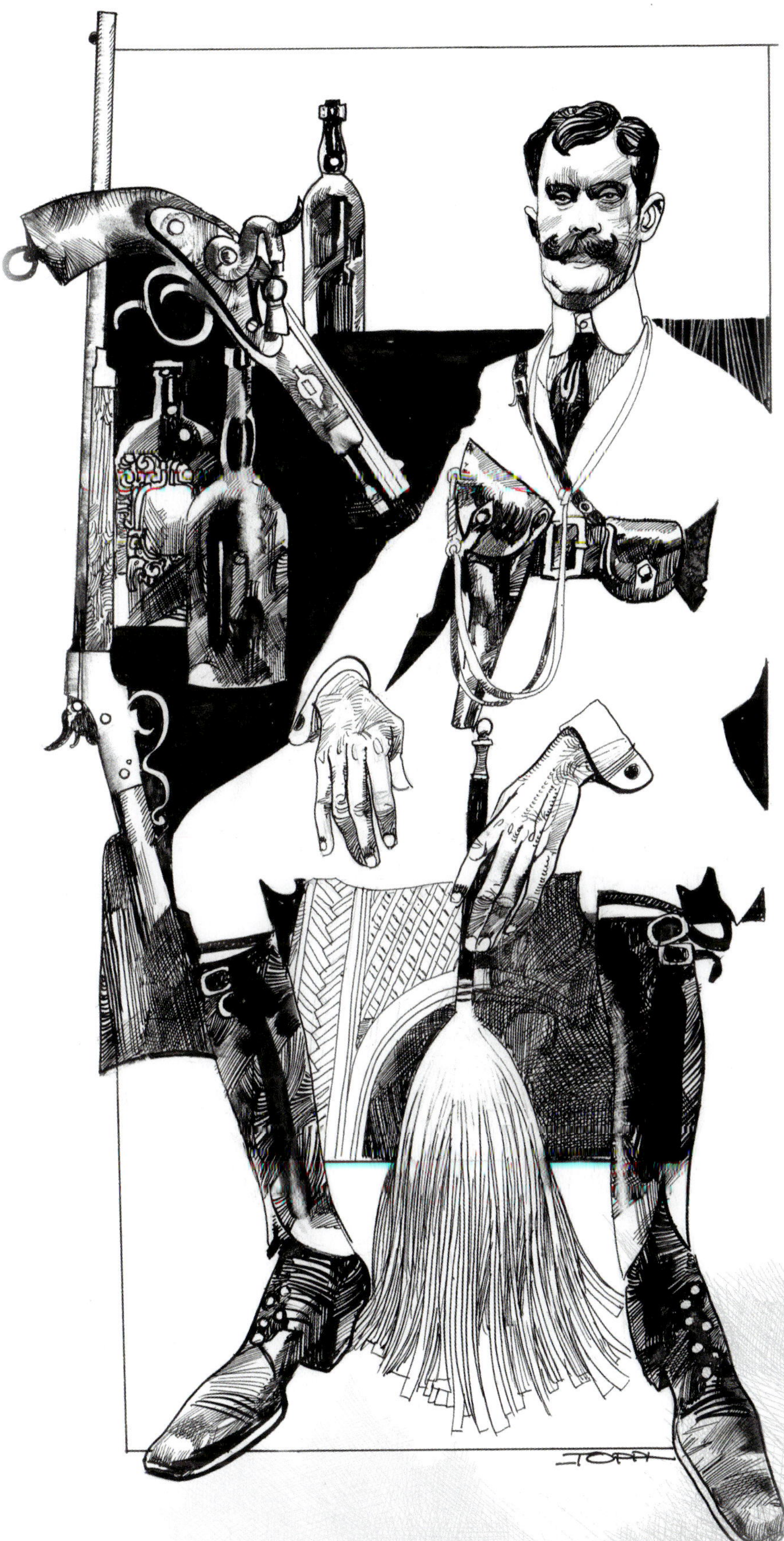

He arrived one cursed morning, pistol slung over his shoulder, with his army of native porters and henchmen. He scarcely needed to fight and behaved as if he were already in conquered territory. He took the largest hut for himself and immediately began living lavishly. He belched raucously, pissed loudly, and was constantly drunk. He slicked his hair back with brilliantine, sprayed himself with cologne, distributed blows from his riding crop, and reserved the village's virgins for his own personal use. He looked dapper, he smelled terrible. There was no need for revolt to be rid of him; gangrene took care of that.

ILLUSTRATION FOR THE NOVELLA
LA SEDIA DI N'GOMBI BY EDGAR WALLACE,
PUBLISHED IN *CORTO MALTESE* NO.9, 1984.

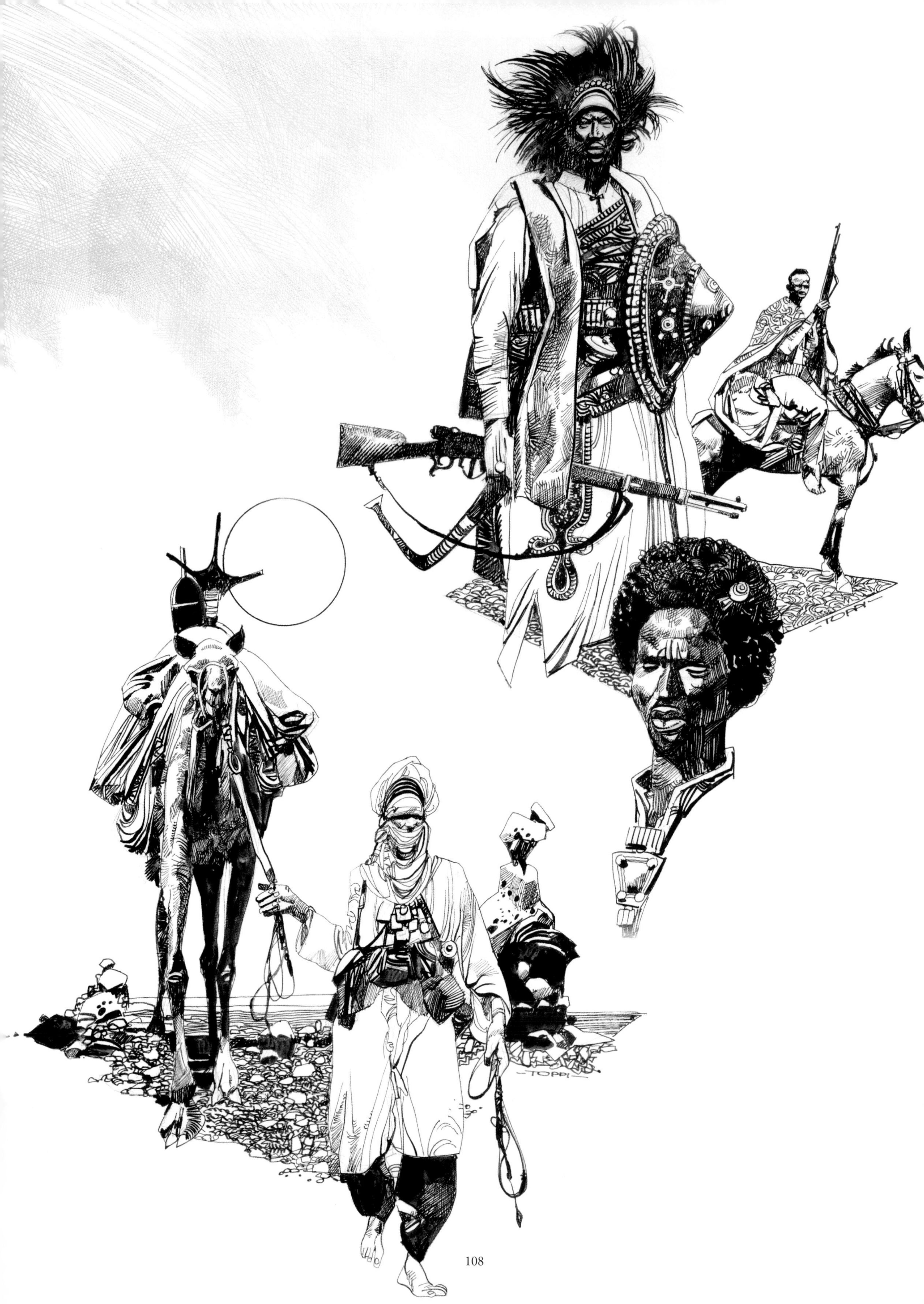

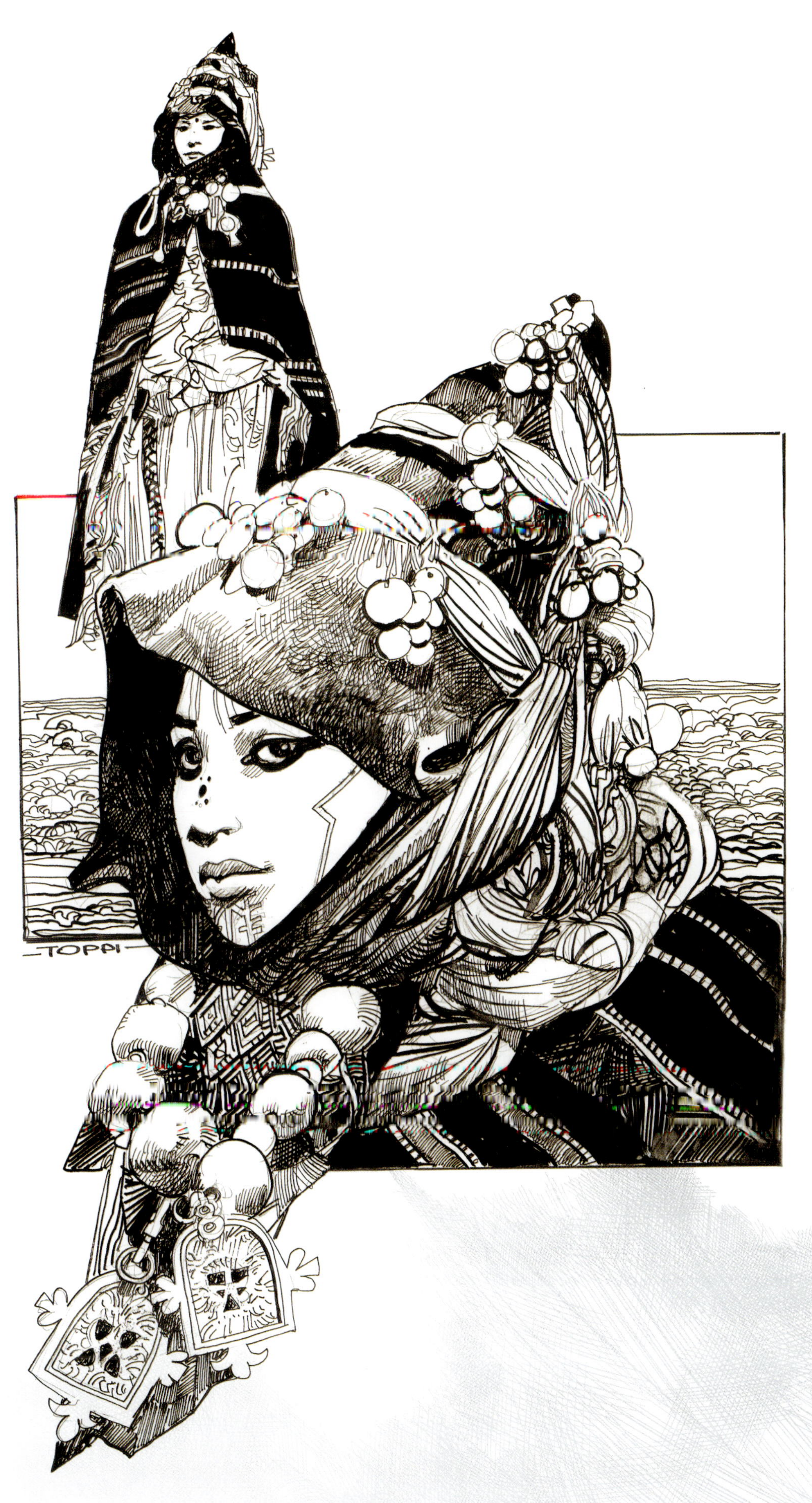

Last Tango in Sarajevo

It was the War to End all Wars, they said.

In truth, it was the first slaughter of modern times, after which many other massacres would follow. The 20th Century was born in horrible convulsions. These convulsions have never truly ceased. It is true that our times are more and more modern.

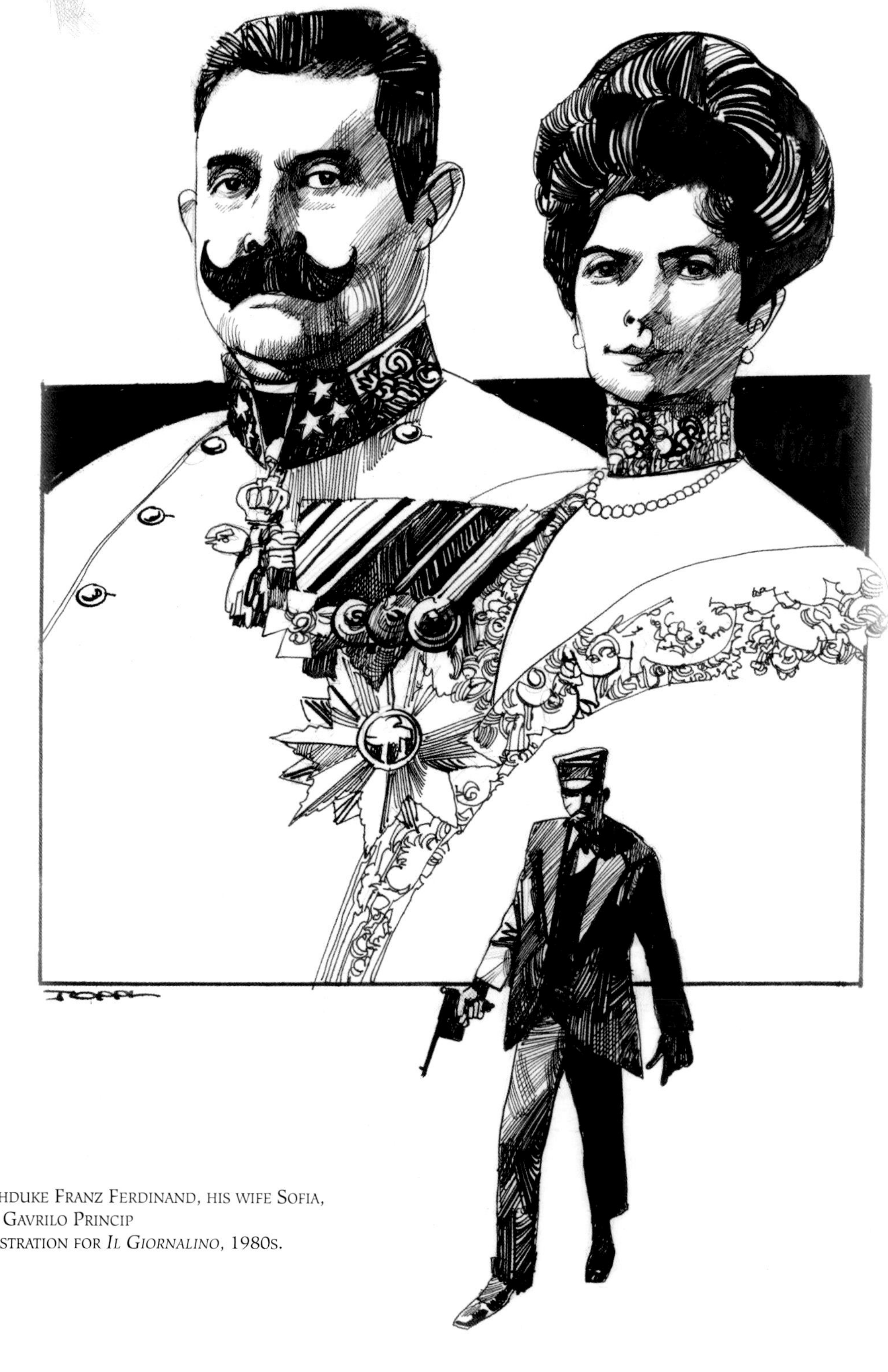

Archduke Franz Ferdinand, his wife Sofia, and Gavrilo Princip
Illustration for *Il Giornalino*, 1980s.

Her Ladyship the Baroness distracted herself with parties, waltzes, organdy ruffles, champagne bubbles, and toasts proposed to "our beloved soldiers, future victors." She would become drunk on sparkling wine, lilting music, and wealthy gentlemen. She would have someone briefly summarize what the newspapers were saying, punctuating the report with some witty pirouette before quickly returning to the hasty preparations for that evening's ball. She had but one subject of irritation: the constant difficulty in finding competent lackeys. Her entire household staff had been sent to the trenches.

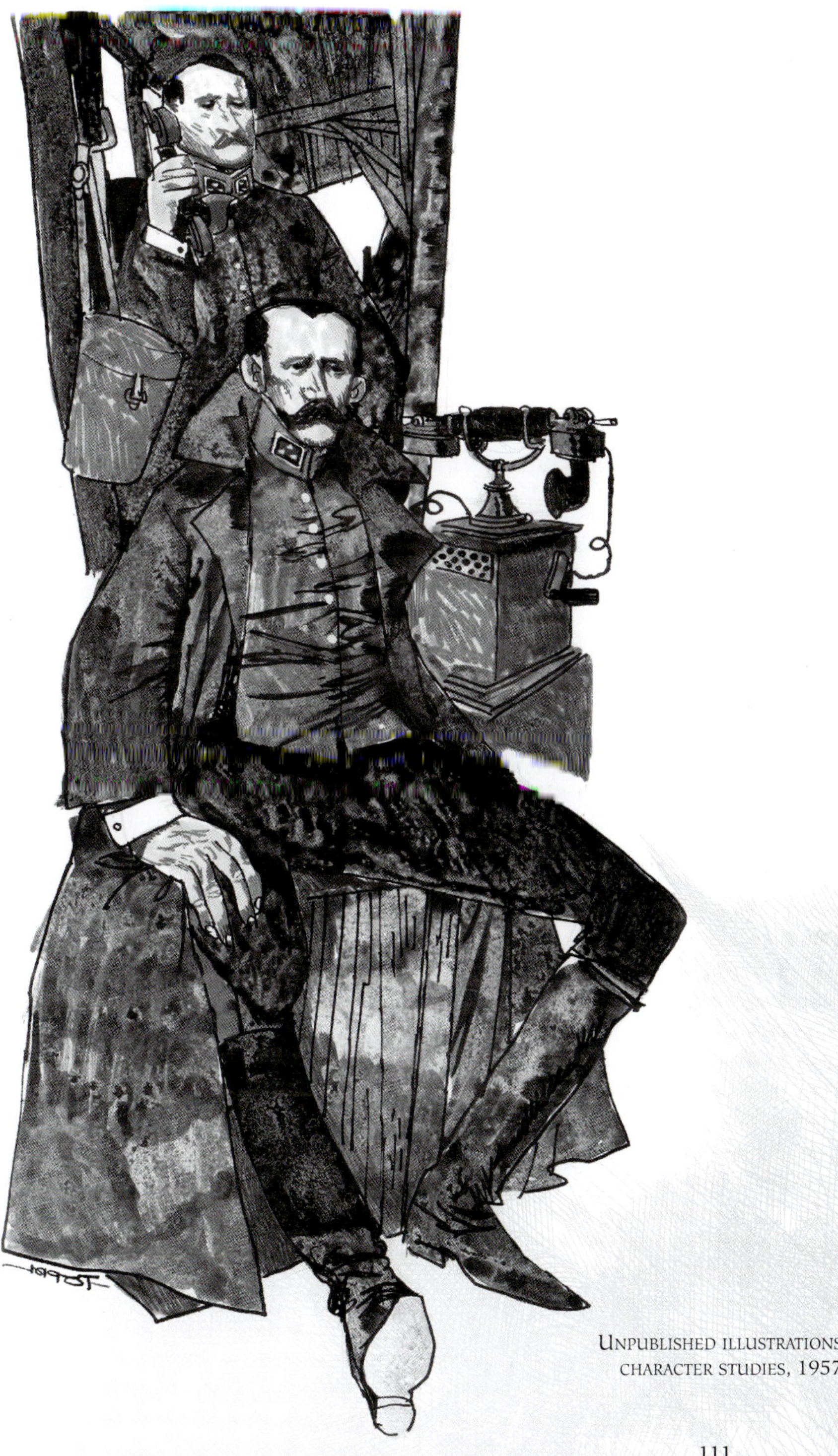

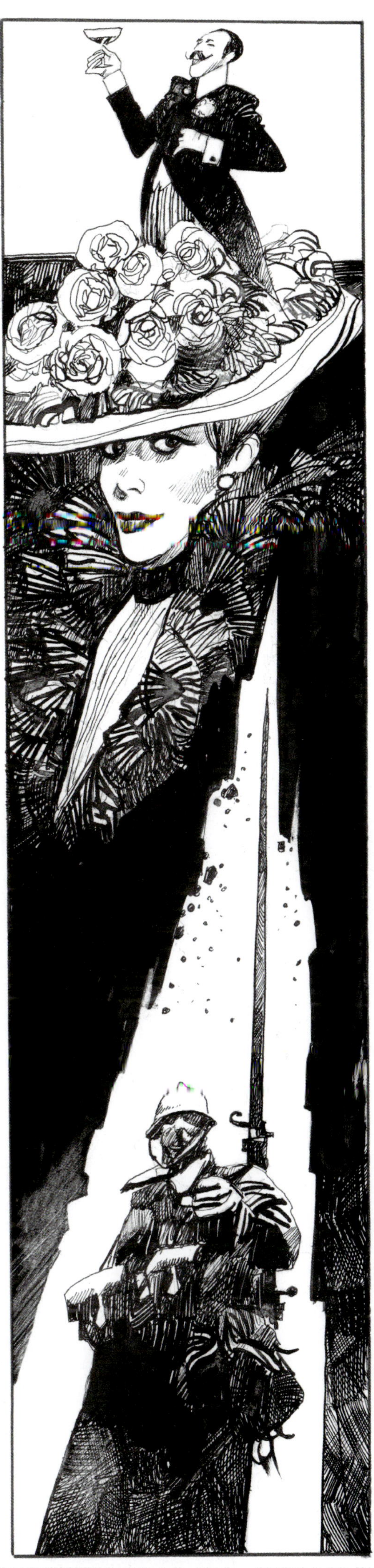

Unpublished illustrations, character studies, 1957.

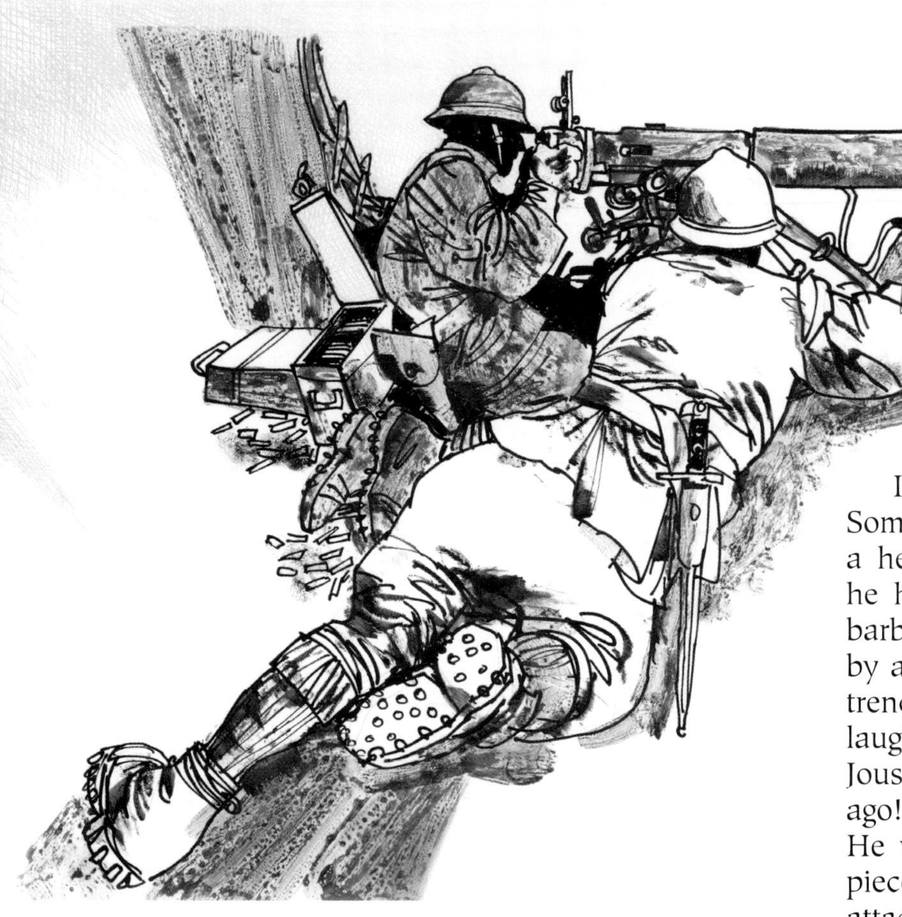

In civilian life, he had been a gardener. Someone told him: "So you know how to trim a hedge! Do I have a job for you!" Today, he has traded his oleanders and cedars for barbed wire. Armed with clippers, protected by a helmet and a steel apron, he clears the trenches. His helm and armor make his friends laugh. "Hey, knight! You're in the wrong war! Jousts and tournaments were a few centuries ago!" He lets them laugh, he doesn't answer. He waits for the next stray bullet, the next piece of flying shrapnel, the next bayonet attack. Soon, some of them won't be laughing so hard.

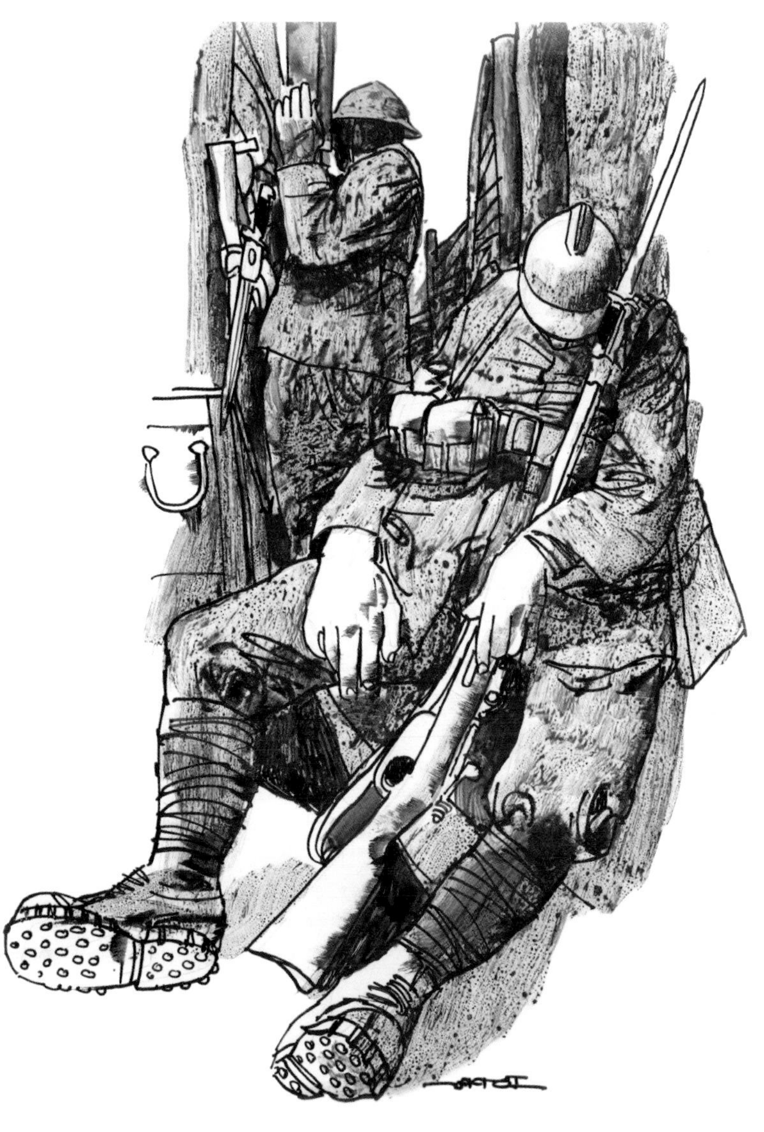

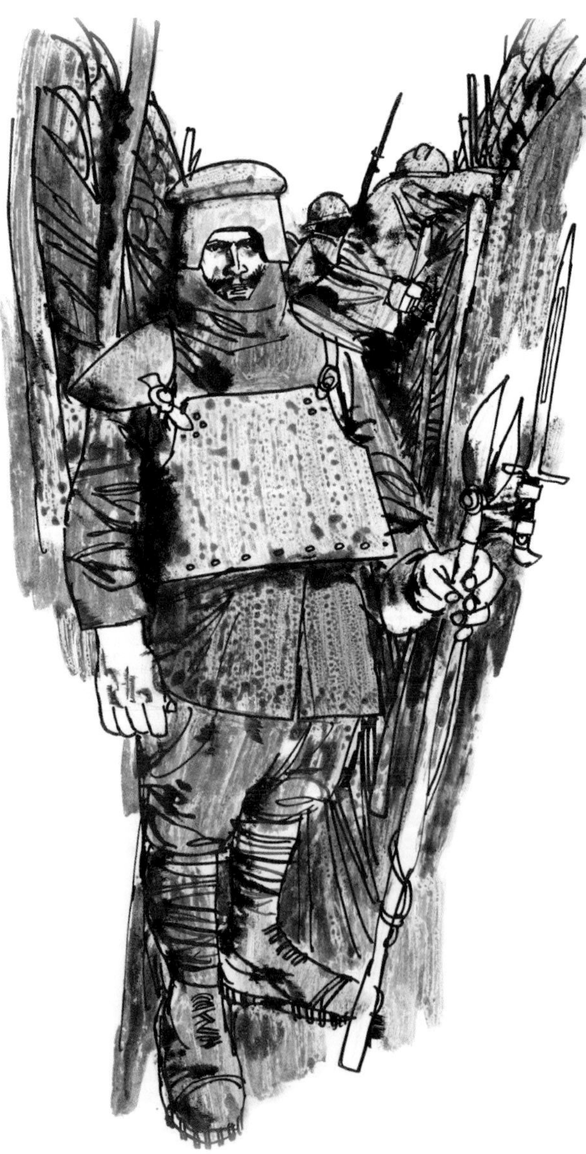

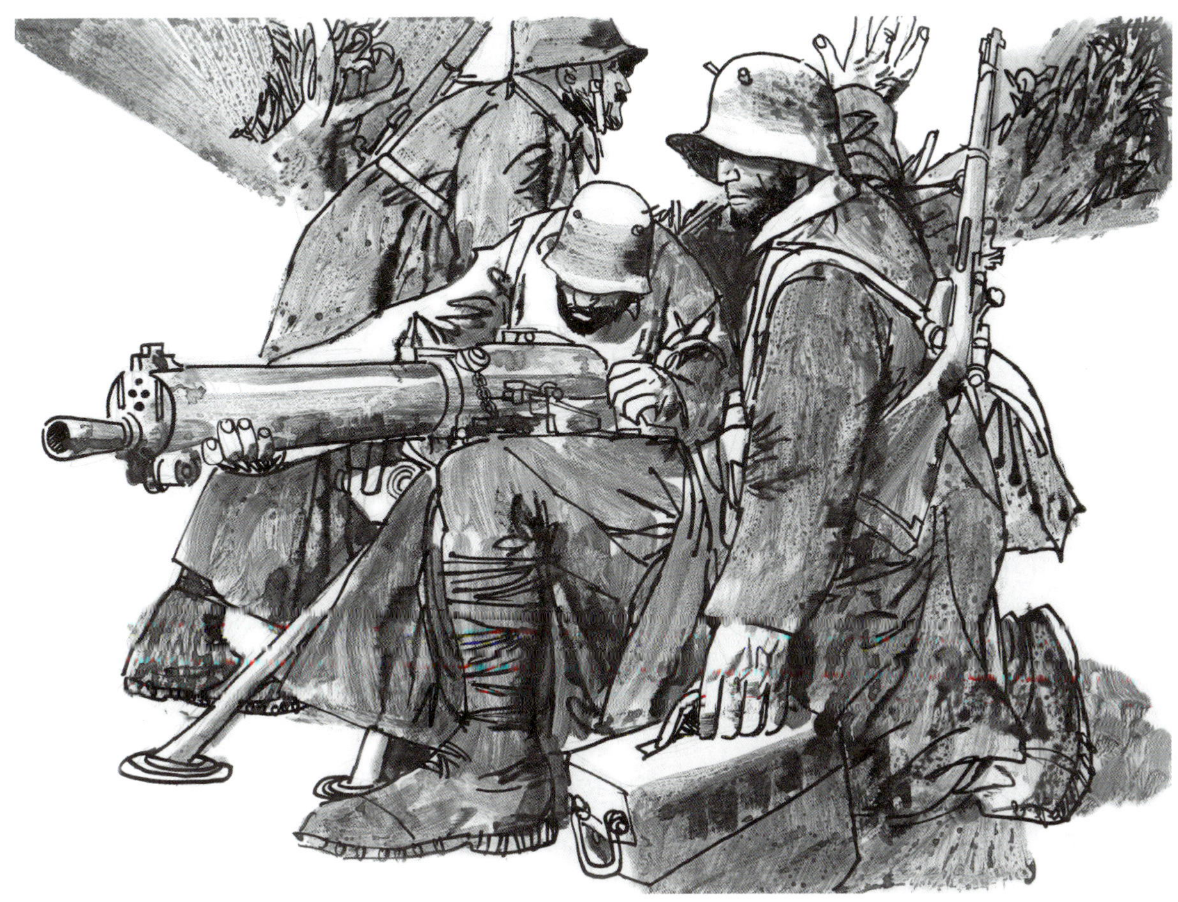

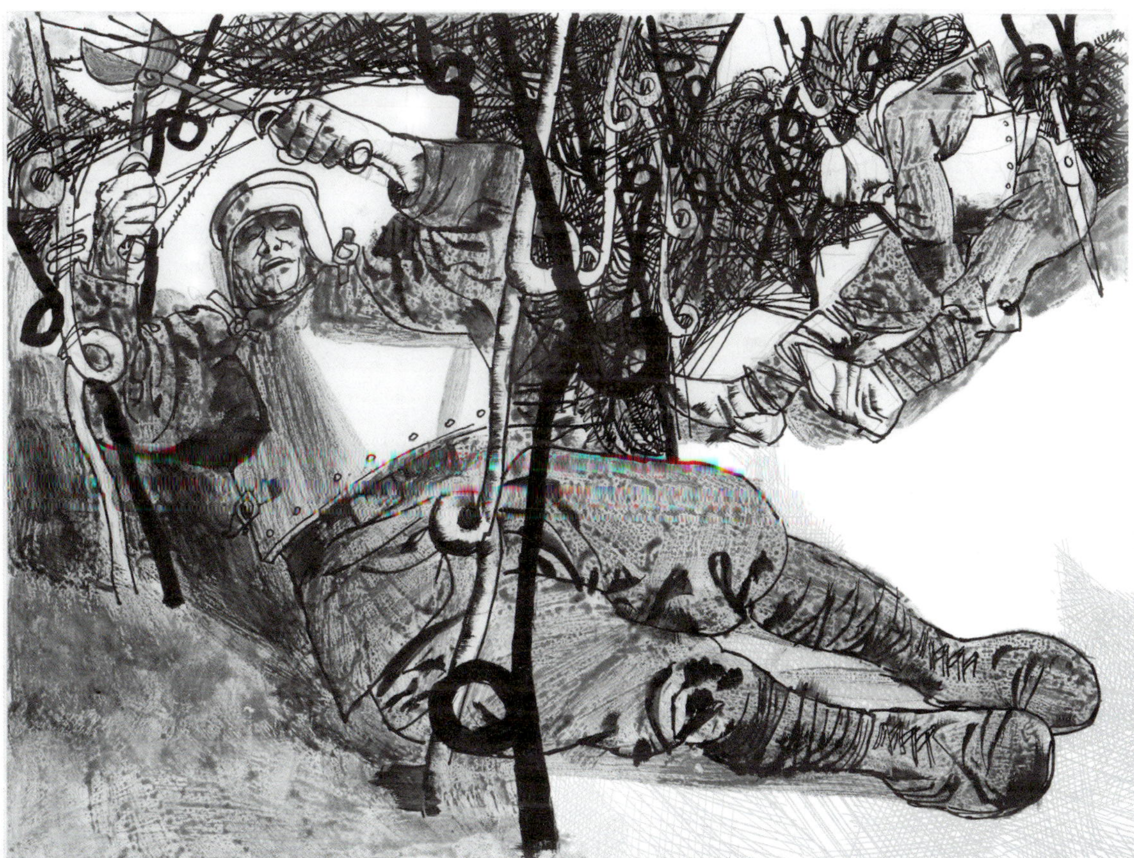

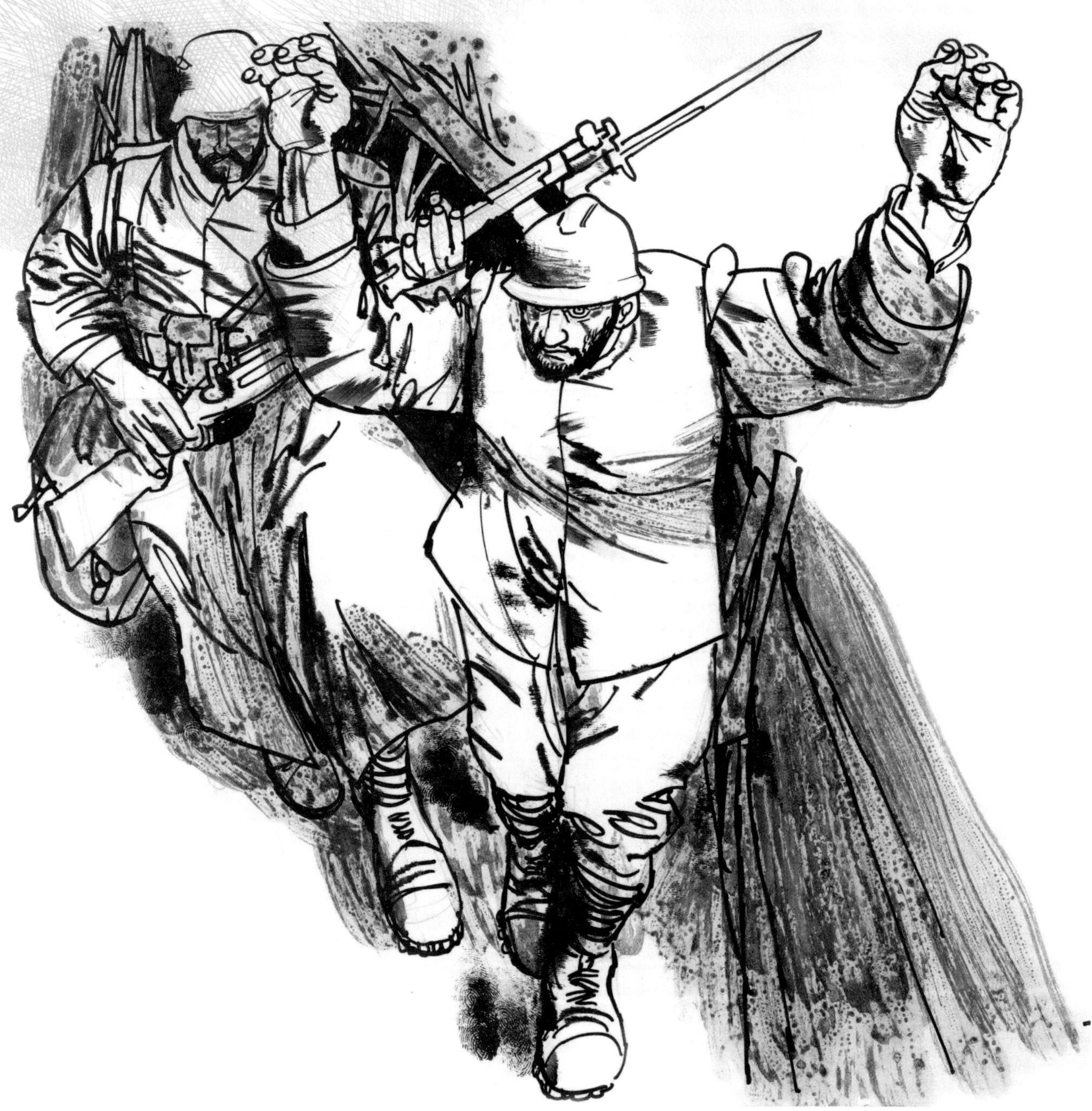

They don't know it yet, but they will make it back home. Haggard, lost, incapable of speech, but whole. For the rest of their lives, they will remain silent about the feeling of guilt for a sin they did not commit: for having survived, while others died. The screams, the moans, the groans, the deafening clamor of the mortar shells: they will be silent from here on out, although they sense that, inside themselves, they will never again know silence. For now, they are simply afraid. They don't know it yet, but they will feel guilty for having saved their own skin. They trembled with cold and dread, they drank their ration of hooch, and watched the men next to them fall one by one.

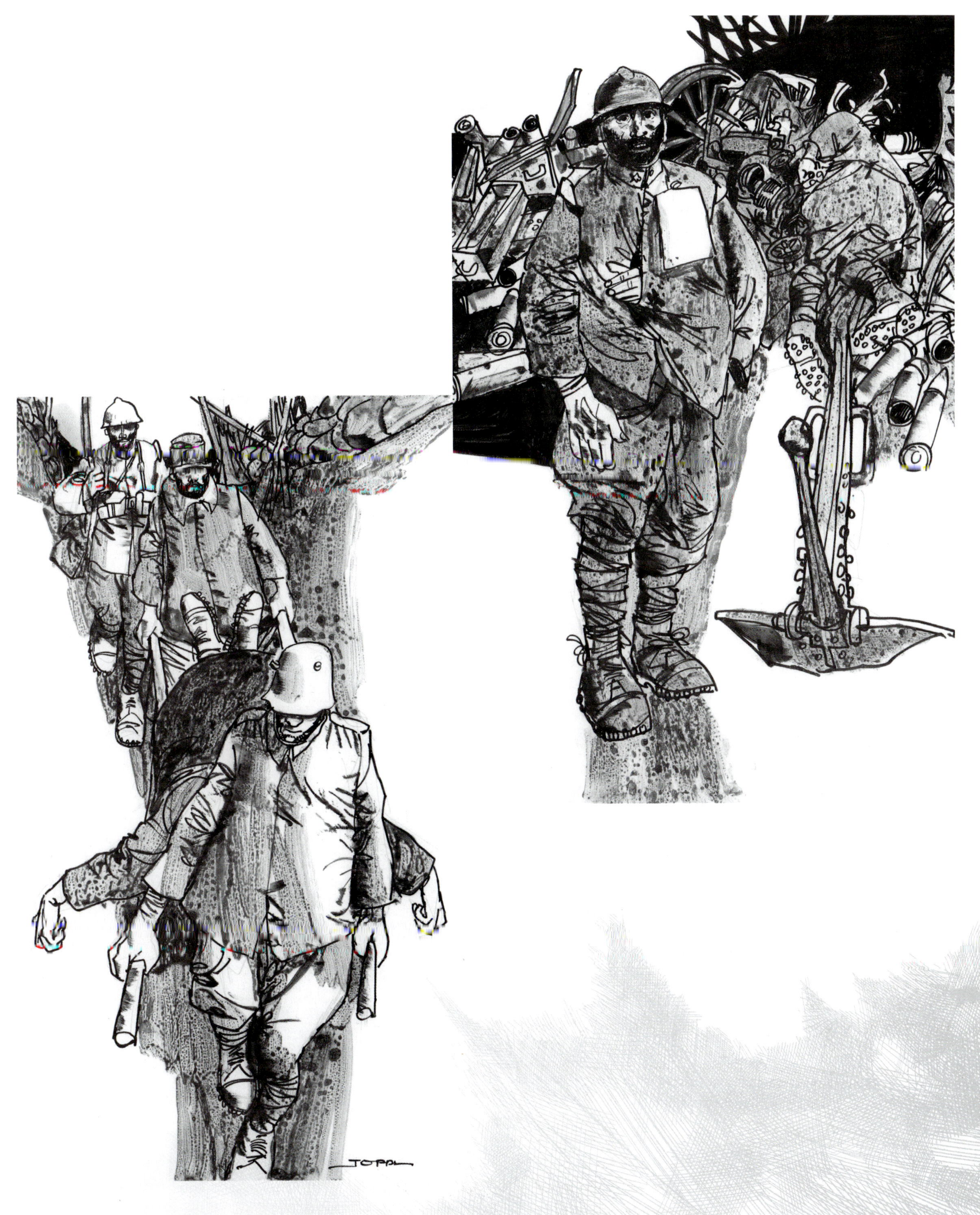

These pages: Unpublished illustrations, character studies, 1957.

The Red Baron's dog was incontinent. After his head wound in July 1917, Manfred would expound at length about the brave animal's urinary deficiencies. He would complain about no longer being able to bring it with him in his Fokker Triplane due to the risk of splashing when he would attempt any kind of acrobatics — looping or diving too sharply.

As a result, he had to resign himself to leaving it on the ground. On April 21, 1918, above Vaux-sur-Somme, the Red Baron was shot out of the sky. And the dog? Incontinent, perhaps, but still alive, at least.

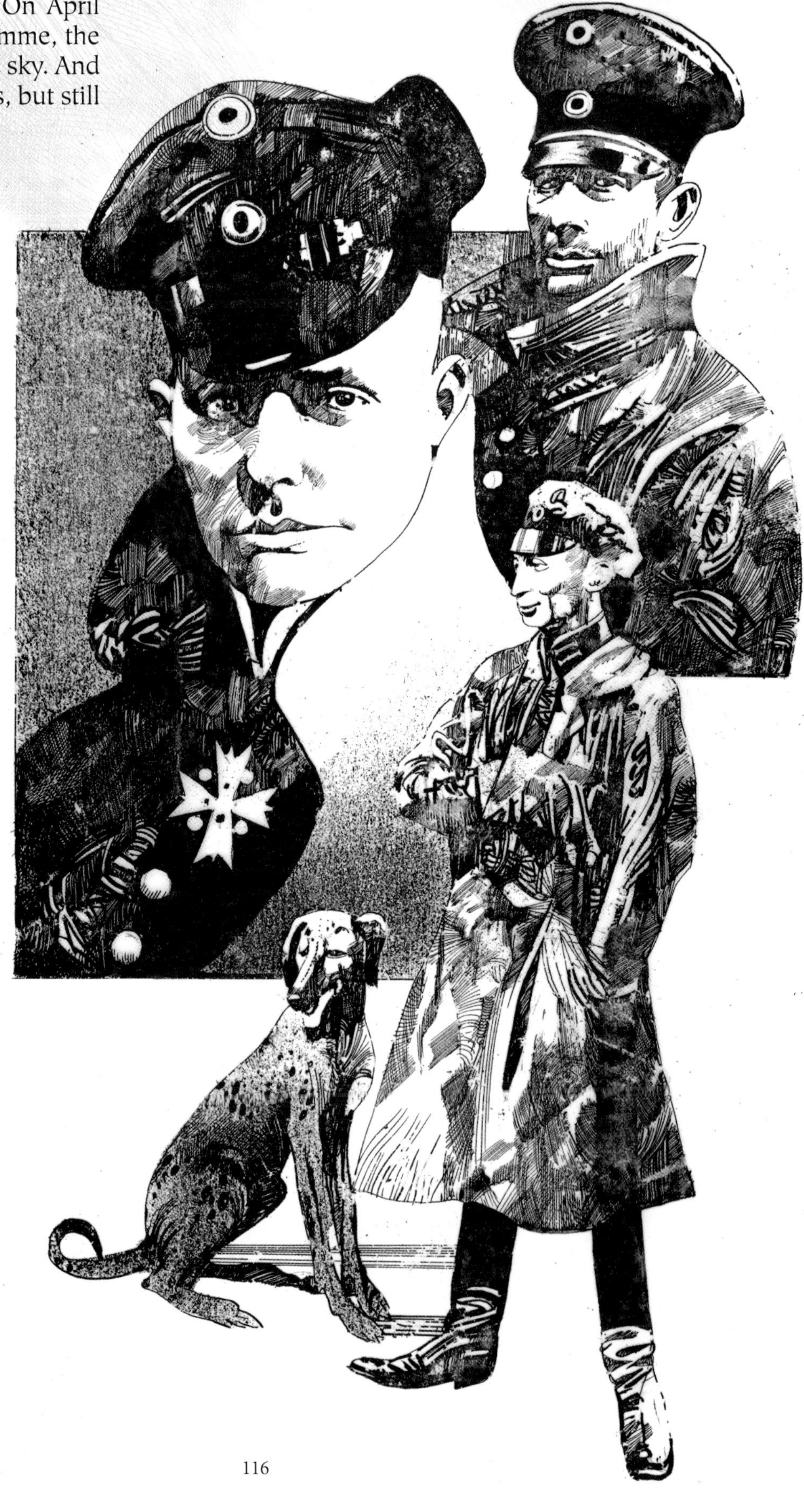

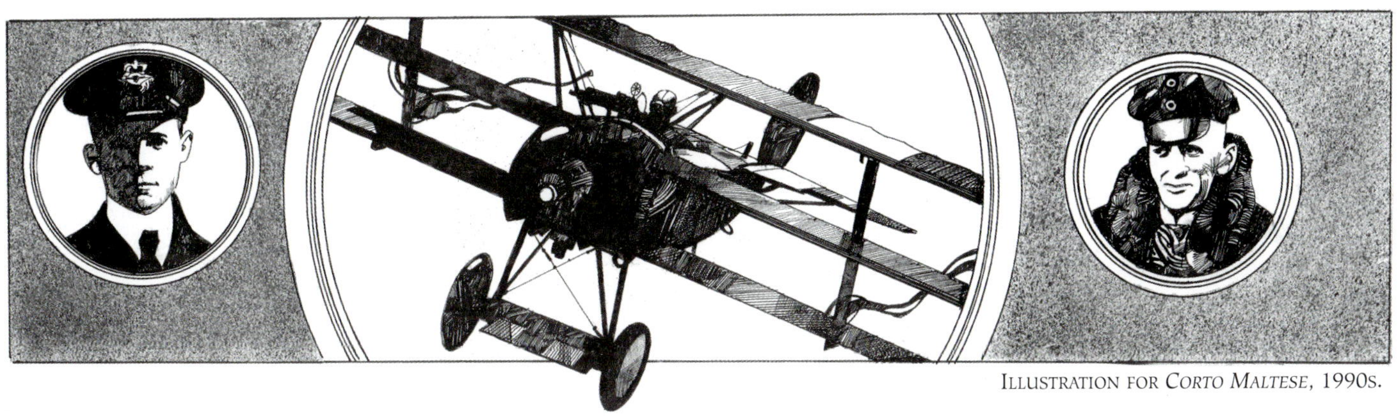

ILLUSTRATION FOR *CORTO MALTESE*, 1990S.

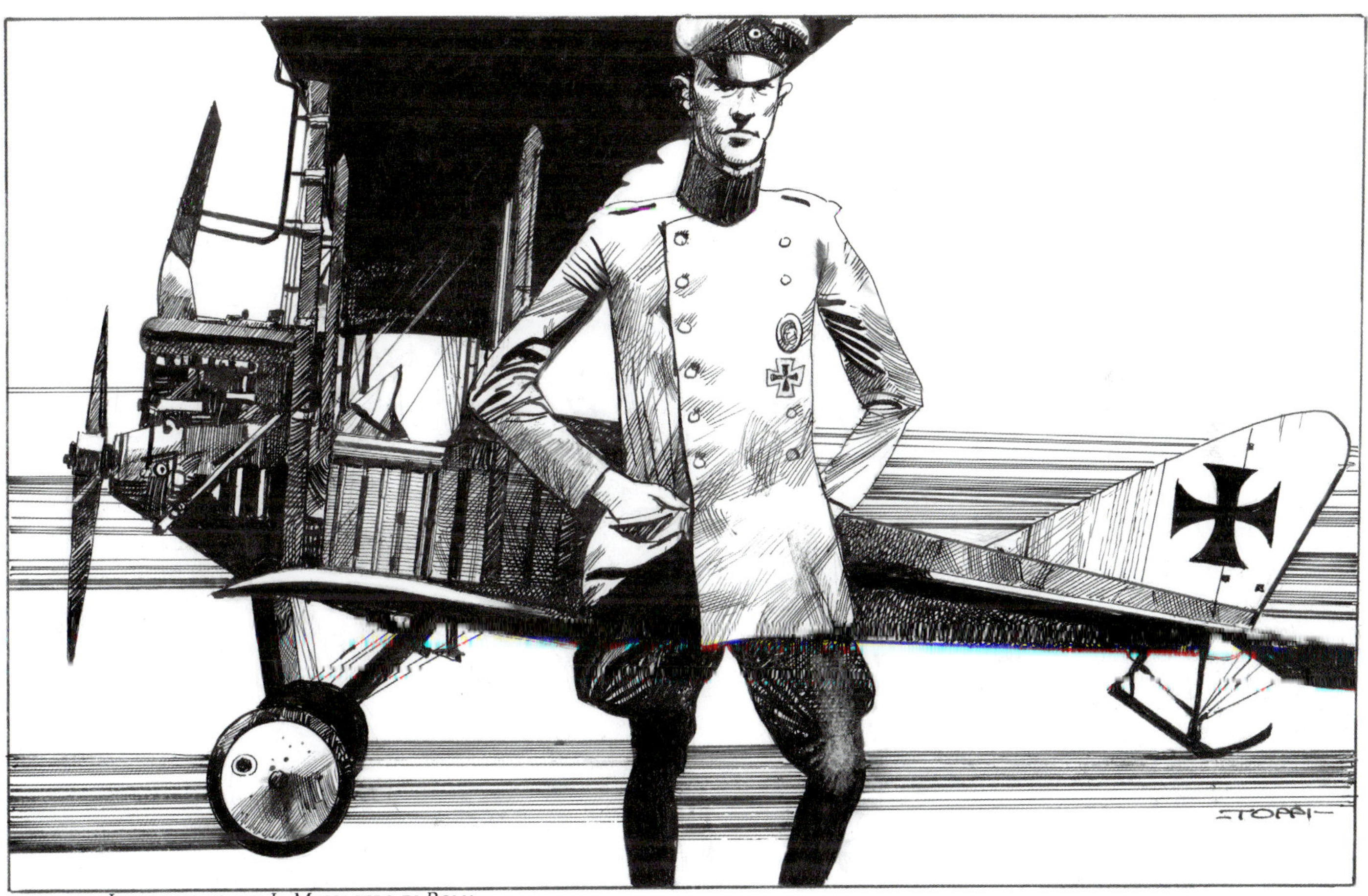

ILLUSTRATION FOR *IL MESSAGERO DI ROMA*,
1990S.

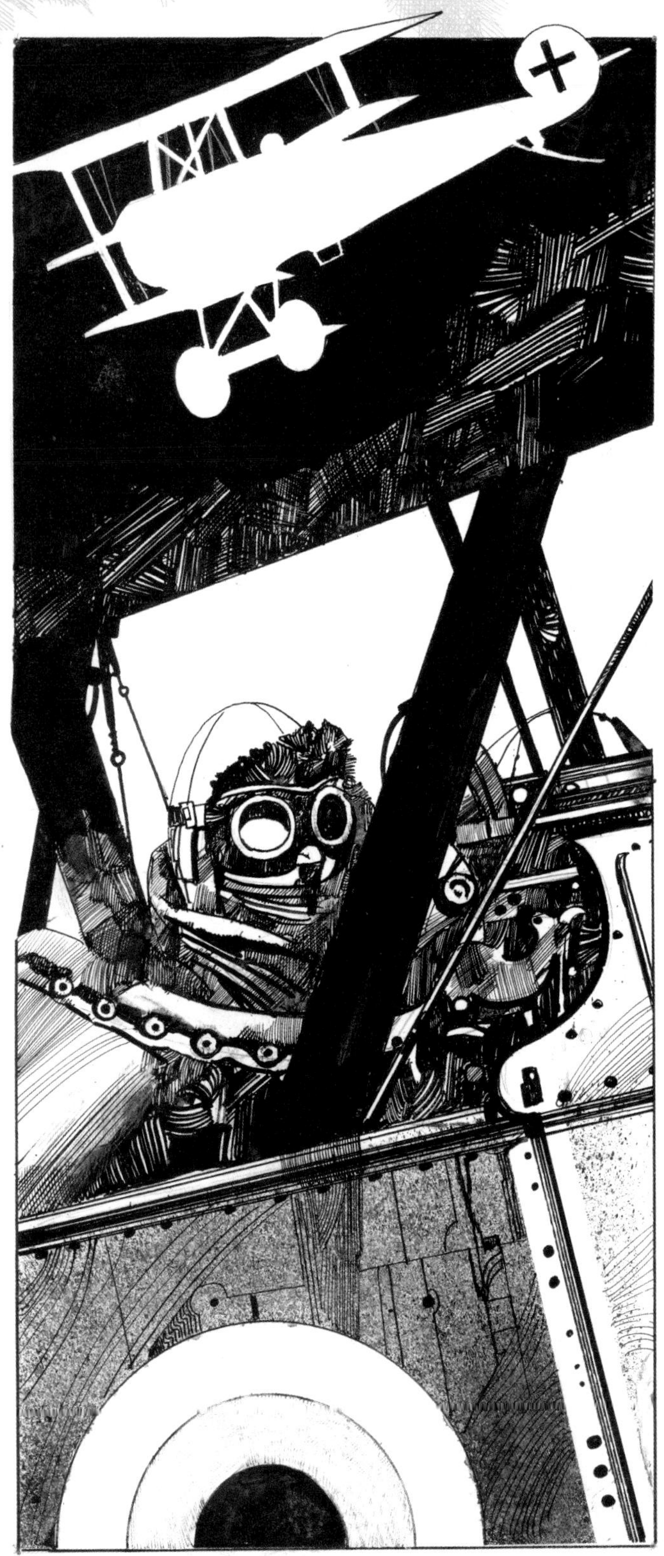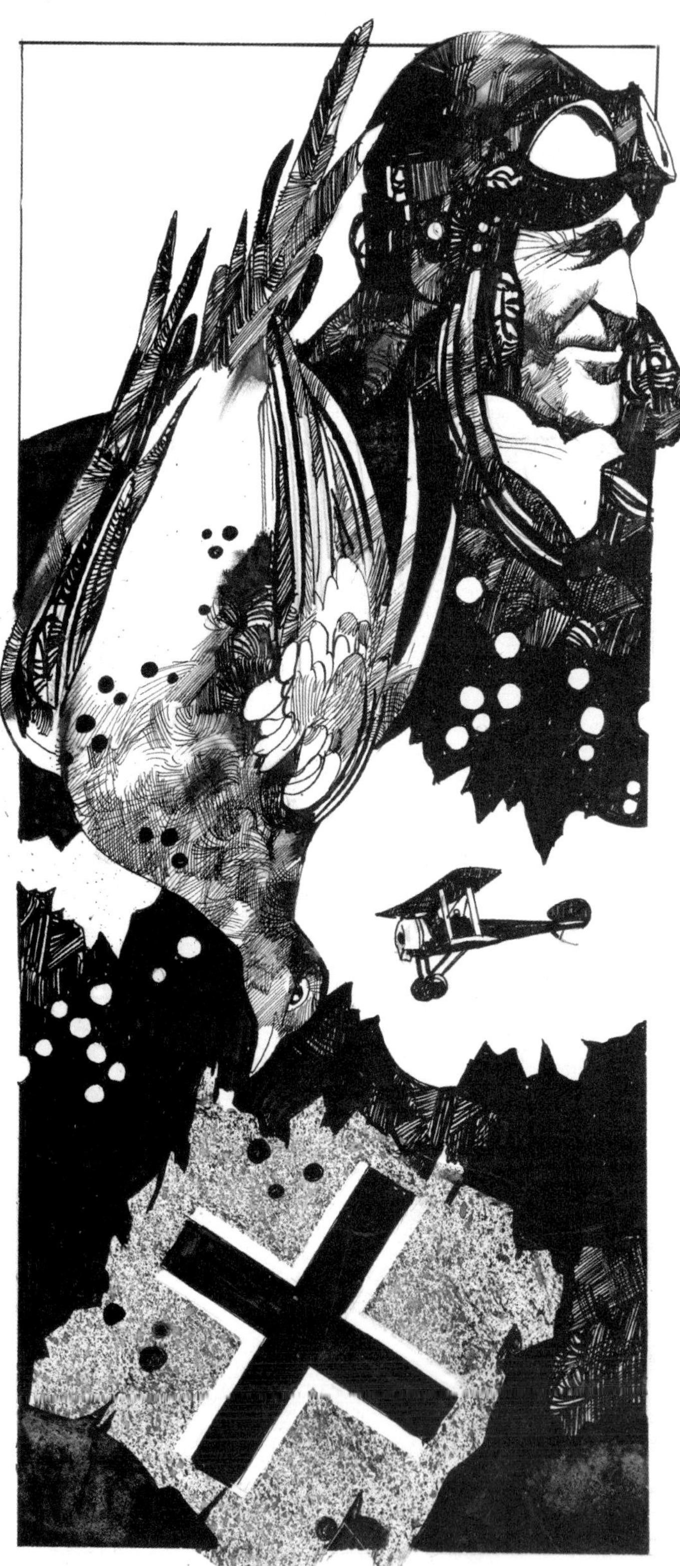

ILLUSTRATIONS FOR *CORTO MALTESE*, 1990s.

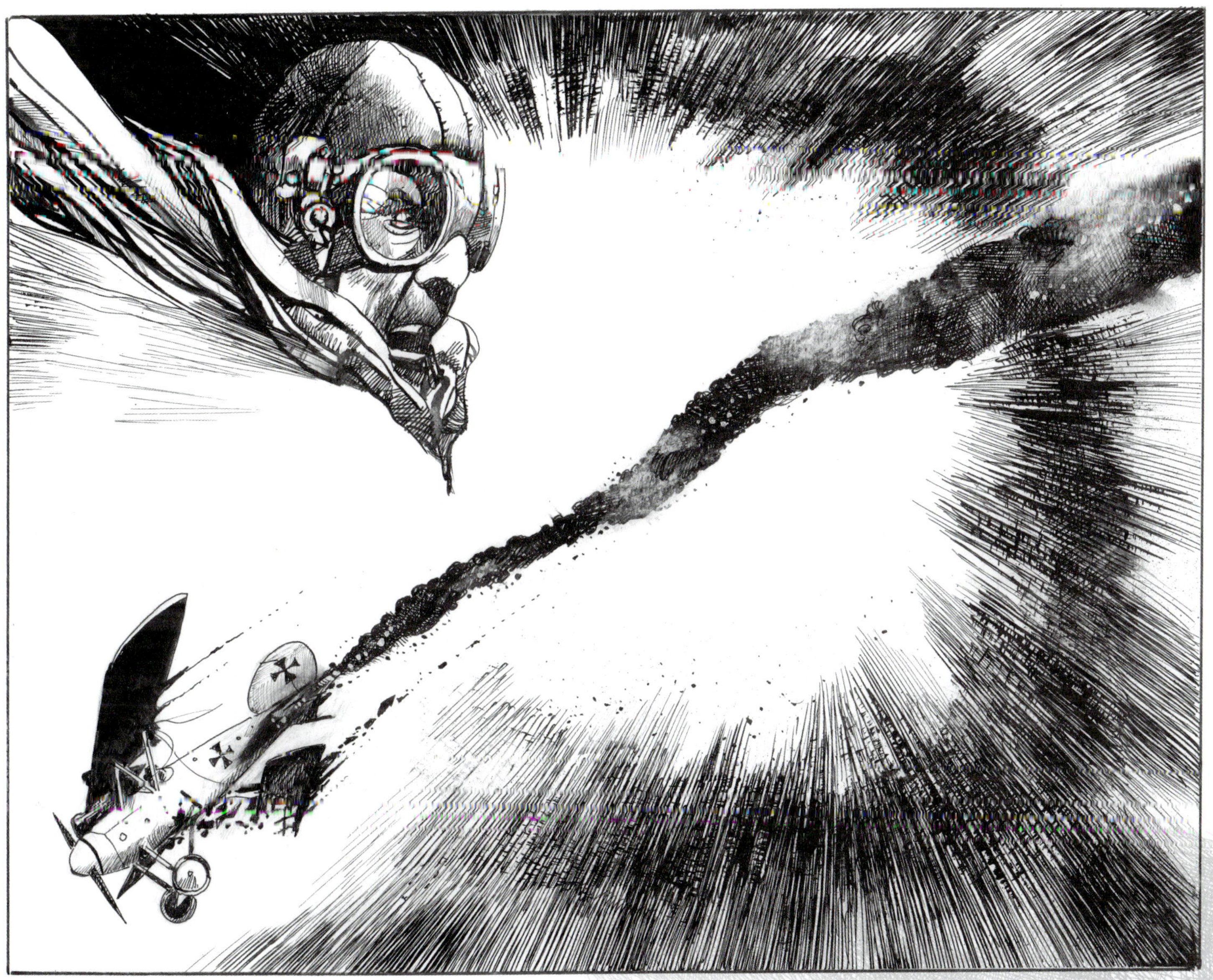

ILLUSTRATION FOR *IL MESSAGERO DI ROMA*, 1990s.

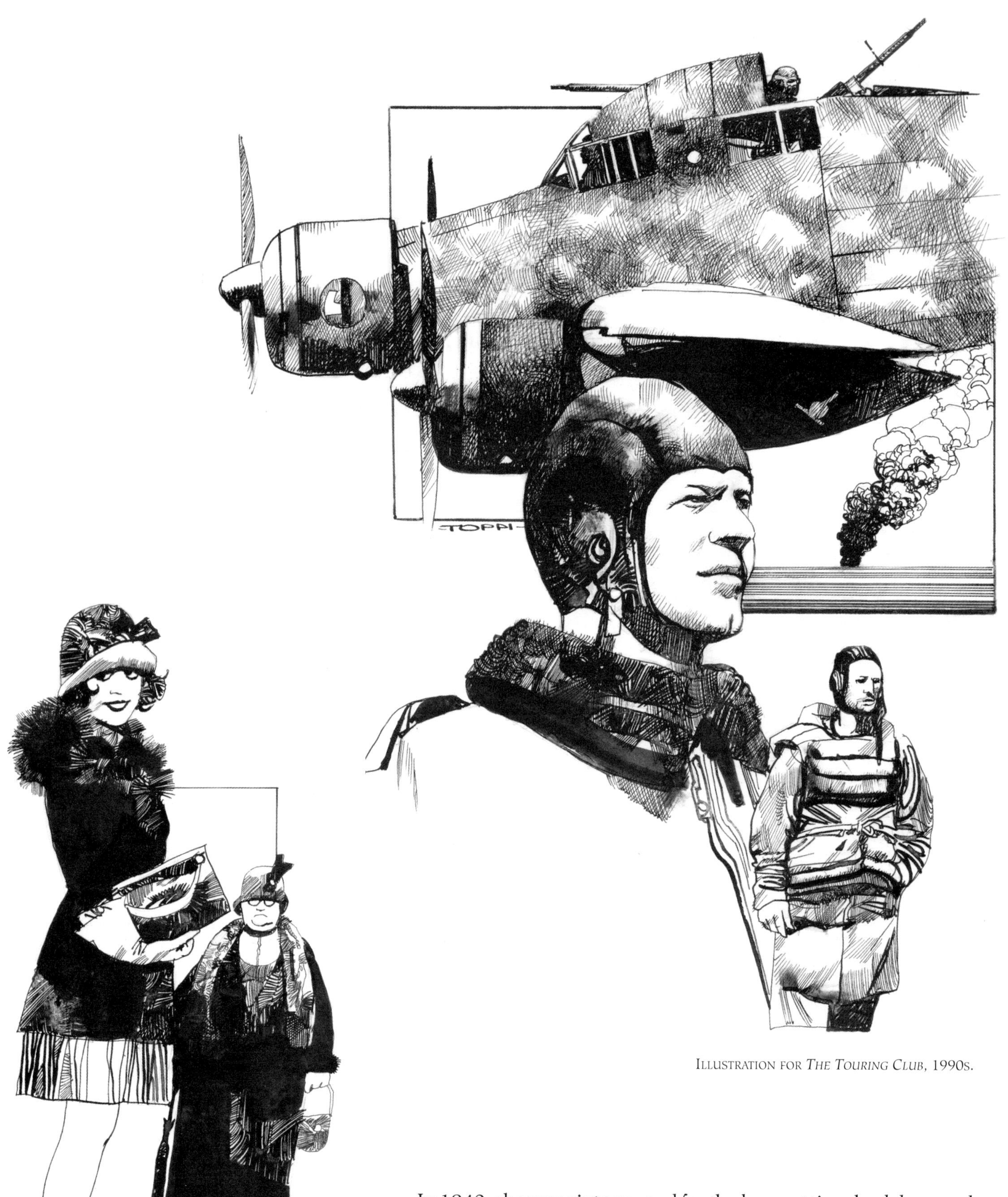

ILLUSTRATION FOR *THE TOURING CLUB*, 1990s.

ILLUSTRATIONS FOR IL GIORNALINO, 1990s.

In 1940, she was sixteen, and for the longest time had dreamed of marrying an aviator. As she would leave Sunday mass, from the corner of her eye, she would gaze at the impeccable uniforms of the Air Force officers. She would thrill at the slightest mention of heroes, demigods, knights in shining armor. Her mother hardly shared such starry-eyed schoolgirl daydreams that left her daughter languorous and idle. She dreamed of marrying an aviator; she ended up settling for a gentle butcher.

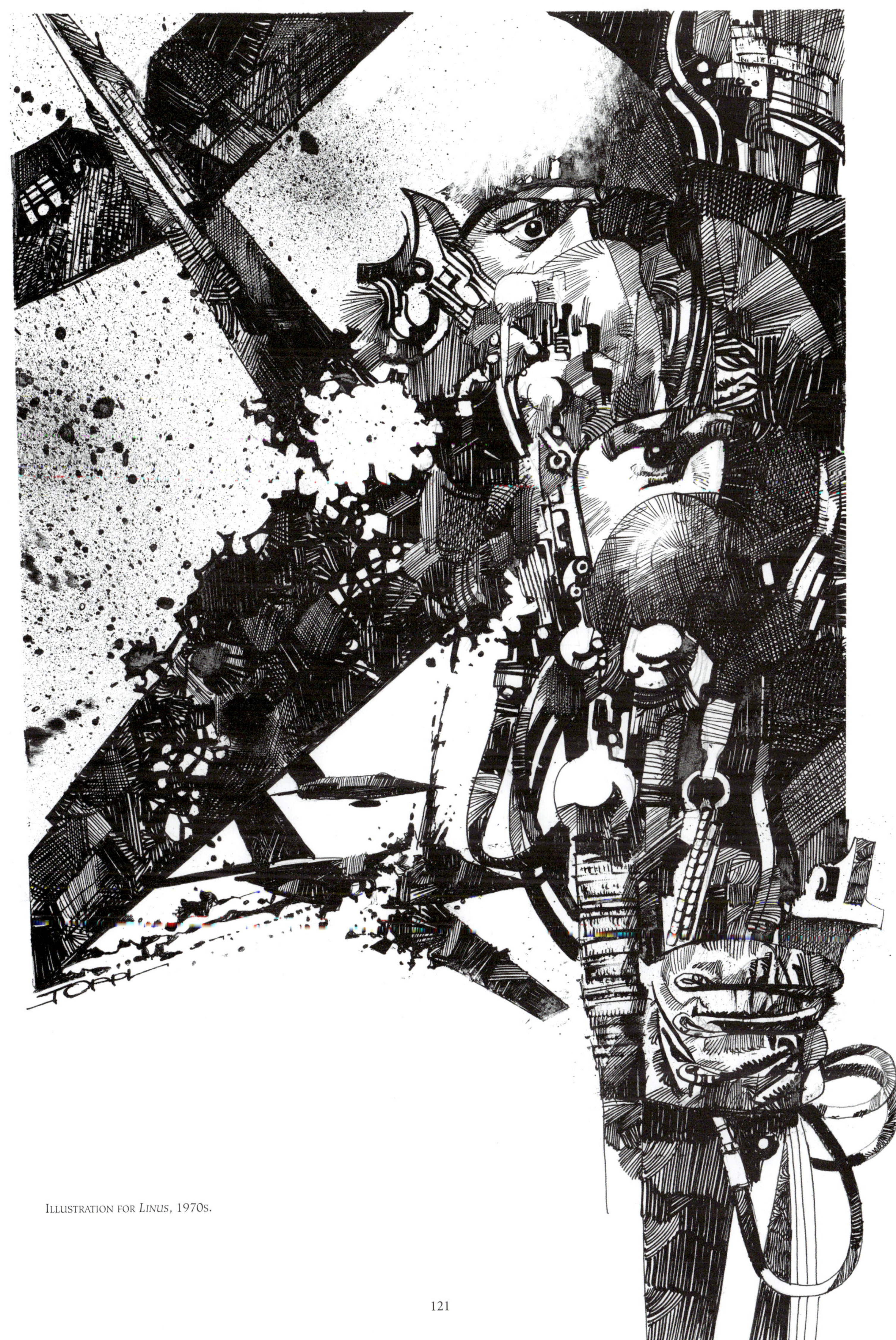

ILLUSTRATION FOR *LINUS*, 1970S.

Woman is the future of mankind,

Or so they say...

A great deal can be said about Aphrodite's appetites.
She married the blacksmith Hephaestus, ugly and lame; and she took Ares,
massive, belligerent, and cruel, for a lover. After whom, she hooked up with Dionysus,
notorious drunkard, then Hermes, thief, liar, and patron of merchants.
How reassuring.

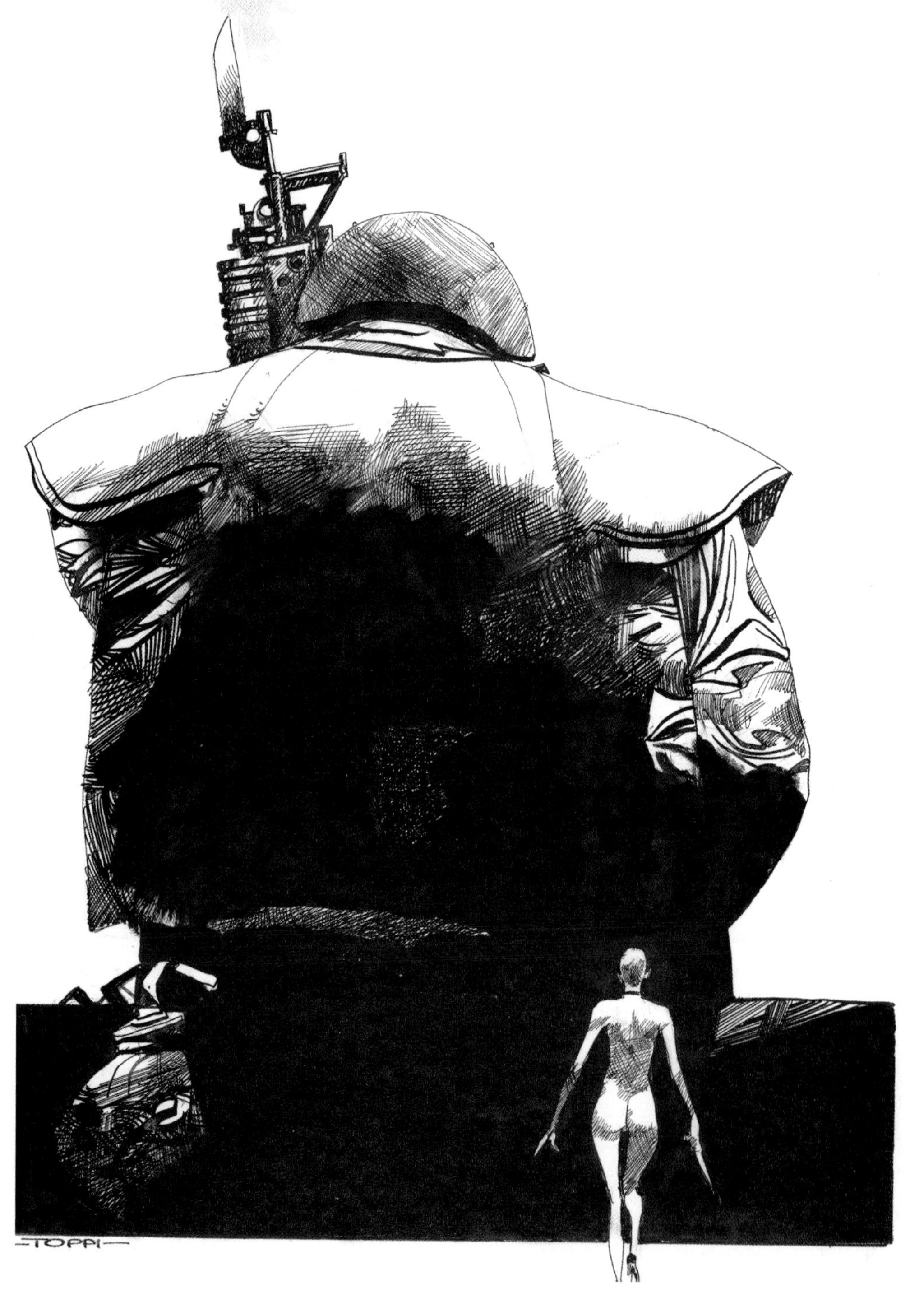

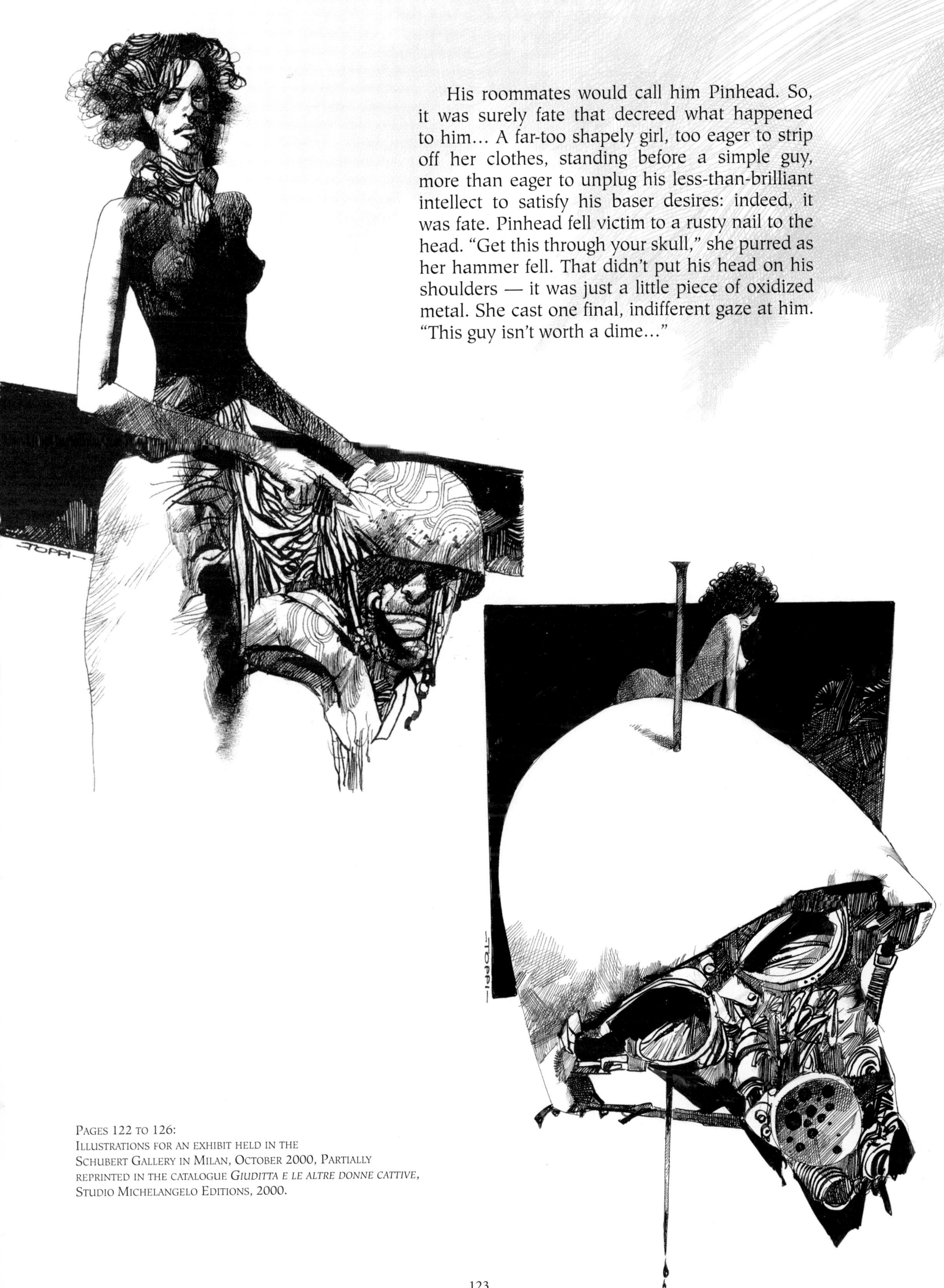

His roommates would call him Pinhead. So, it was surely fate that decreed what happened to him... A far-too shapely girl, too eager to strip off her clothes, standing before a simple guy, more than eager to unplug his less-than-brilliant intellect to satisfy his baser desires: indeed, it was fate. Pinhead fell victim to a rusty nail to the head. "Get this through your skull," she purred as her hammer fell. That didn't put his head on his shoulders — it was just a little piece of oxidized metal. She cast one final, indifferent gaze at him. "This guy isn't worth a dime..."

PAGES 122 TO 126:
ILLUSTRATIONS FOR AN EXHIBIT HELD IN THE
SCHUBERT GALLERY IN MILAN, OCTOBER 2000, PARTIALLY
REPRINTED IN THE CATALOGUE *GIUDITTA E LE ALTRE DONNE CATTIVE*,
STUDIO MICHELANGELO EDITIONS, 2000.

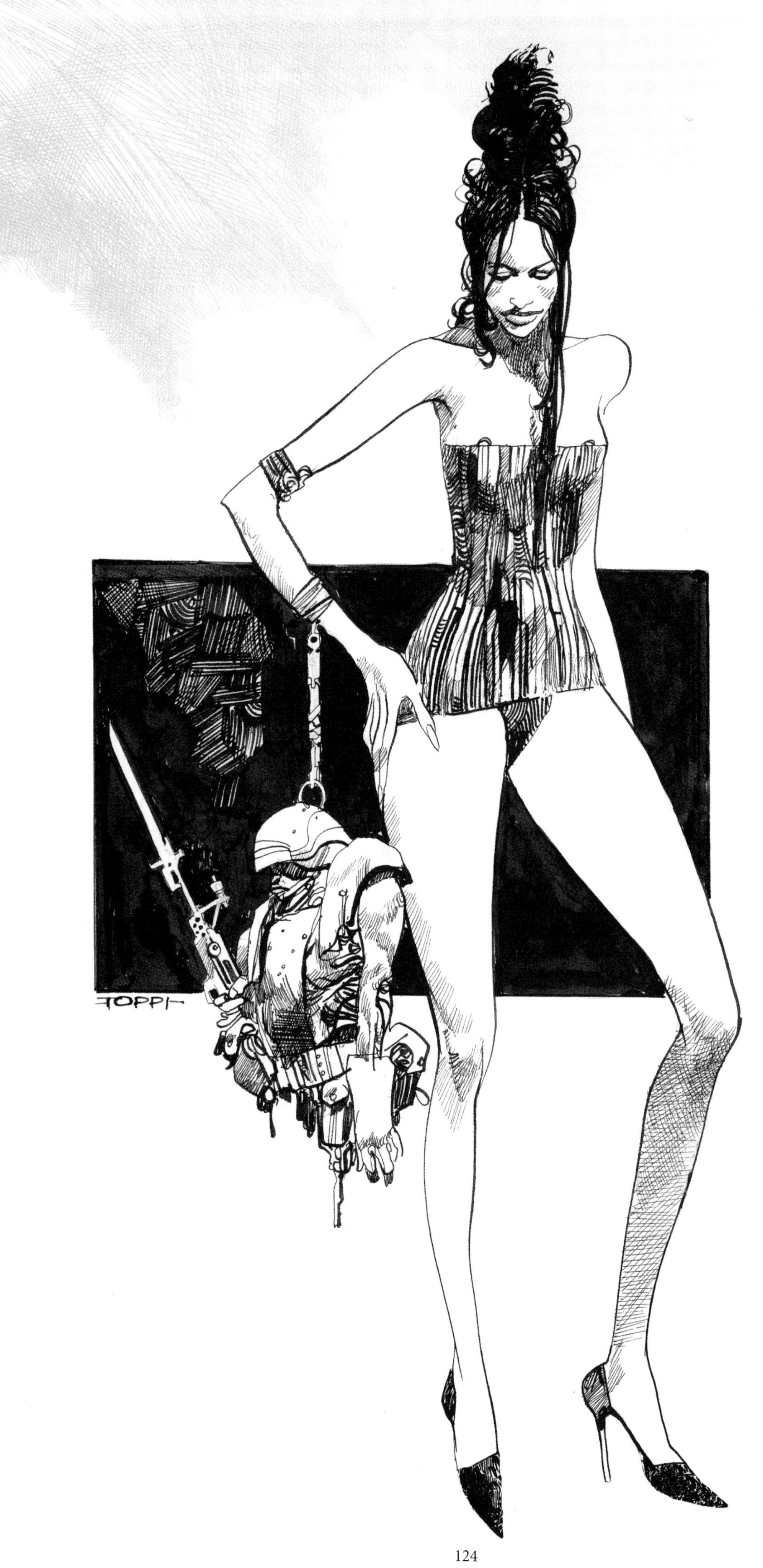
TOPPI

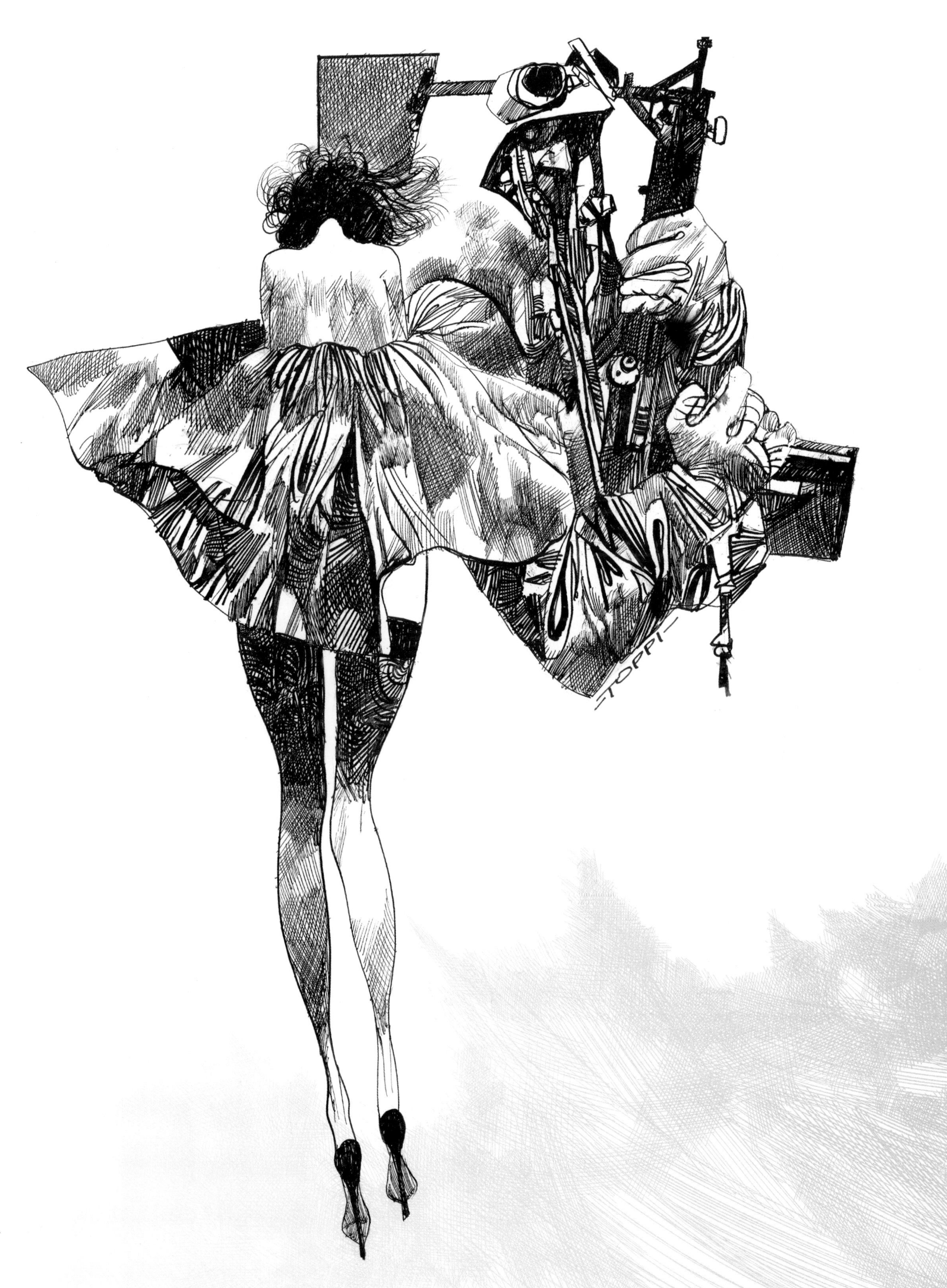

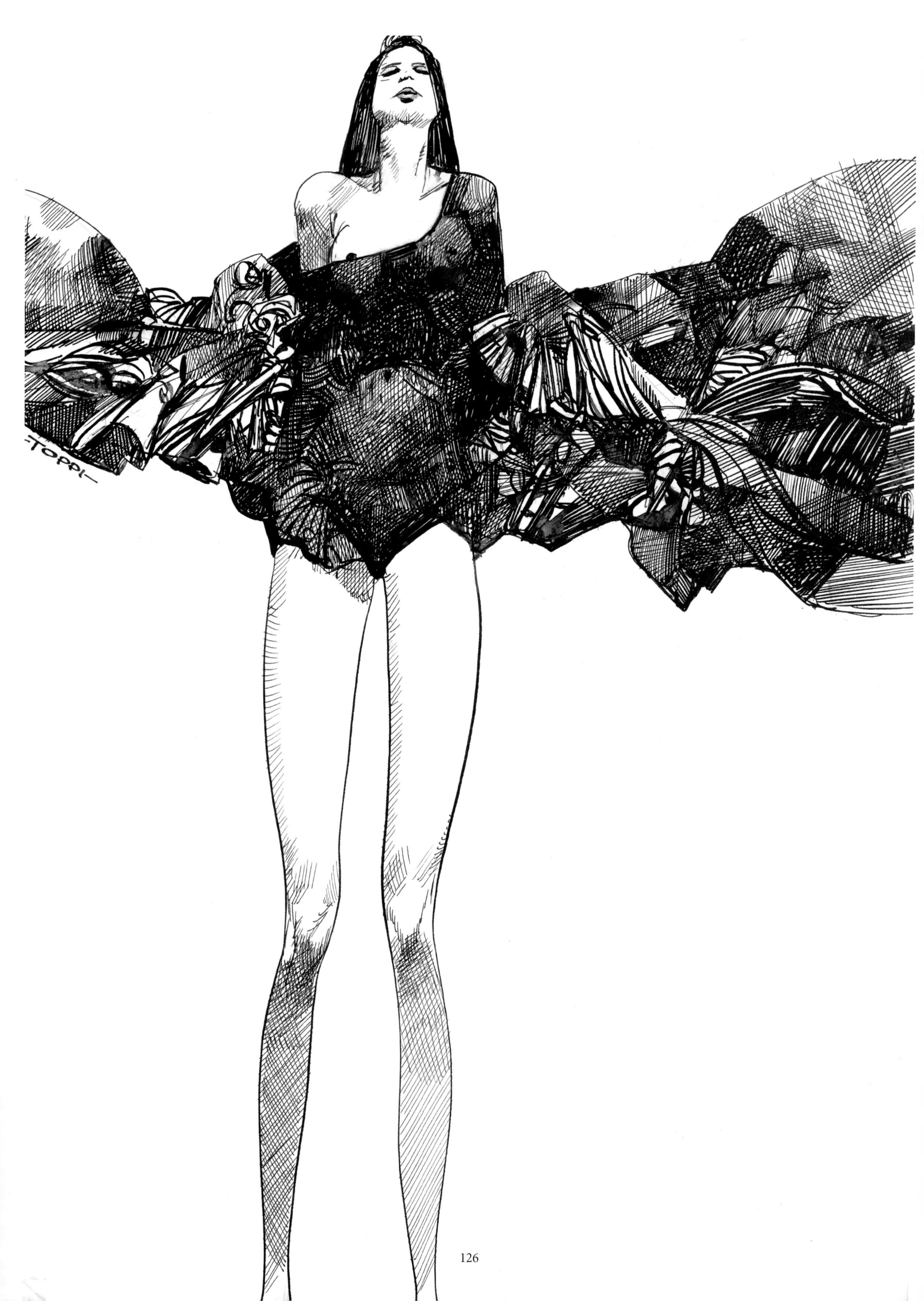

TOPPI

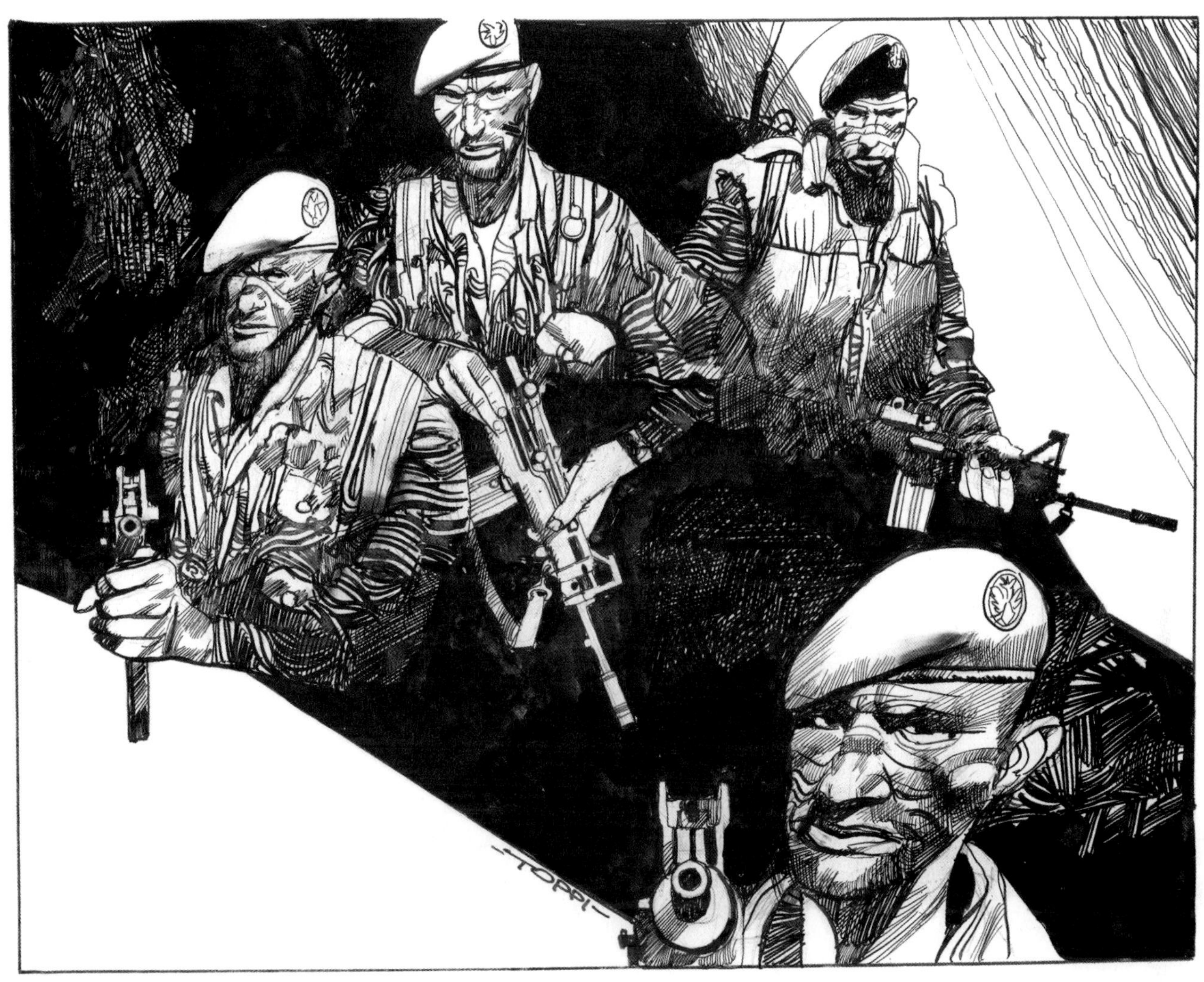

ILLUSTRATIONS FOR *IL MESSAGERO DI ROMA*, 1990S.

They called them "the horrible ones." Not because they were uglier than the next guy (although they were anything but handsome), but because they spread horror wherever they went. The dictionary confirms it: "horror" and "horrible" both come from the same root word. Horror is the essence of the ghastly: they are indifferent to fear, abomination is their home. Their soul is contorted: so they adopt a countenance that resembles it. Their face is a mask, but there is nothing behind it.

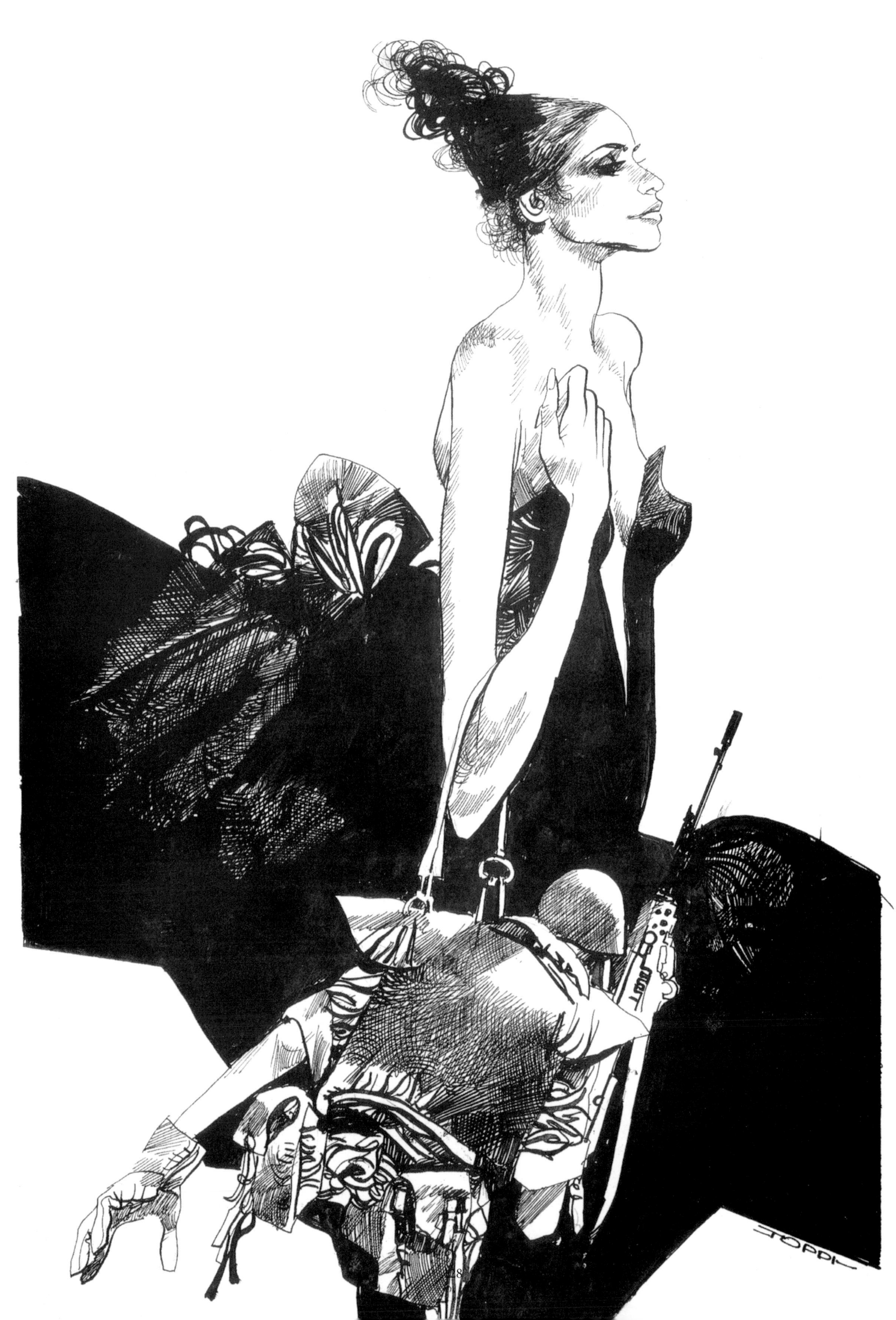

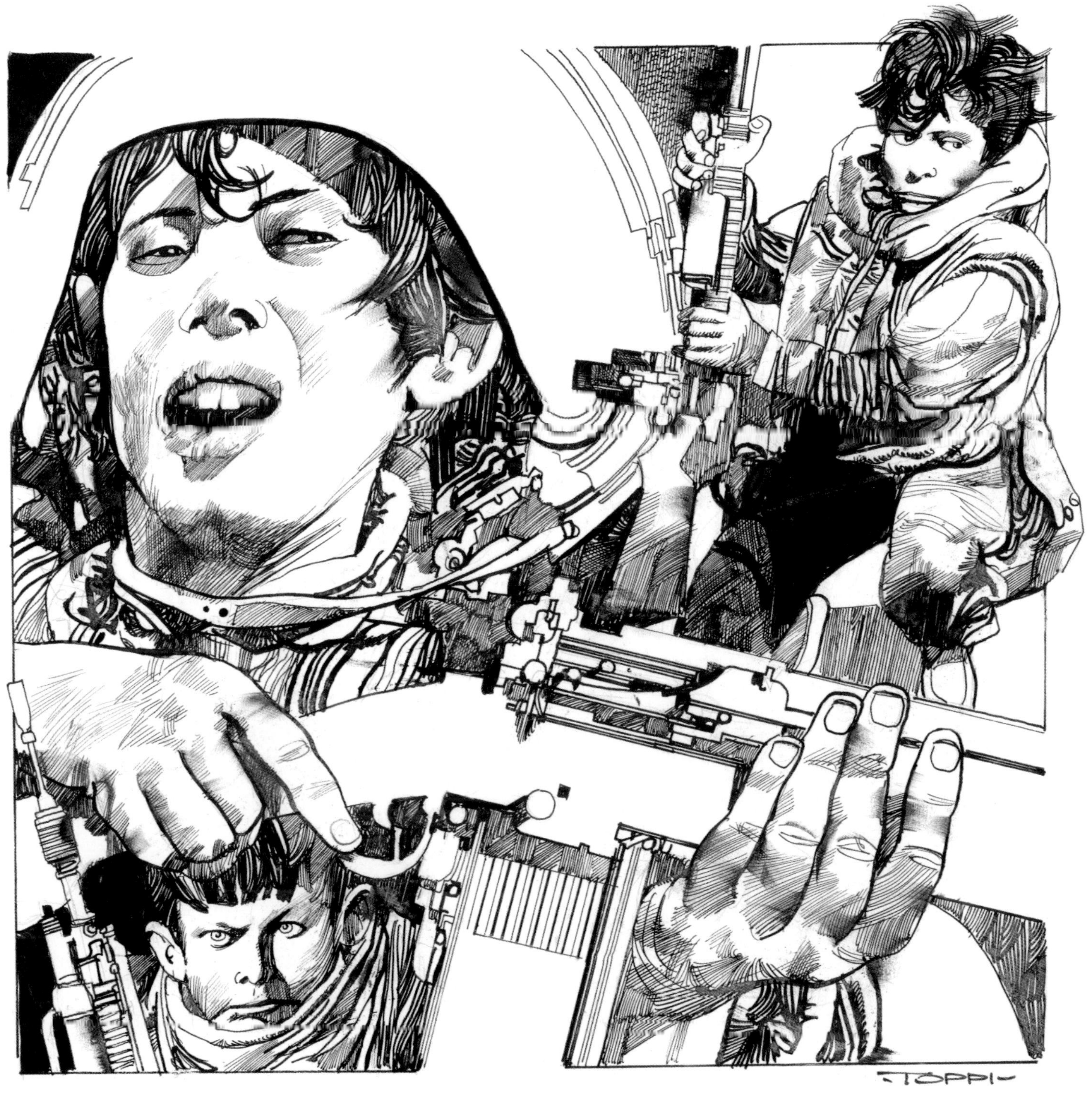

PAGES 129 AND 130: ILLUSTRATIONS FOR THE NOVELLA *LA CACCIA* BY N. BALESTRINI IN *CORTO MALTESE MAGAZINE*, NO.15, 1984.

PREVIOUS PAGE: ILLUSTRATION FOR *GIUDITTA E LE ALTRE DONNE CATTIVE*, 2000.

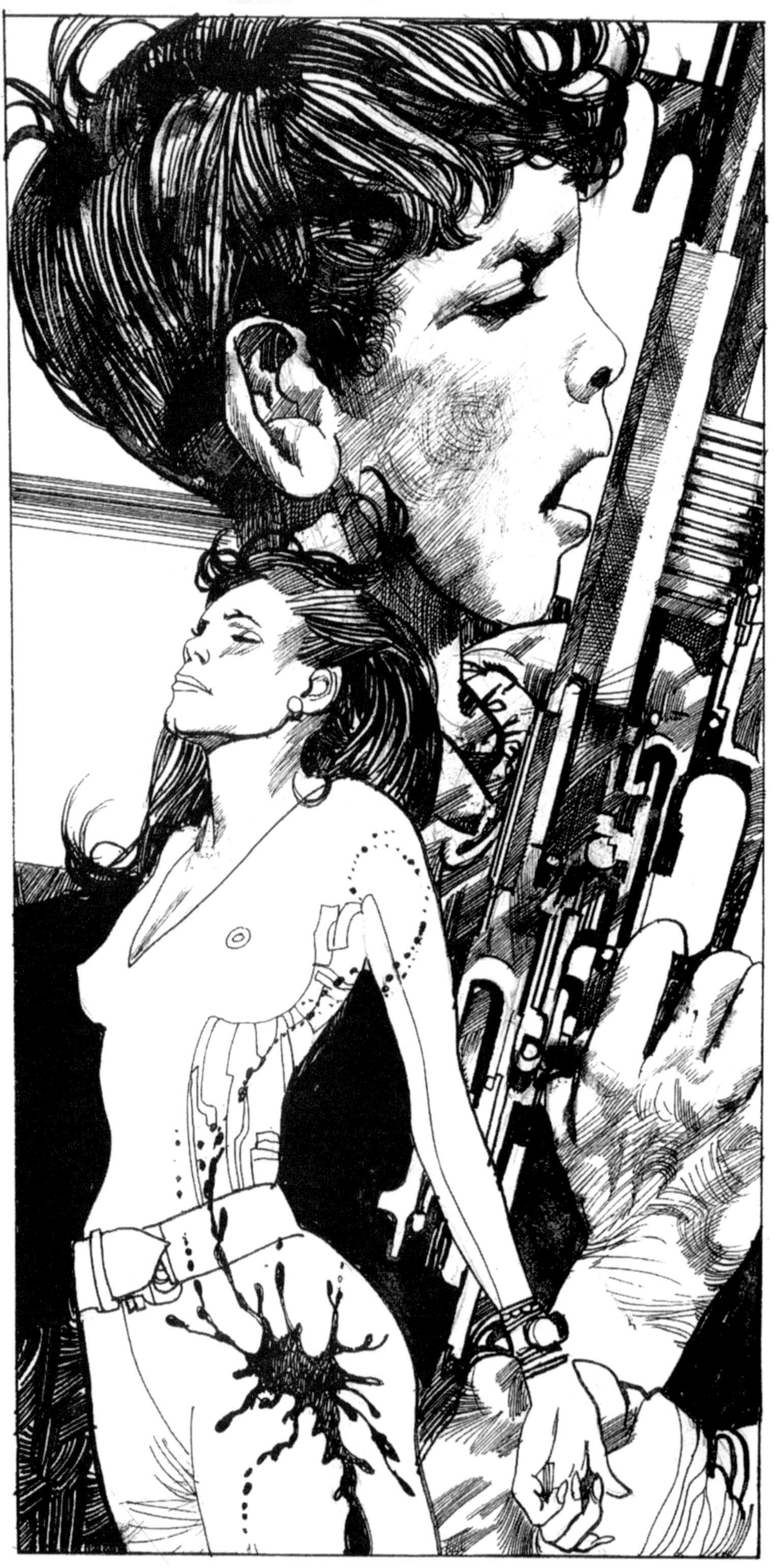

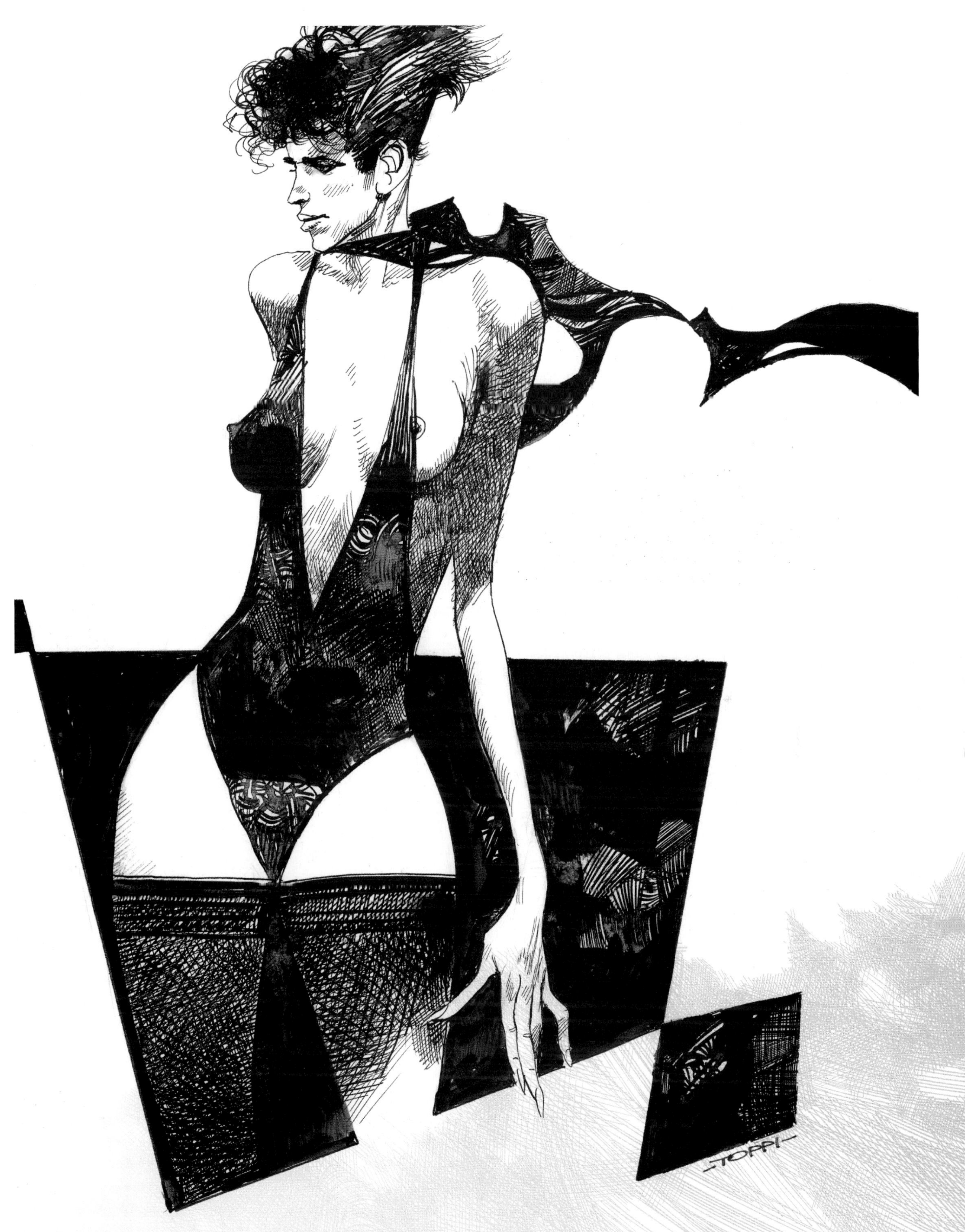

ILLUSTRATION FOR *GIUDITTA E LE ALTRE DONNE CATTIVE*, 2000.

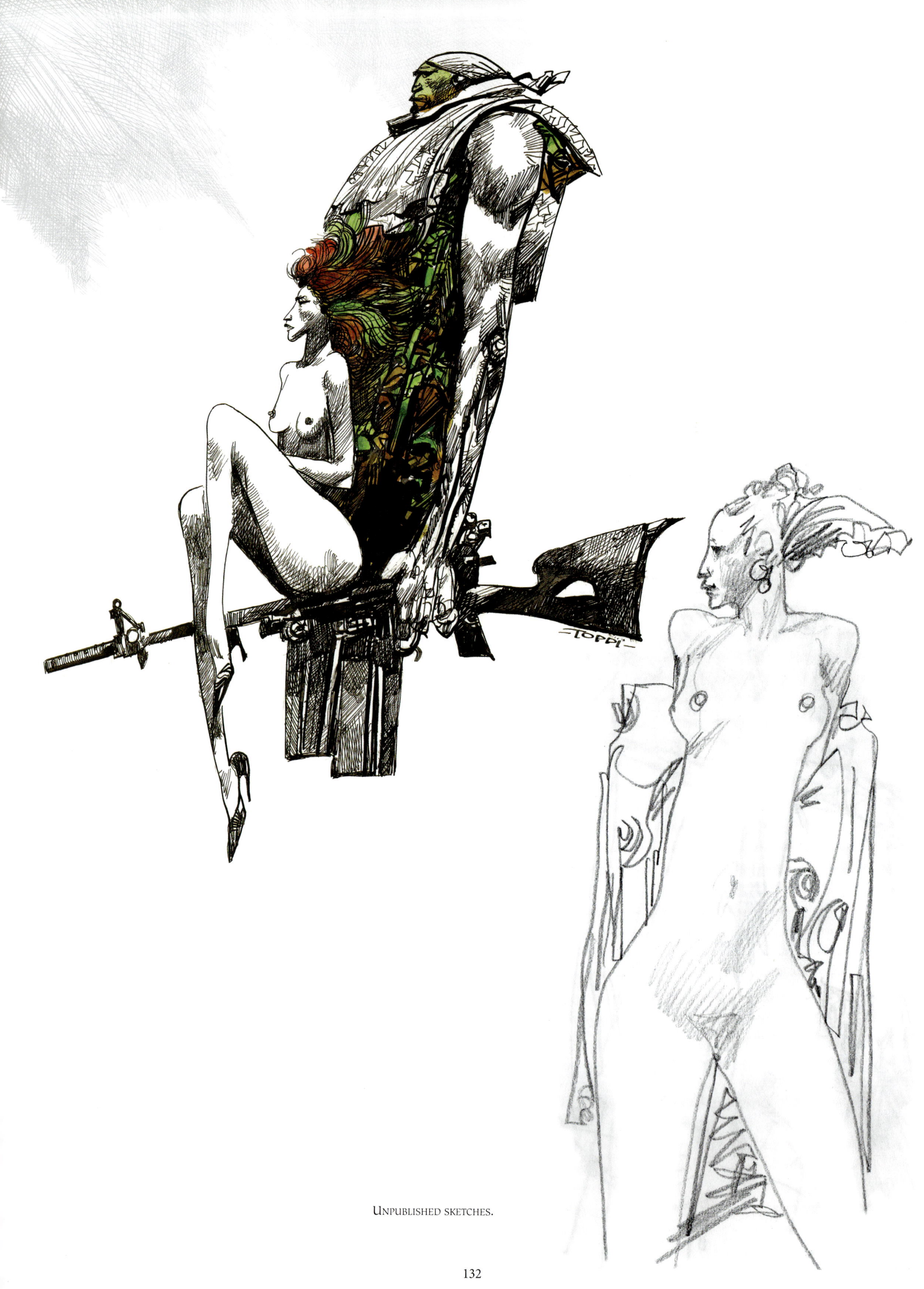

UNPUBLISHED SKETCHES.

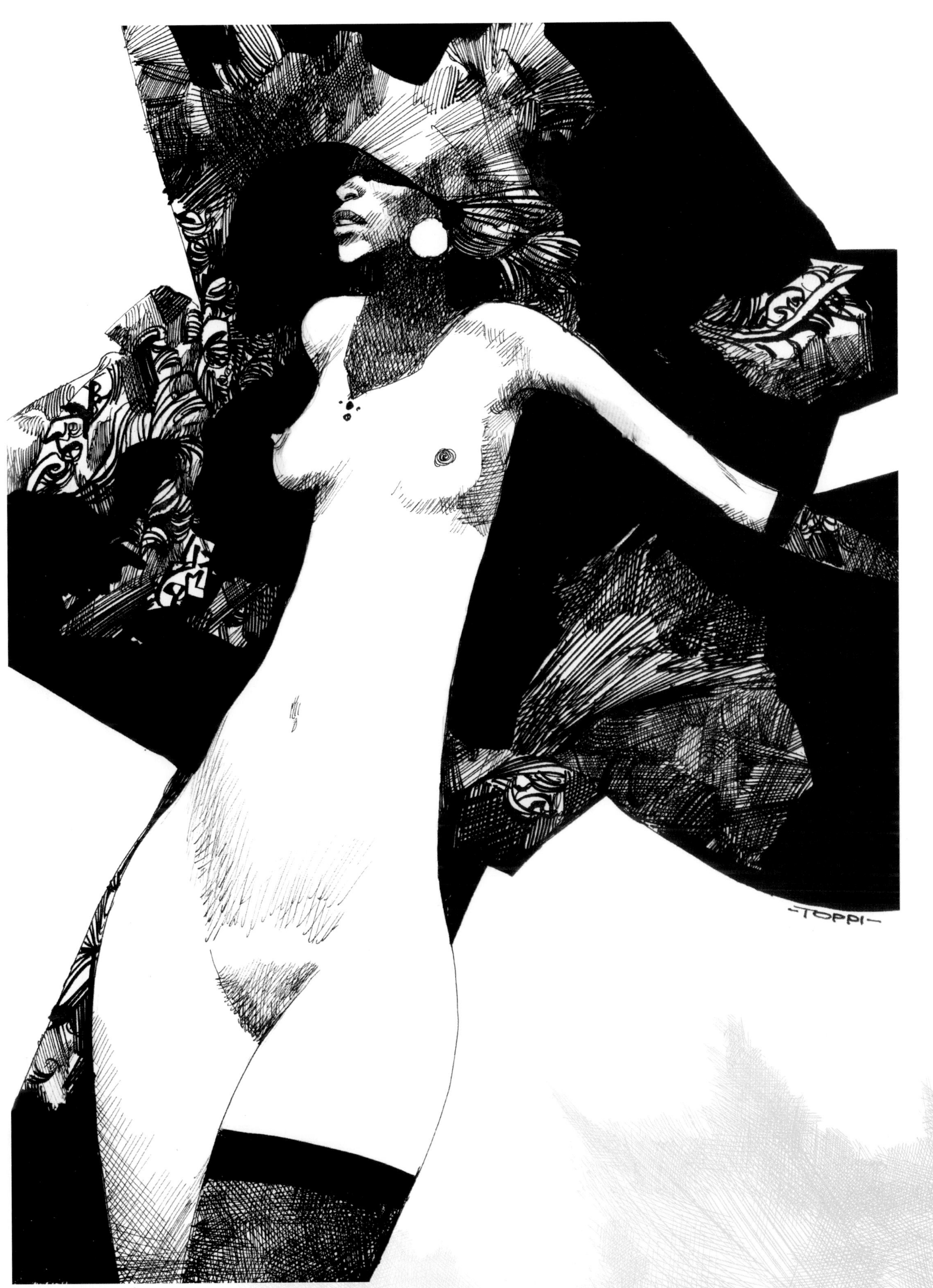

-TOPPI-

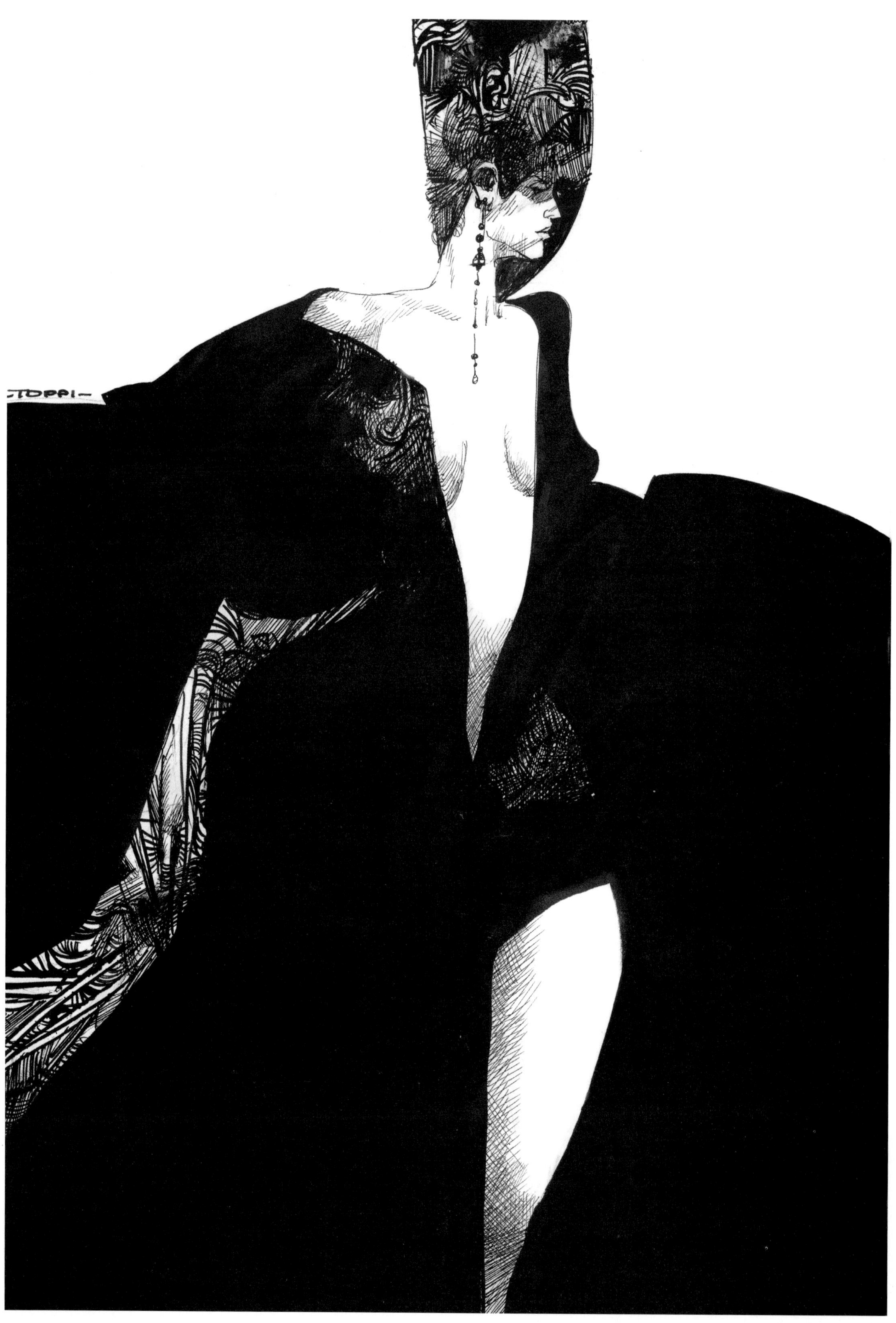

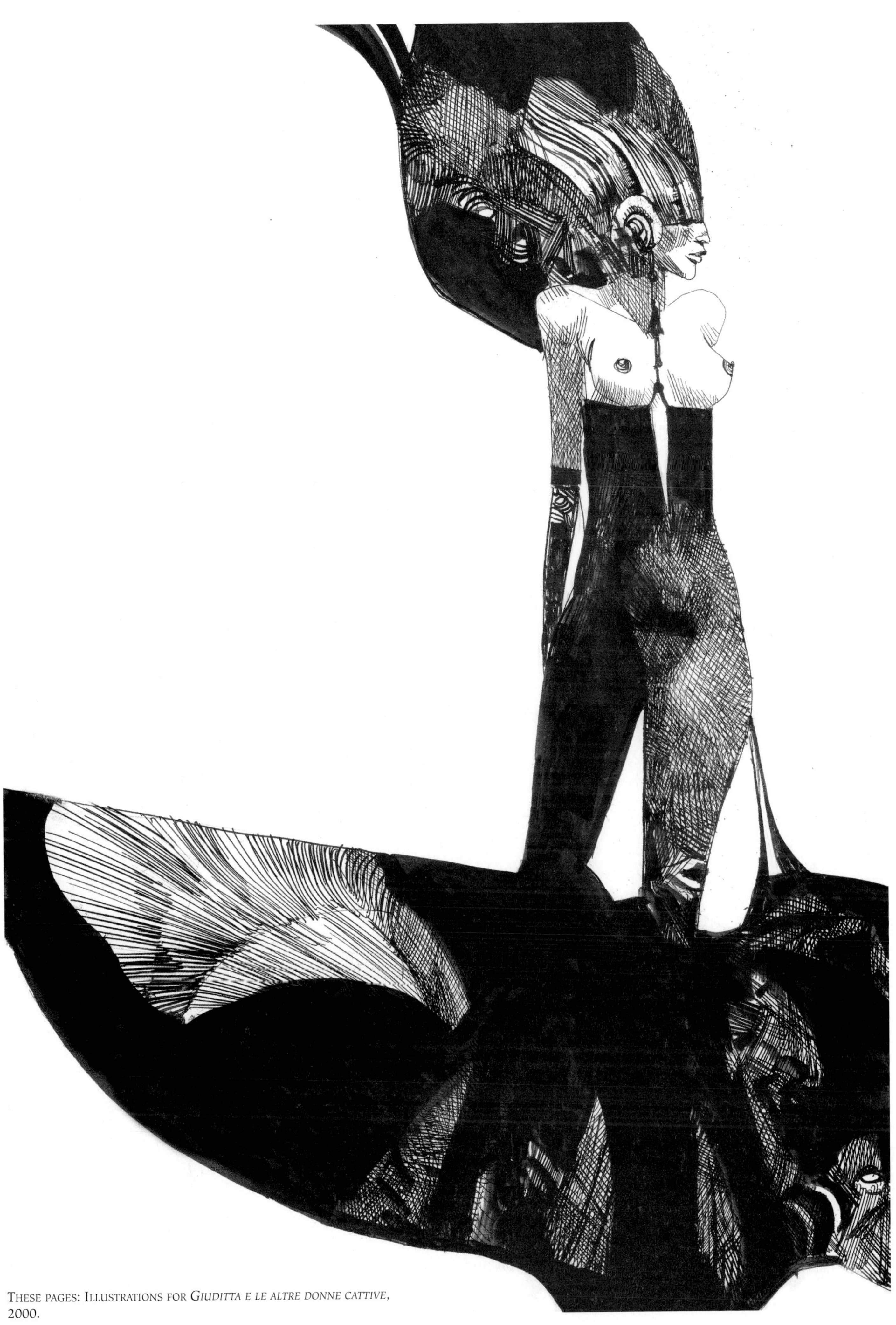

"Vade retro, Satana!" Twice he repeated this cry. He held his dying comrade close to his chest. Tears obscured his vision. He felt himself robbed of all he held dear. He was absolutely furious: he had been promised manly comradery, and behold, this infernal creature was stalking towards them! He mumbled hymns, exorcised with frantic gestures to this Gorgon he had glimpsed in the darkness, and lightly touched the cotton shirt of his now-inert fellow warrior. Get that woman out of here! Make her leave! Make her forget us! "What are you talking about, comrade? There is no woman here; only death is coming."

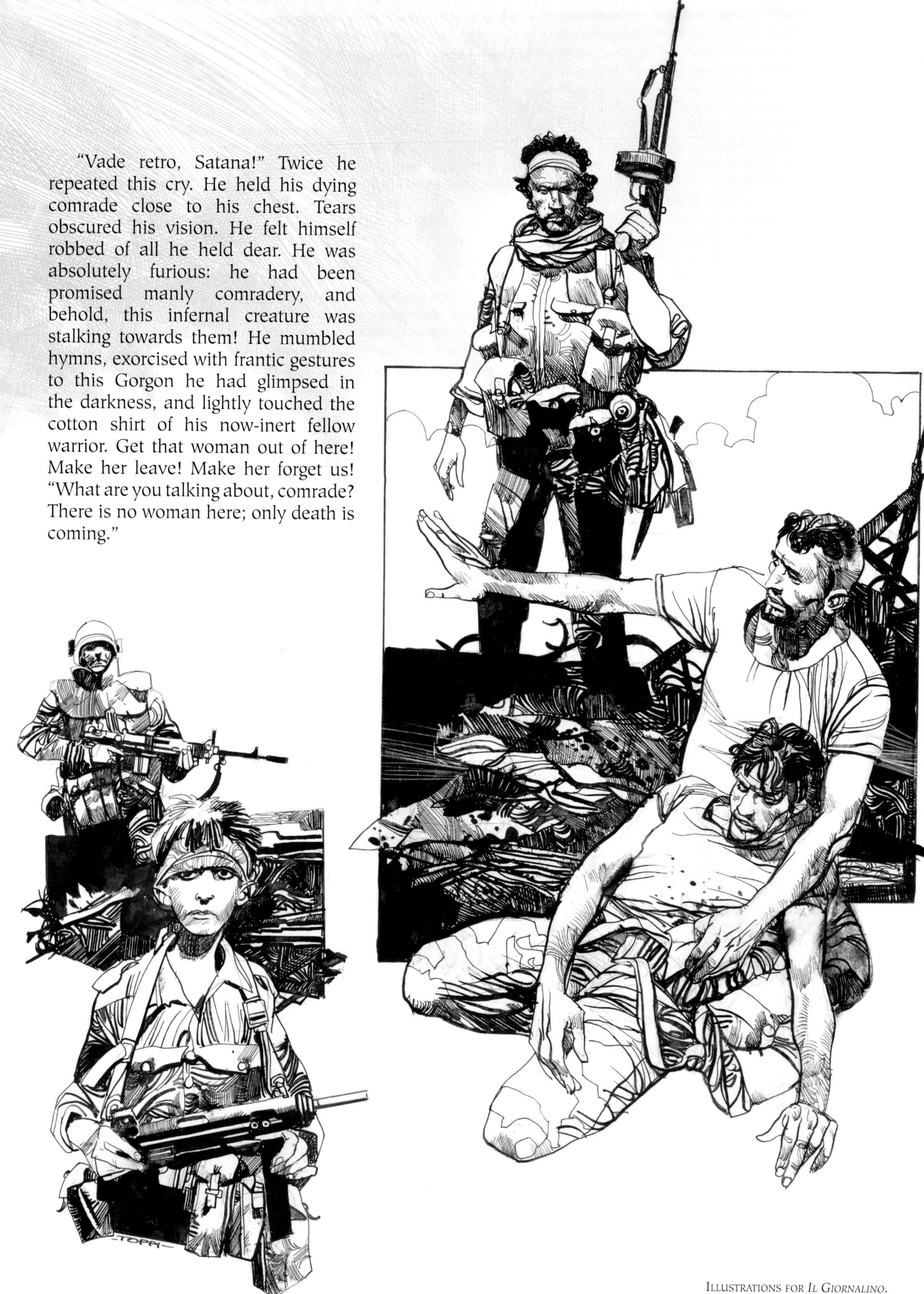

136

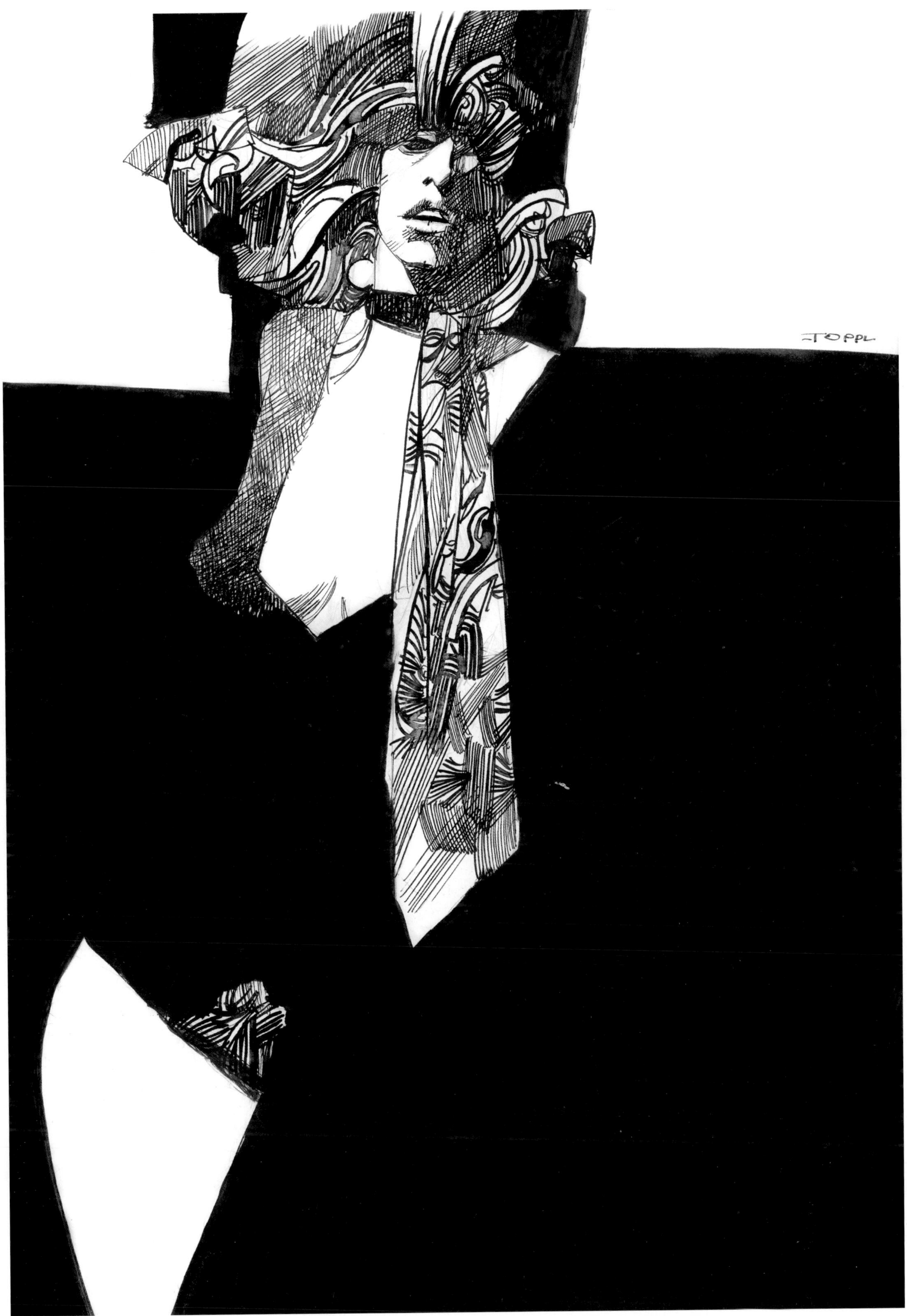

Illustration for *Giuditta e le altre donne cattive*, 2000.

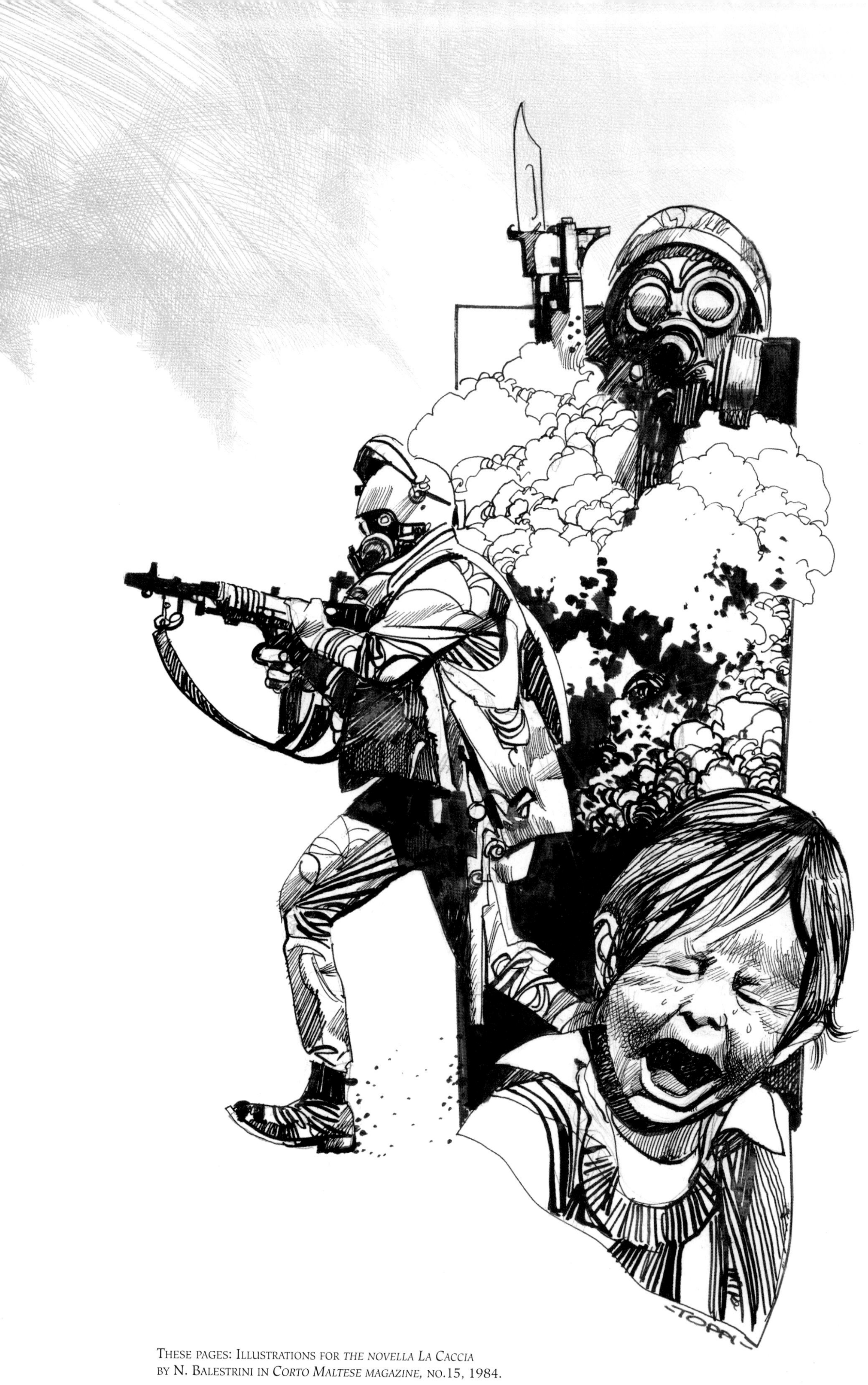

These pages: Illustrations for *the novella La Caccia* by N. Balestrini in *Corto Maltese magazine*, no.15, 1984.

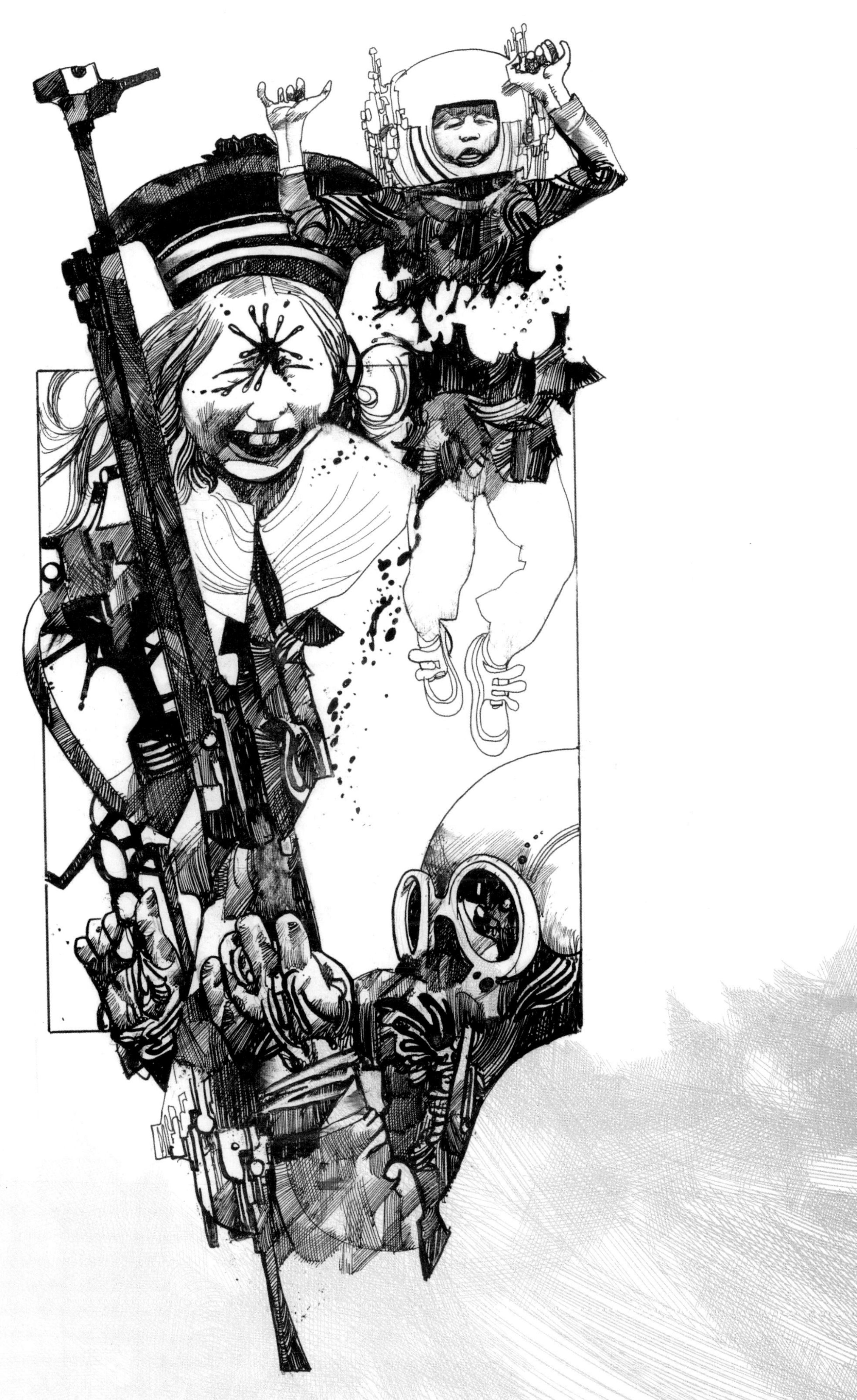

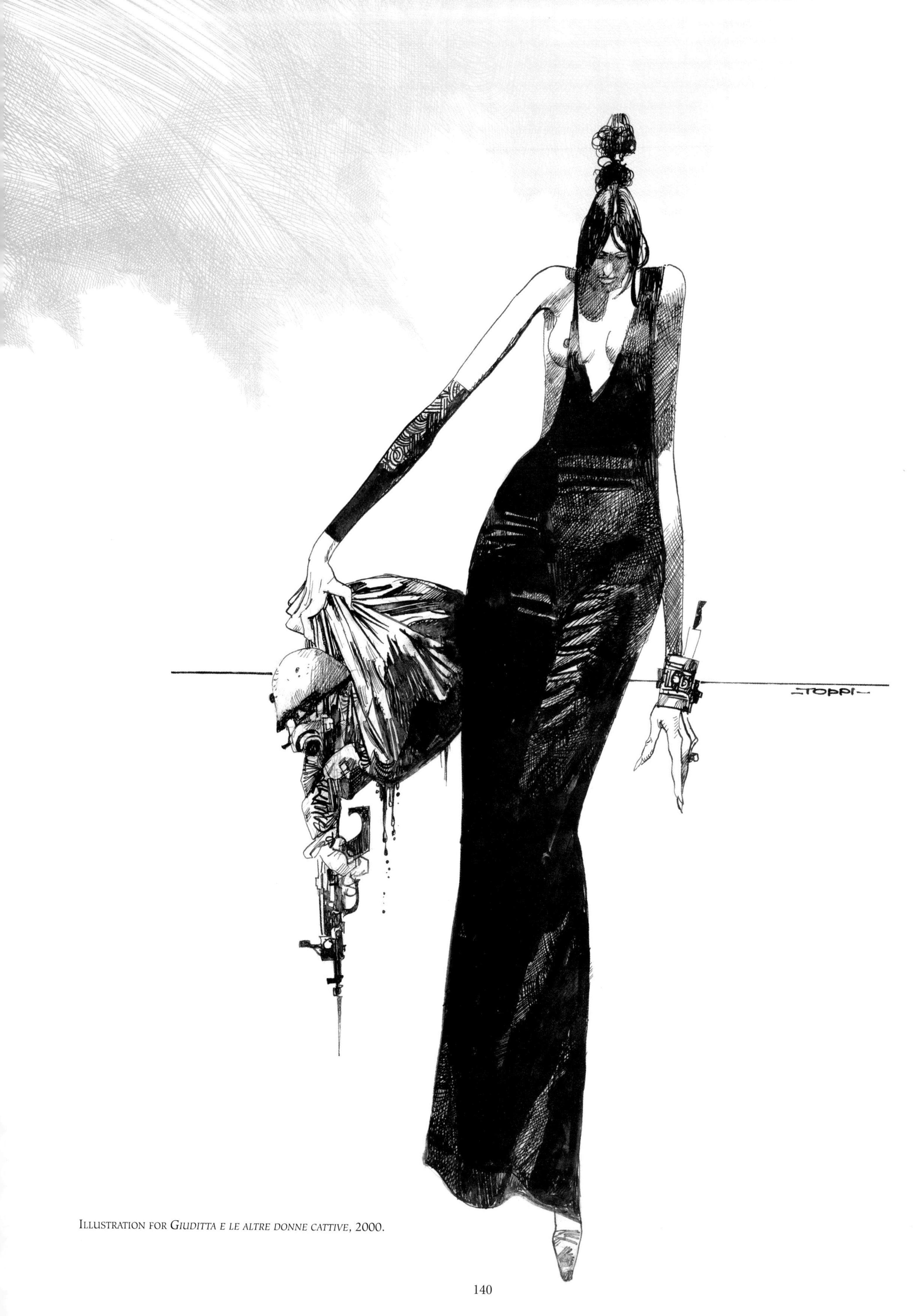

Illustration for *Giuditta e le altre donne cattive*, 2000.

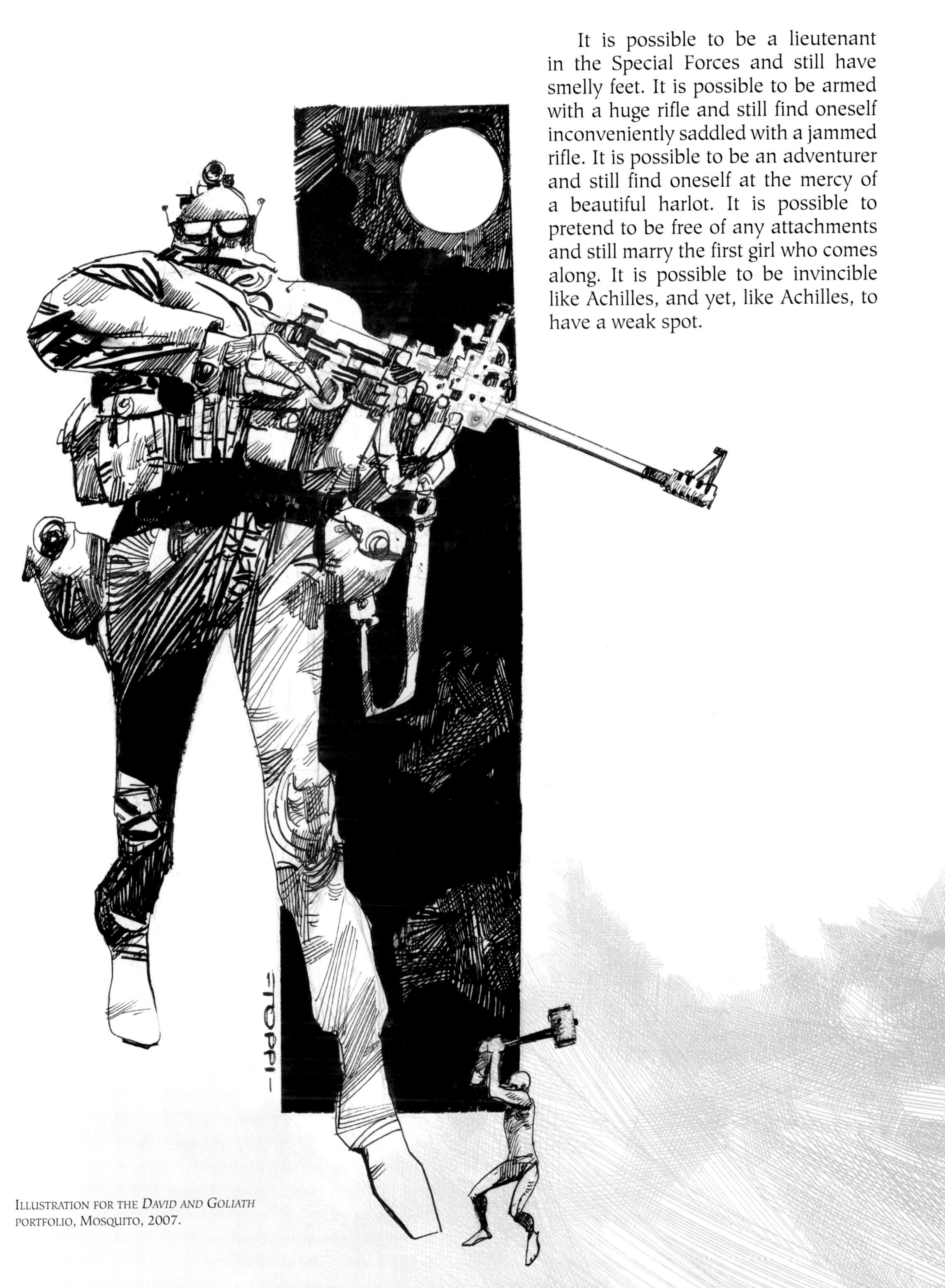

It is possible to be a lieutenant in the Special Forces and still have smelly feet. It is possible to be armed with a huge rifle and still find oneself inconveniently saddled with a jammed rifle. It is possible to be an adventurer and still find oneself at the mercy of a beautiful harlot. It is possible to pretend to be free of any attachments and still marry the first girl who comes along. It is possible to be invincible like Achilles, and yet, like Achilles, to have a weak spot.

Illustration for the *David and Goliath* portfolio, Mosquito, 2007.

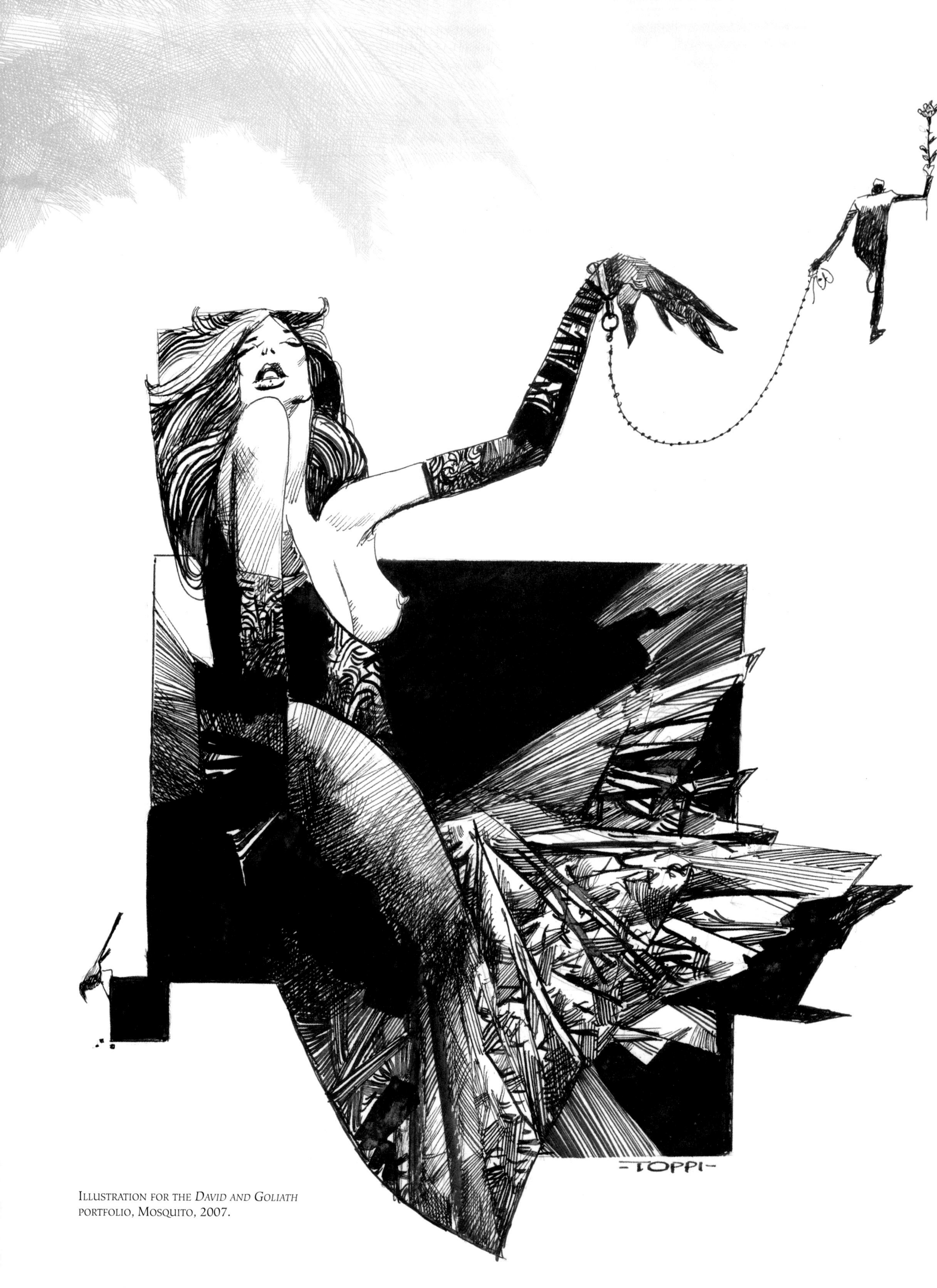

ILLUSTRATION FOR THE *DAVID AND GOLIATH*
PORTFOLIO, MOSQUITO, 2007.

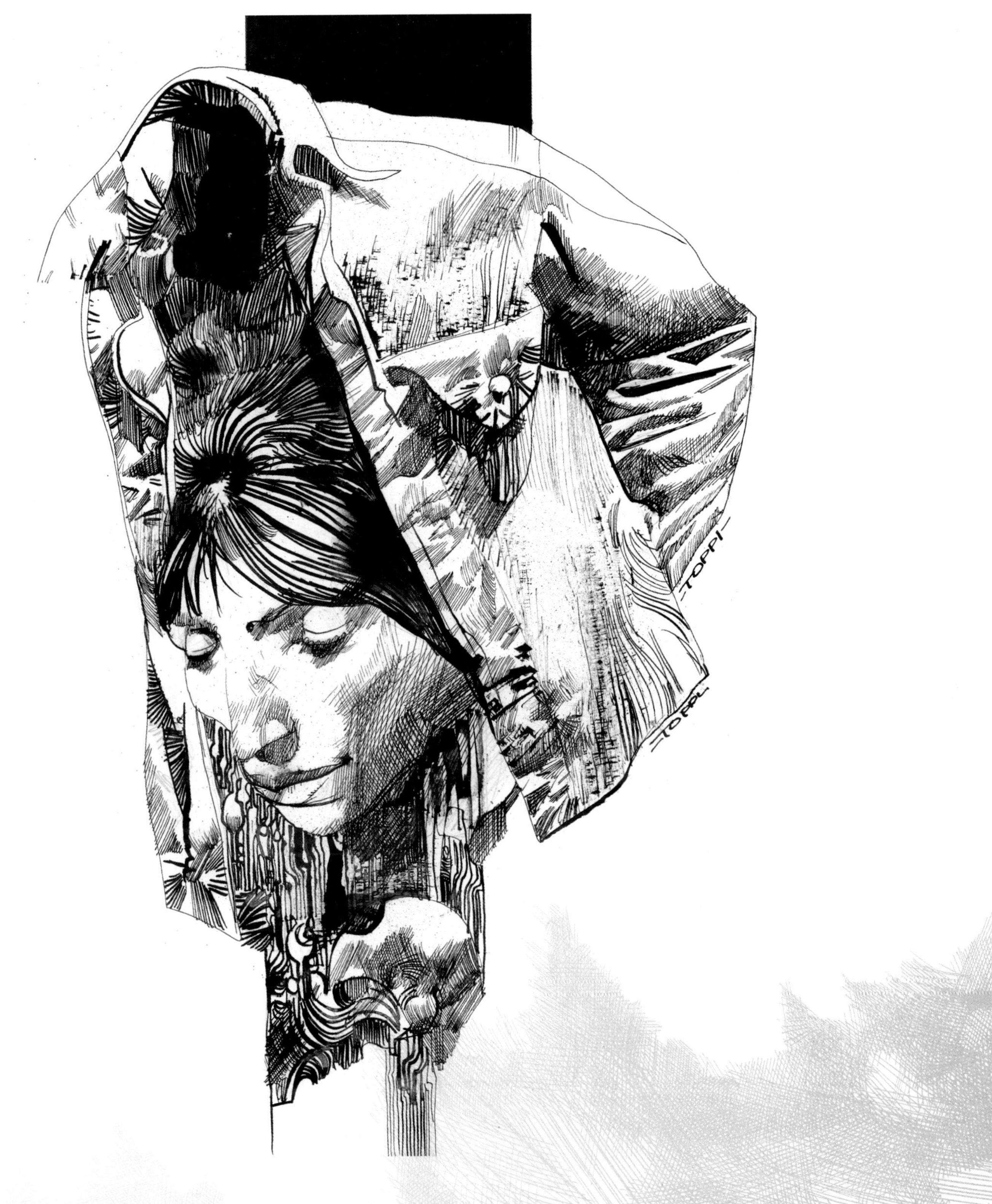

Illustration from 2000.

About the Author

Sergio Toppi was born in Milan, Italy, on October 11, 1932. As a self-taught artist, he began his career in illustration working for the renowned Italian publisher UTET on numerous notable advertising campaigns. Adapting his style to fit the needs of each commission, he excelled at capturing documentary accuracy as well as caricatural cartooning. His first sequential work was featured in *Corriere dei Piccoli* ("The Children's Gazette"), featuring the character Il Mago Zurli ("The Zurli Wizard"). In the decades that followed, his subsequent work evolved in artistry, garnering numerous accolades throughout the European industry. He primarily focused on short, self-contained stories for various French and Italian publications, including the experimental monthly *Alter Alter*, the adventure magazine *Orient Express*, and well-known comics magazines such as *Linus*, *Corto Maltese*, and *Un Uomo Un'avventura* in Italy, and *L'Histoire de France en Bandes Dessinées* and *La Découverte du Monde* in France. Collected exclusively in Europe by the French publisher Mosquito, his body of work has been recognized as a masterful example of illustration and sequential storytelling that has influenced many of the biggest names in the industry worldwide. His art has been displayed in the "Masters of the European Comic Book" exhibit at the Bibliothèque Nationale in Paris and in the Museum of Comic Art in Angoulême.

Toppi passed away on August 21, 2012, in the city of his birth.

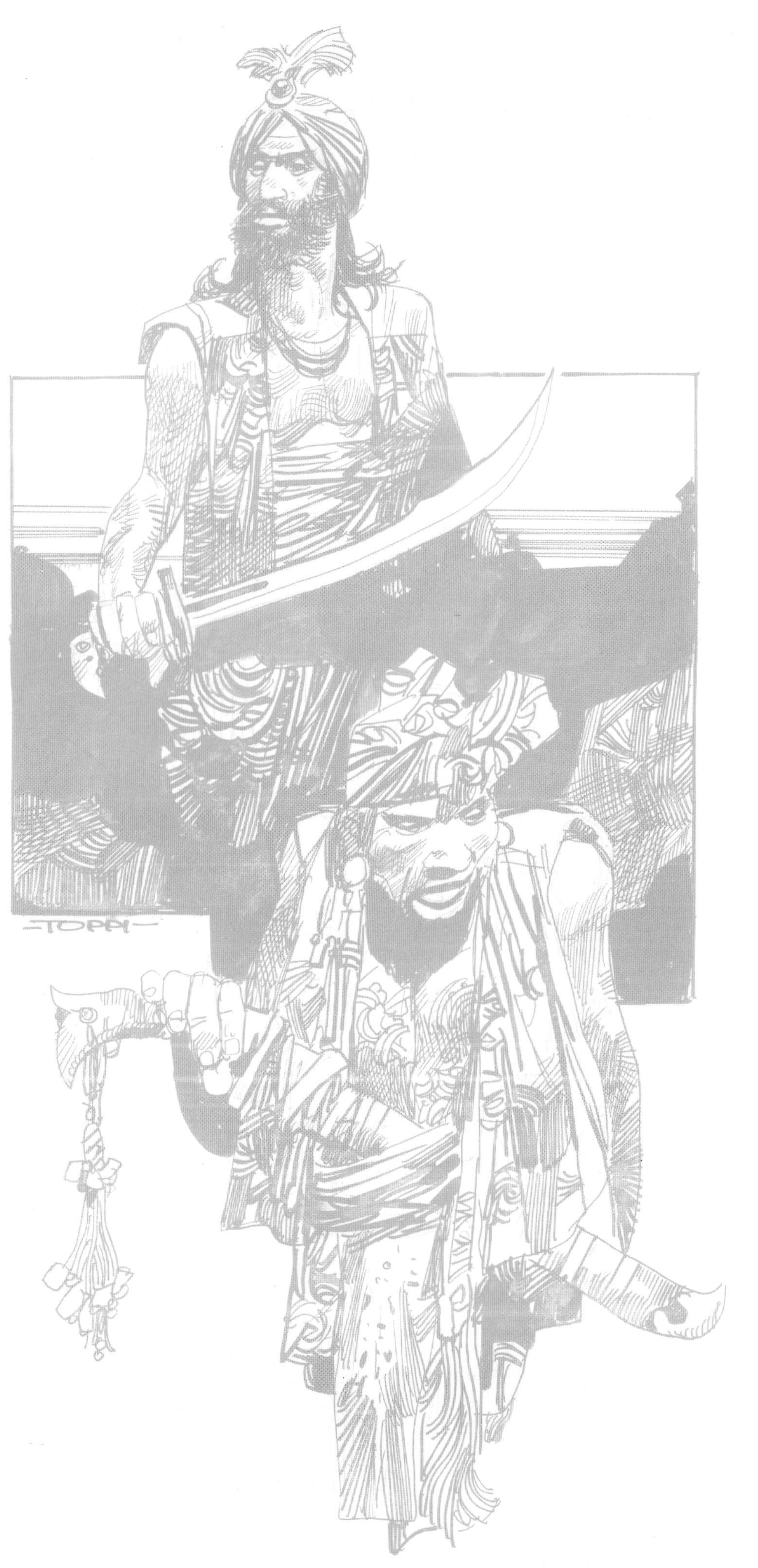